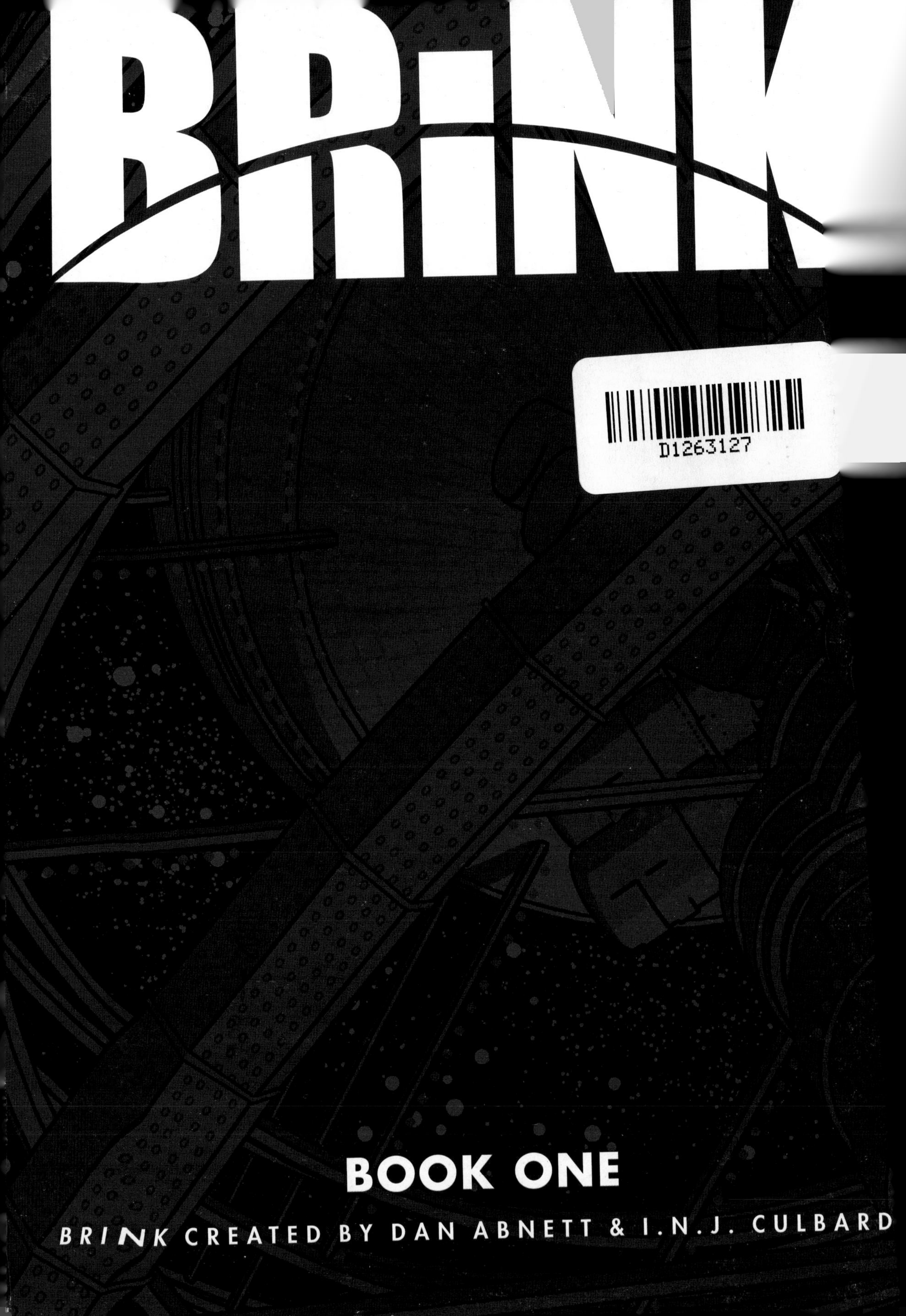

BRINK

BOOK ONE

BRINK CREATED BY DAN ABNETT & I.N.J. CULBARD

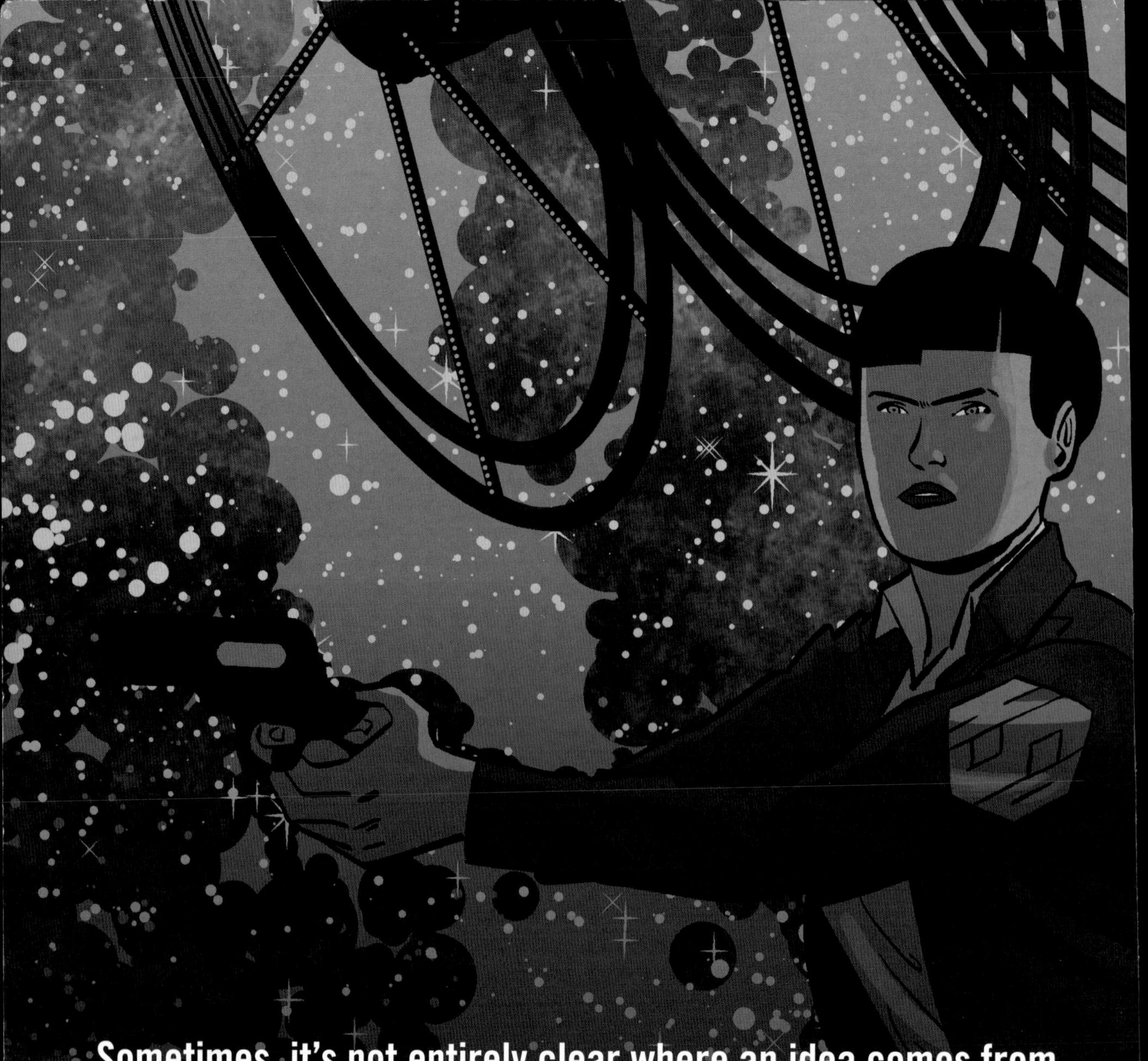

Sometimes, it's not entirely clear where an idea comes from.

I first worked with Ian Culbard on *The New Deadwardians*, a series for DC Vertigo that I had devised. I knew and admired his work, and suggested him as artist. Even though the story was mapped out before he arrived, it developed as we got chatting. We began long, regular conversations and, if nothing else, they established a degree of understanding, so I quickly knew how much (or little) to give him in a script, and he knew what I was looking for in his art.

We've since collaborated on a number of different projects, most notably *Wild's End* for Boom! The one thing they've all had in common is that the ideas have been ours. They've grown from conversations. They've all been original to us, even if we can't precisely say how they formed.

As we were both long-time contributors to *2000 AD*, it seemed appropriate for us to produce a series for the Mighty Tharg together. That series was *Brink*, the first volume of which is contained in this book. It's full on space-set SF, which was a change of pace for us, but it's also a horror story, a police procedural, and a mystery. That particular cocktail was again the product of our conversations. One moment, we were rambling, and the next we exclaimed, 'That's it! That's the idea!'

Brink was very well received by the readers. Apart from the obvious pleasures of Ian's distinctive art work and brilliant storytelling, readers seemed to enjoy the story method itself. It's character-driven and carried by

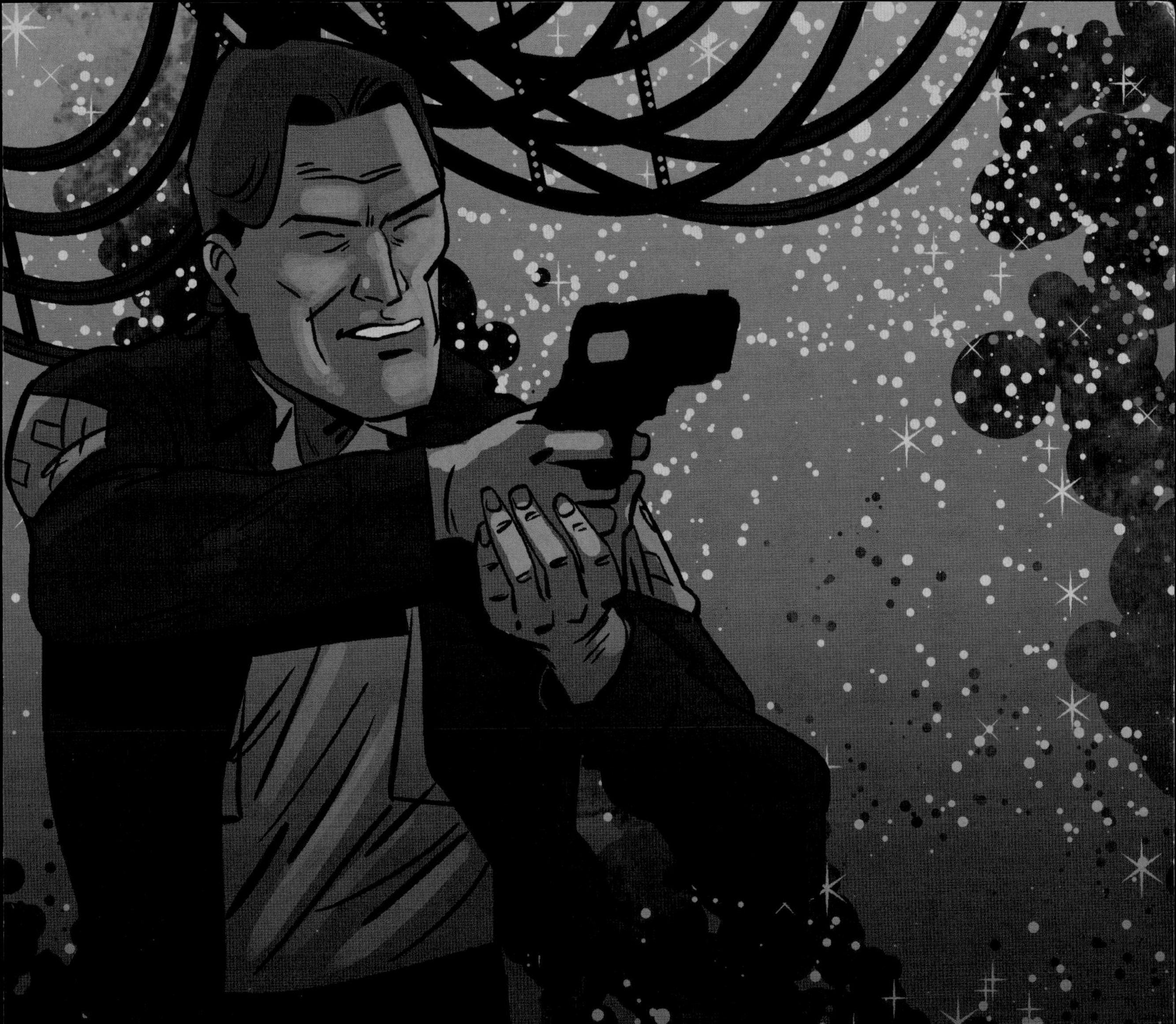

dialogue. There is no narration. Information is delivered via 'tags' that work like footnotes to fill in raw exposition. This meant the dialogue could be extremely conversational and naturalistic. It's (deceptively) slow-burn, and paced unlike other *2000 AD* stories. It's also nothing like anything else I've written.

You're about to read it, so no spoilers, but I will say that there's a twisting of comprehension as the characters gradually, creepily, realise that ideas have permeated their world that make no sense on the surface yet seem to be true and real. Life for these humans living on the 'Brink' - artificial stations and habitats to which they have been exiled following the death of Earth - is slowly becoming unzipped. It is a genuine otherness, or simply a psychological breakdown triggered by this remote, unforgiving, castaway life?

The mystery underpinning the drama is... where are these ideas coming from?

And, as I mentioned at the start, that's not always easy to figure out.

Dan Abnett

Somewhere on the brink,

March 2017

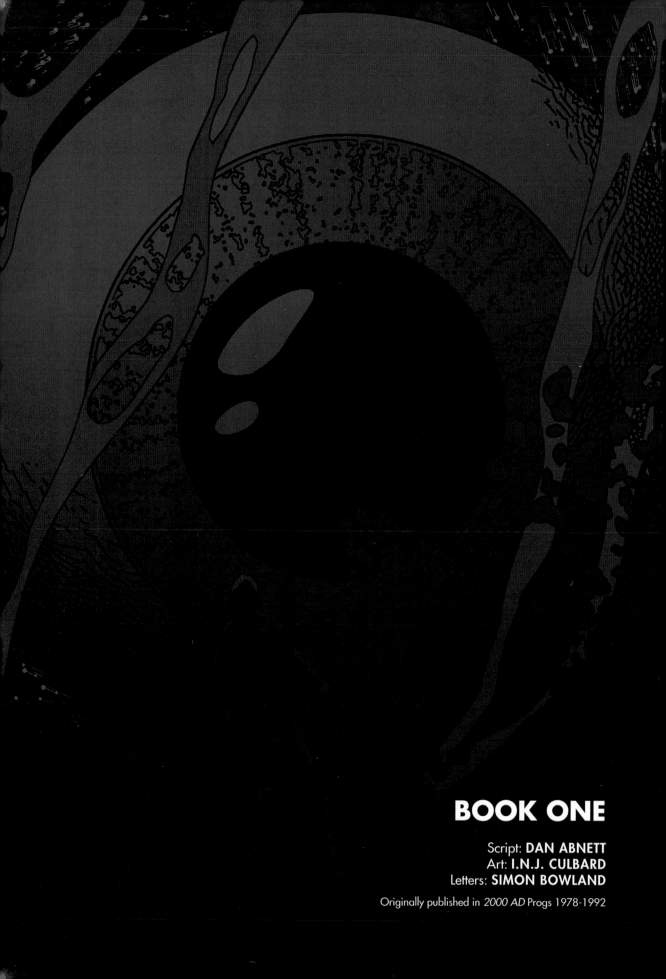

BOOK ONE

Script: **DAN ABNETT**
Art: **I.N.J. CULBARD**
Letters: **SIMON BOWLAND**

Originally published in *2000 AD* Progs 1978-1992

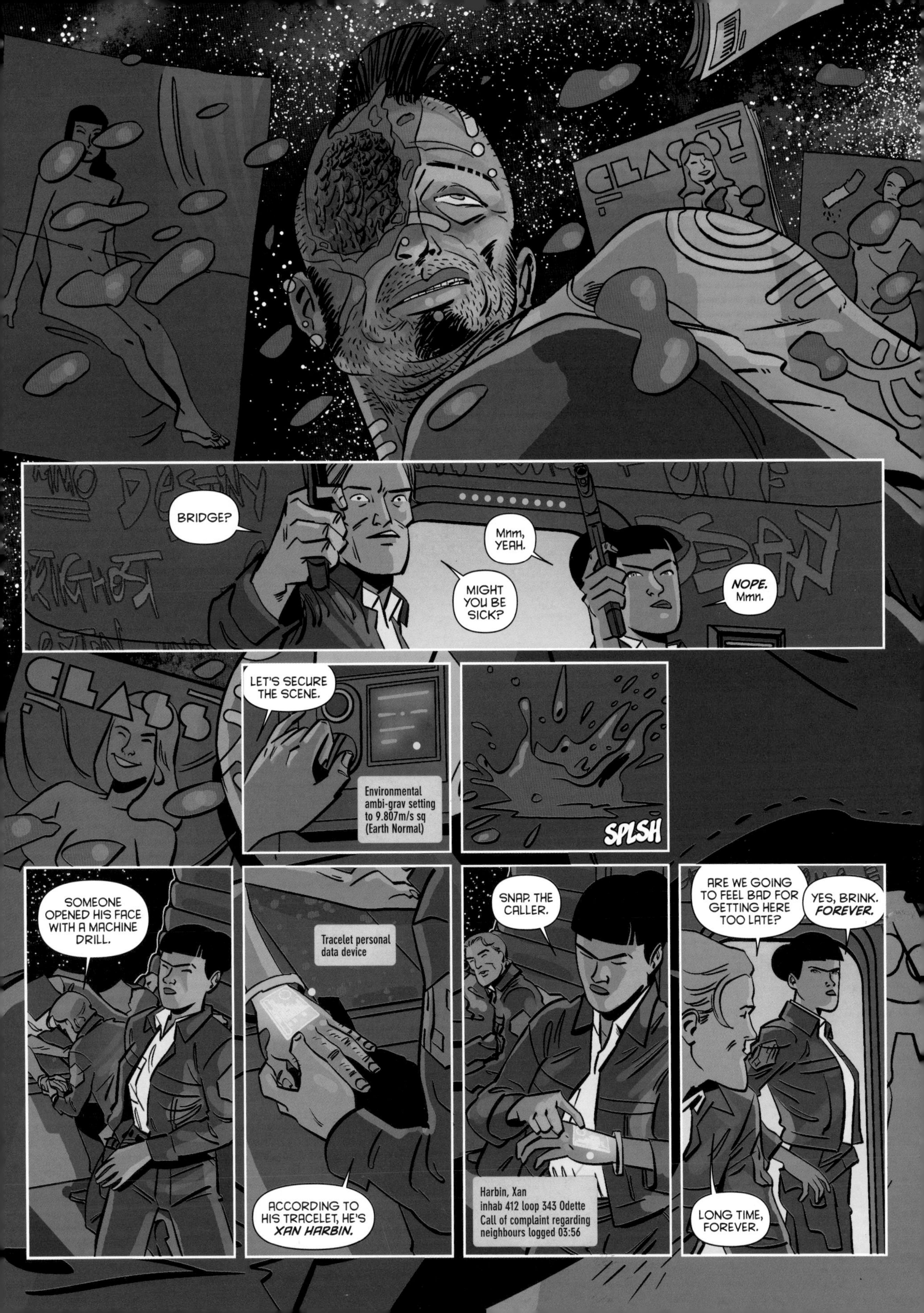
BRIDGE?
Mnm, YEAH.
MIGHT YOU BE SICK?
NOPE. Mmn.
LET'S SECURE THE SCENE.
Environmental ambi-grav setting to 9.807m/s sq (Earth Normal)
SPLSH
SOMEONE OPENED HIS FACE WITH A MACHINE DRILL.
Tracelet personal data device
ACCORDING TO HIS TRACELET, HE'S XAN HARBIN.
SNAP. THE CALLER.
Harbin, Xan
inhab 412 loop 343 Odette
Call of complaint regarding neighbours logged 03:56
ARE WE GOING TO FEEL BAD FOR GETTING HERE TOO LATE?
YES, BRINK. FOREVER.
LONG TIME, FOREVER.

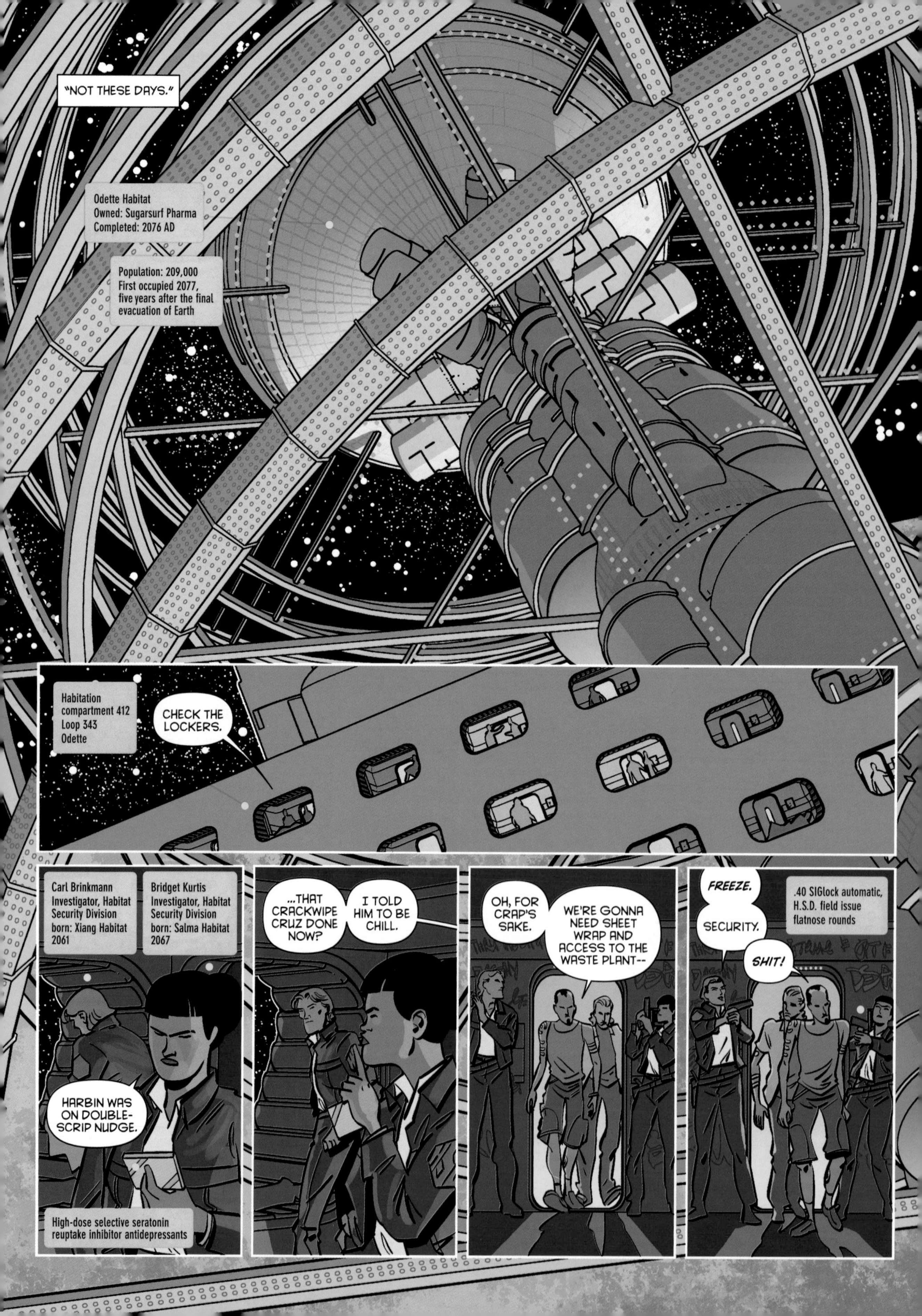

"NOT THESE DAYS."
Odette Habitat
Owned: Sugarsurf Pharma
Completed: 2076 AD
Population: 209,000
First occupied 2077, five years after the final evacuation of Earth
Habitation compartment 412
Loop 343
Odette
CHECK THE LOCKERS.
Carl Brinkmann
Investigator, Habitat Security Division
born: Xiang Habitat 2061
Bridget Kurtis
Investigator, Habitat Security Division
born: Salma Habitat 2067
HARBIN WAS ON DOUBLE-SCRIP NUDGE.
High-dose selective seratonin reuptake inhibitor antidepressants
...THAT CRACKWIPE CRUZ DONE NOW?
I TOLD HIM TO BE CHILL.
OH, FOR CRAP'S SAKE.
WE'RE GONNA NEED SHEET WRAP AND ACCESS TO THE WASTE PLANT--
FREEZE.
SECURITY.
.40 SIGlock automatic, H.S.D. field issue flatnose rounds
SHIT!

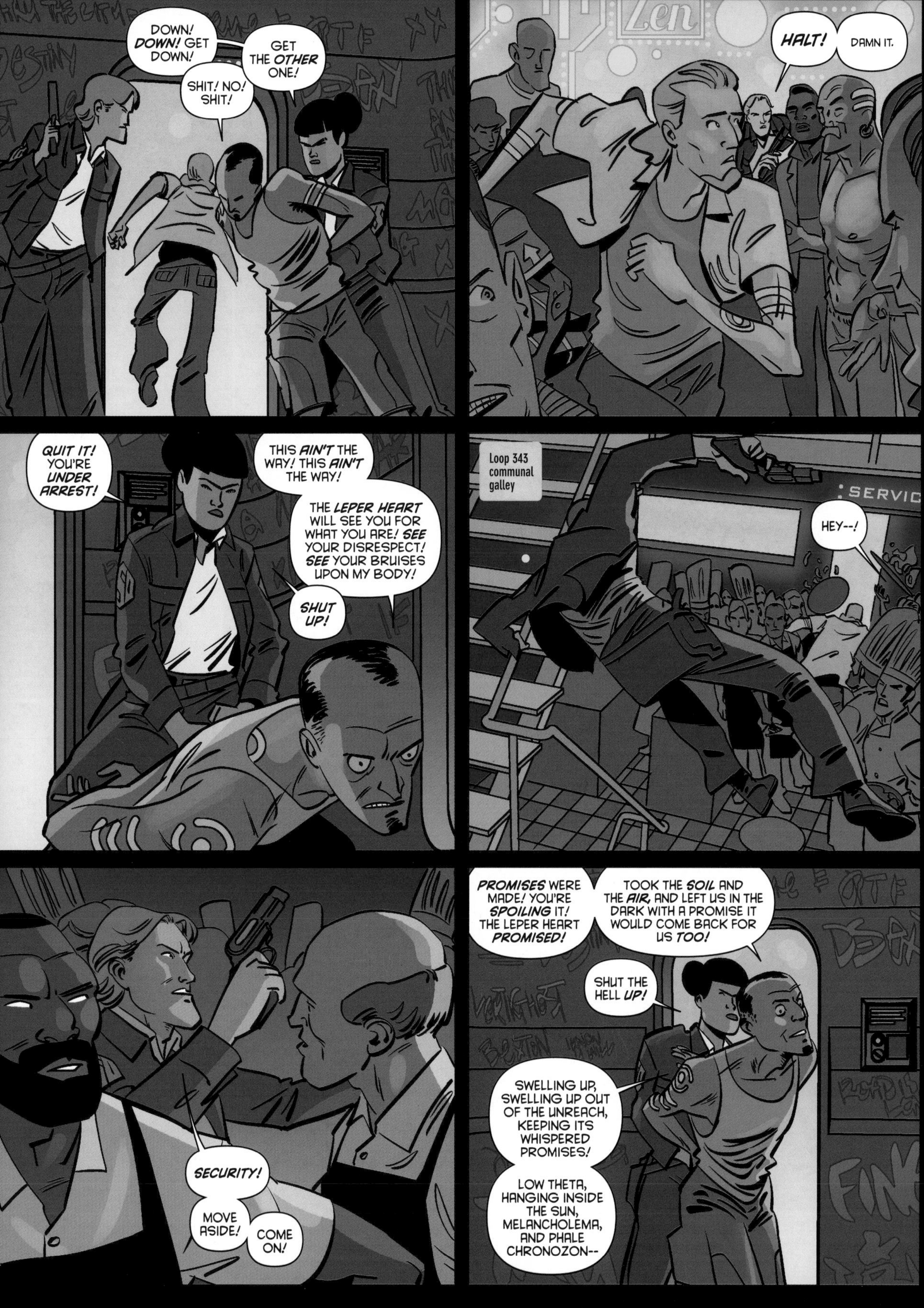
DOWN! DOWN! GET DOWN!
GET THE OTHER ONE!
SHIT! NO! SHIT!
Zen
HALT!
DAMN IT.
QUIT IT! YOU'RE UNDER ARREST!
THIS AIN'T THE WAY! THIS AIN'T THE WAY!
THE LEPER HEART WILL SEE YOU FOR WHAT YOU ARE! SEE YOUR DISRESPECT! SEE YOUR BRUISES UPON MY BODY!
SHUT UP!
Loop 343 communal galley
SERVIC
HEY--!
SECURITY!
MOVE ASIDE!
COME ON!
PROMISES WERE MADE! YOU'RE SPOILING IT! THE LEPER HEART PROMISED!
TOOK THE SOIL AND THE AIR, AND LEFT US IN THE DARK WITH A PROMISE IT WOULD COME BACK FOR US TOO!
SHUT THE HELL UP!
SWELLING UP, SWELLING UP OUT OF THE UNREACH, KEEPING ITS WHISPERED PROMISES!
LOW THETA, HANGING INSIDE THE SUN, MELANCHOLEMA, AND PHALE CHRONOZON--

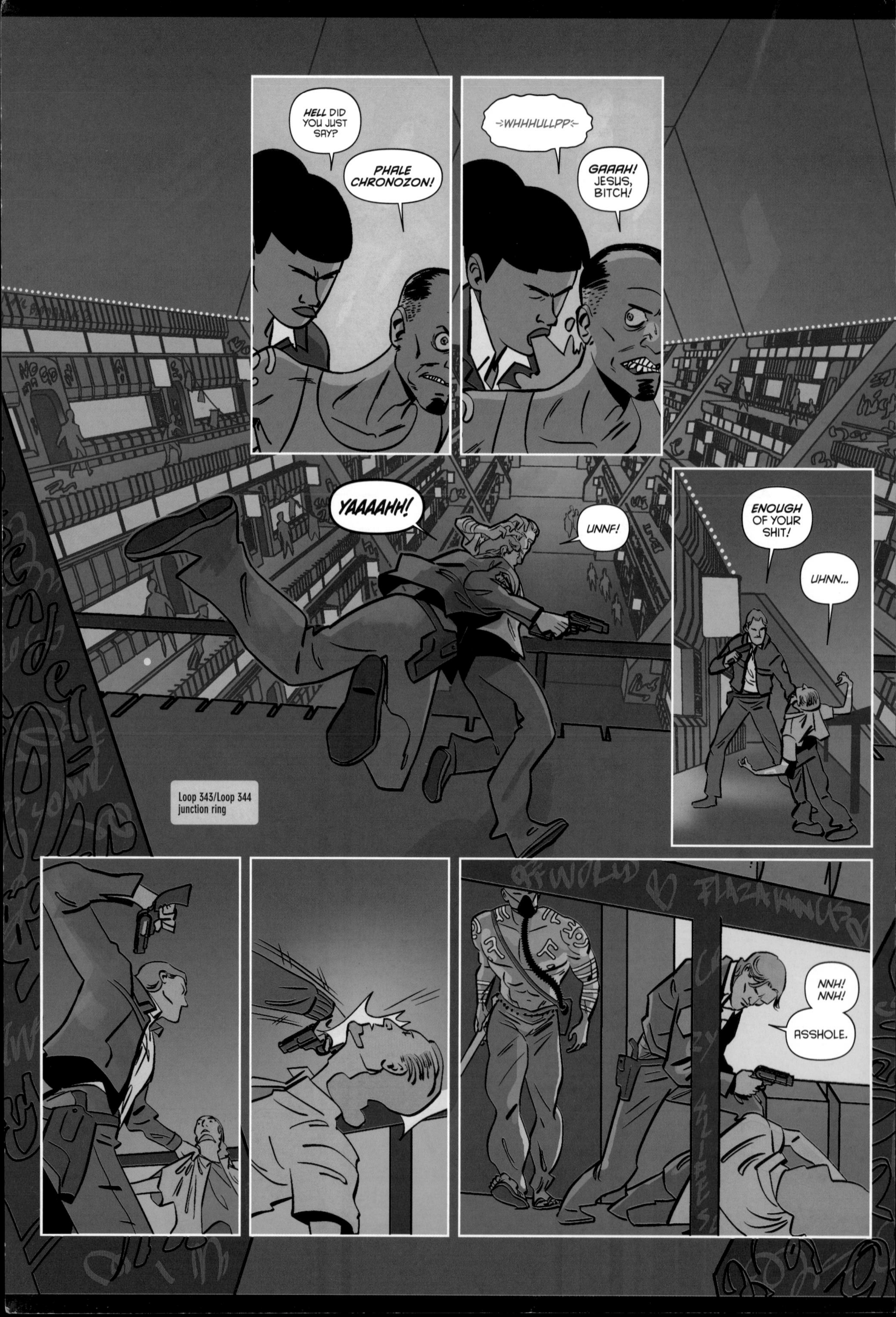

HELL DID YOU JUST SAY?
PHALE CHRONOZON!
-WHHHULLPP-
GAAAH! JESUS, BITCH!
YAAAAHH!
UNNF!
ENOUGH OF YOUR SHIT!
UHNN...
Loop 343/Loop 344 junction ring
NNH! NNH!
ASSHOLE.

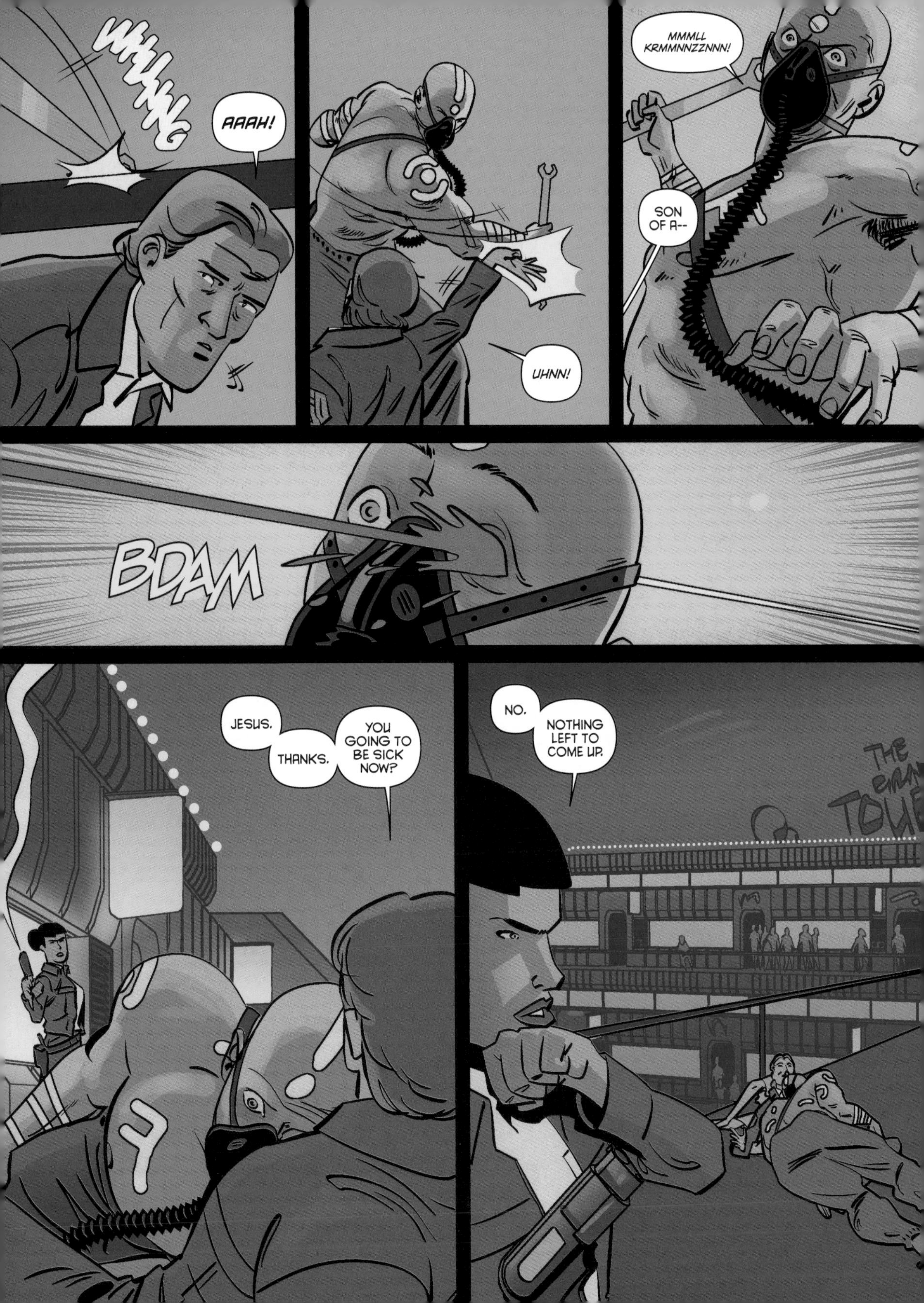
WHANG
AAAH!
UHNN!
MMMLL KRMMNNZZNNN!
SON OF A--
BDAM
JESUS.
THANKS.
YOU GOING TO BE SICK NOW?
NO.
NOTHING LEFT TO COME UP.

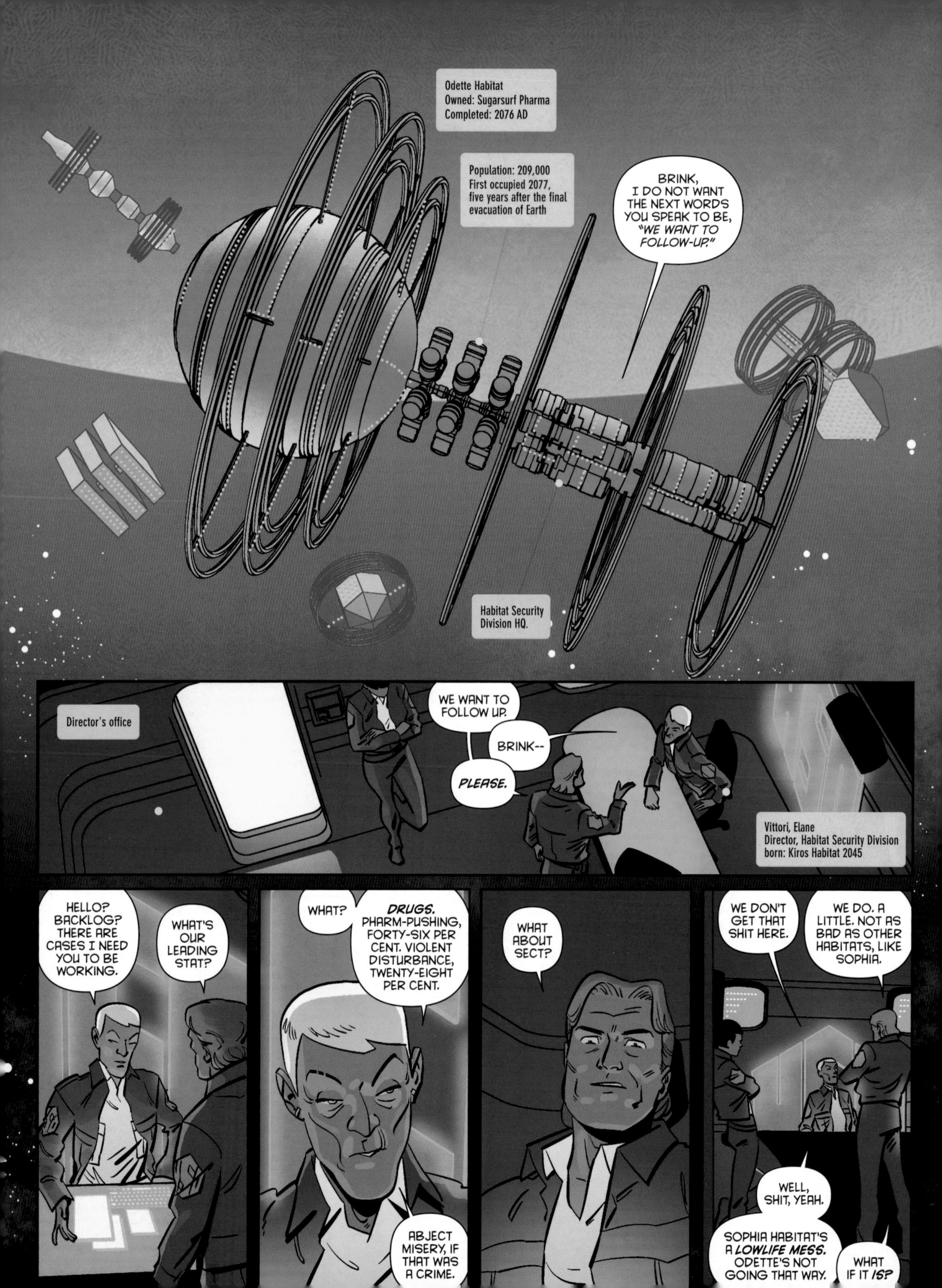

Odette Habitat
Owned: Sugarsurf Pharma
Completed: 2076 AD
Population: 209,000
First occupied 2077, five years after the final evacuation of Earth
BRINK, I DO NOT WANT THE NEXT WORDS YOU SPEAK TO BE, "WE WANT TO FOLLOW-UP."
Habitat Security Division HQ.
Director's office
WE WANT TO FOLLOW UP.
BRINK--
PLEASE.
Vittori, Elane
Director, Habitat Security Division
born: Kiros Habitat 2045
HELLO? BACKLOG? THERE ARE CASES I NEED YOU TO BE WORKING.
WHAT'S OUR LEADING STAT?
WHAT?
DRUGS. PHARM-PUSHING, FORTY-SIX PER CENT. VIOLENT DISTURBANCE, TWENTY-EIGHT PER CENT.
ABJECT MISERY, IF THAT WAS A CRIME.
WHAT ABOUT SECT?
WE DON'T GET THAT SHIT HERE.
WE DO. A LITTLE. NOT AS BAD AS OTHER HABITATS, LIKE SOPHIA.
WELL, SHIT, YEAH.
SOPHIA HABITAT'S A LOWLIFE MESS. ODETTE'S NOT GOING THAT WAY.
WHAT IF IT IS?

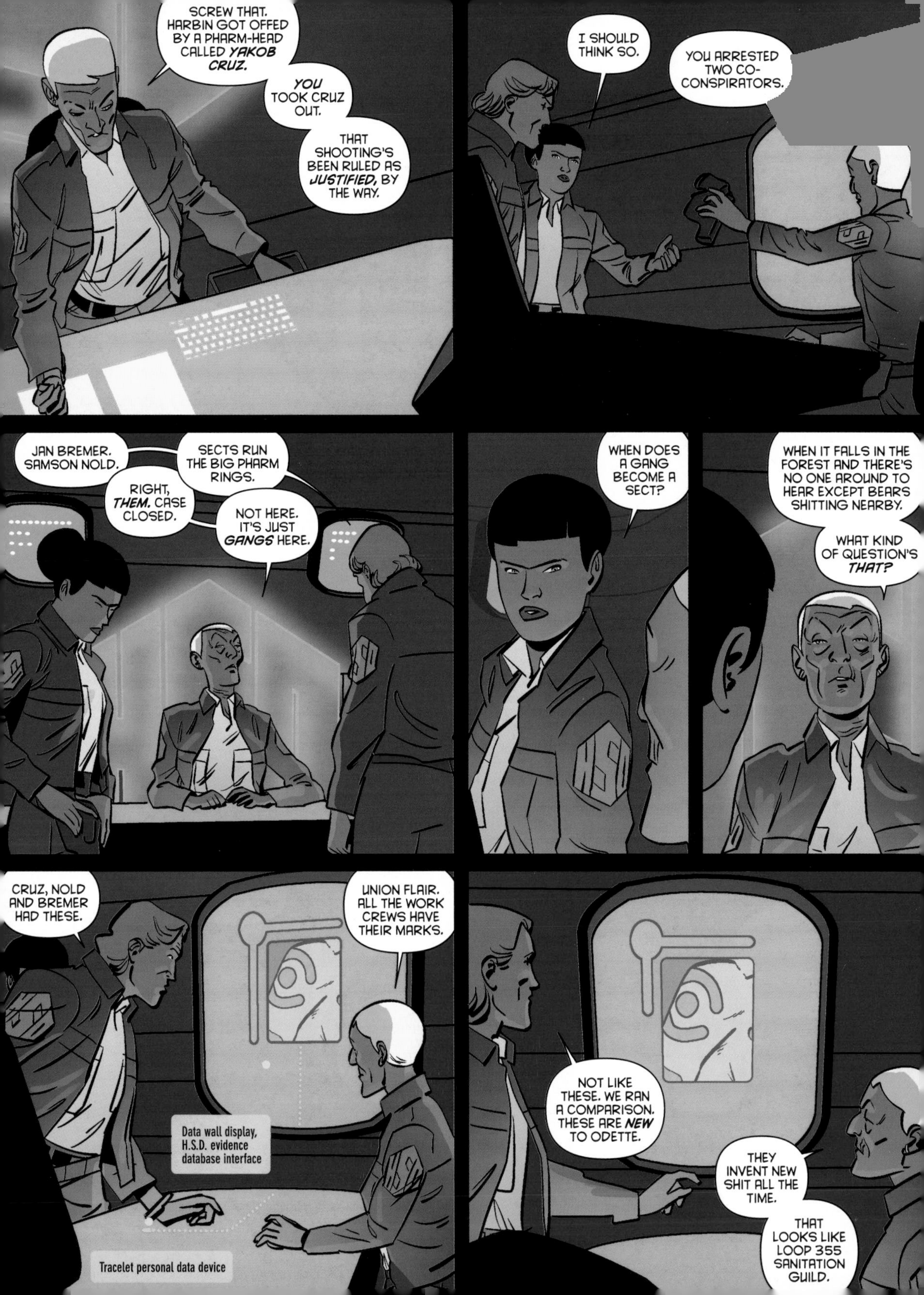
SCREW THAT. HARBIN GOT OFFED BY A PHARM-HEAD CALLED *YAKOB CRUZ.*
YOU TOOK CRUZ OUT.
THAT SHOOTING'S BEEN RULED AS *JUSTIFIED,* BY THE WAY.
I SHOULD THINK SO.
YOU ARRESTED TWO CO-CONSPIRATORS.
JAN BREMER. SAMSON NOLD.
RIGHT, *THEM.* CASE CLOSED.
SECTS RUN THE BIG PHARM RINGS.
NOT HERE. IT'S JUST *GANGS* HERE.
WHEN DOES A GANG BECOME A SECT?
WHEN IT FALLS IN THE FOREST AND THERE'S NO ONE AROUND TO HEAR EXCEPT BEARS SHITTING NEARBY.
WHAT KIND OF QUESTION'S *THAT?*
CRUZ, NOLD AND BREMER HAD THESE.
UNION FLAIR. ALL THE WORK CREWS HAVE THEIR MARKS.
Data wall display, H.S.D. evidence database interface
Tracelet personal data device
NOT LIKE THESE. WE RAN A COMPARISON. THESE ARE *NEW* TO ODETTE.
THEY INVENT NEW SHIT ALL THE TIME.
THAT LOOKS LIKE LOOP 355 SANITATION GUILD.

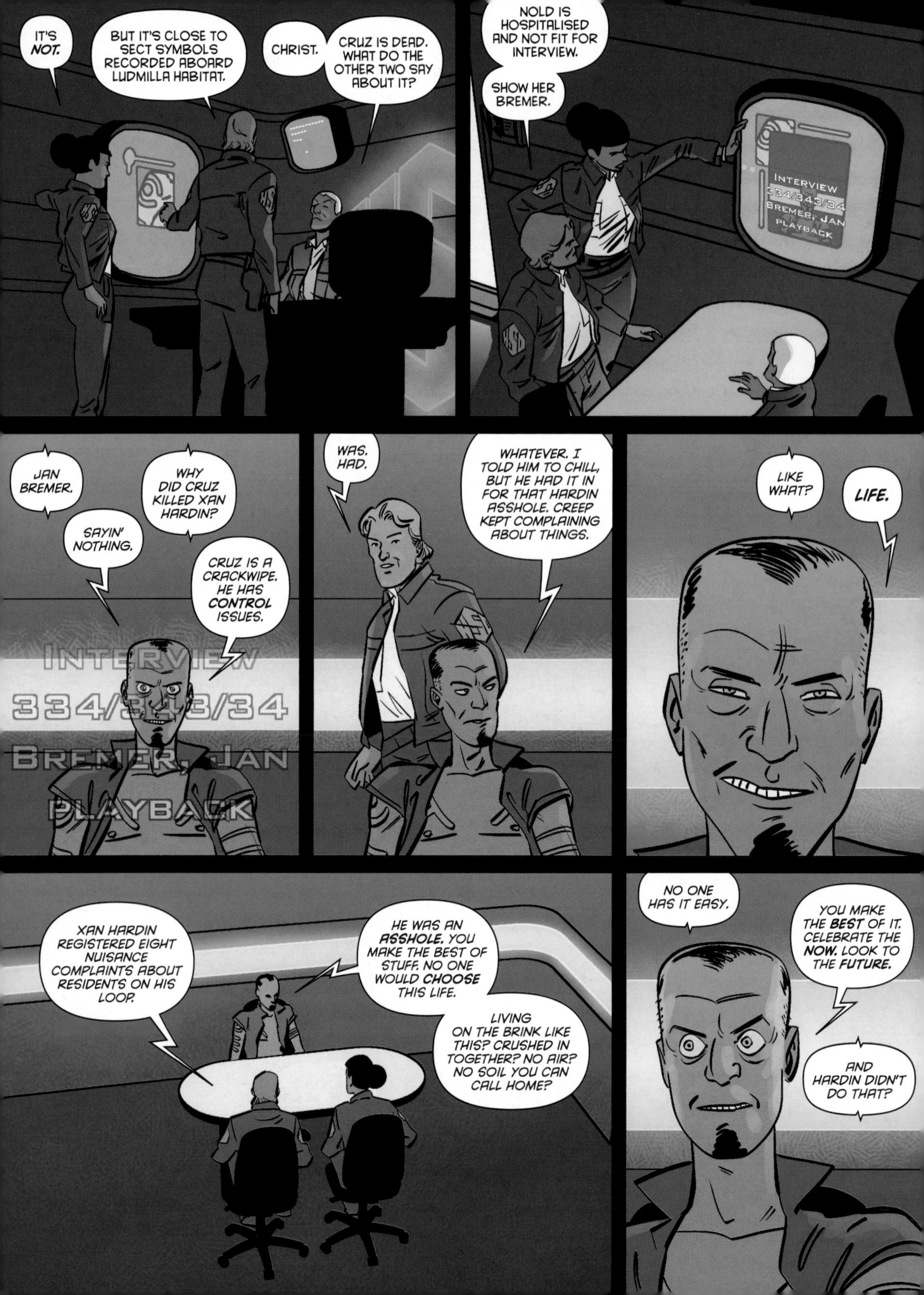
IT'S NOT.
BUT IT'S CLOSE TO SECT SYMBOLS RECORDED ABOARD LUDMILLA HABITAT.
CHRIST.
CRUZ IS DEAD. WHAT DO THE OTHER TWO SAY ABOUT IT?
NOLD IS HOSPITALISED AND NOT FIT FOR INTERVIEW.
SHOW HER BREMER.
INTERVIEW 334/343/34 BREMER, JAN PLAYBACK
JAN BREMER.
WHY DID CRUZ KILLED XAN HARDIN?
SAYIN' NOTHING.
CRUZ IS A CRACKWIPE. HE HAS CONTROL ISSUES.
INTERVIEW
334/343/34
BREMER, JAN
PLAYBACK
WAS. HAD.
WHATEVER. I TOLD HIM TO CHILL, BUT HE HAD IT IN FOR THAT HARDIN ASSHOLE. CREEP KEPT COMPLAINING ABOUT THINGS.
LIKE WHAT?
LIFE.
XAN HARDIN REGISTERED EIGHT NUISANCE COMPLAINTS ABOUT RESIDENTS ON HIS LOOP.
HE WAS AN ASSHOLE. YOU MAKE THE BEST OF STUFF. NO ONE WOULD CHOOSE THIS LIFE.
LIVING ON THE BRINK LIKE THIS? CRUSHED IN TOGETHER? NO AIR? NO SOIL YOU CAN CALL HOME?
NO ONE HAS IT EASY.
YOU MAKE THE BEST OF IT. CELEBRATE THE NOW. LOOK TO THE FUTURE.
AND HARDIN DIDN'T DO THAT?

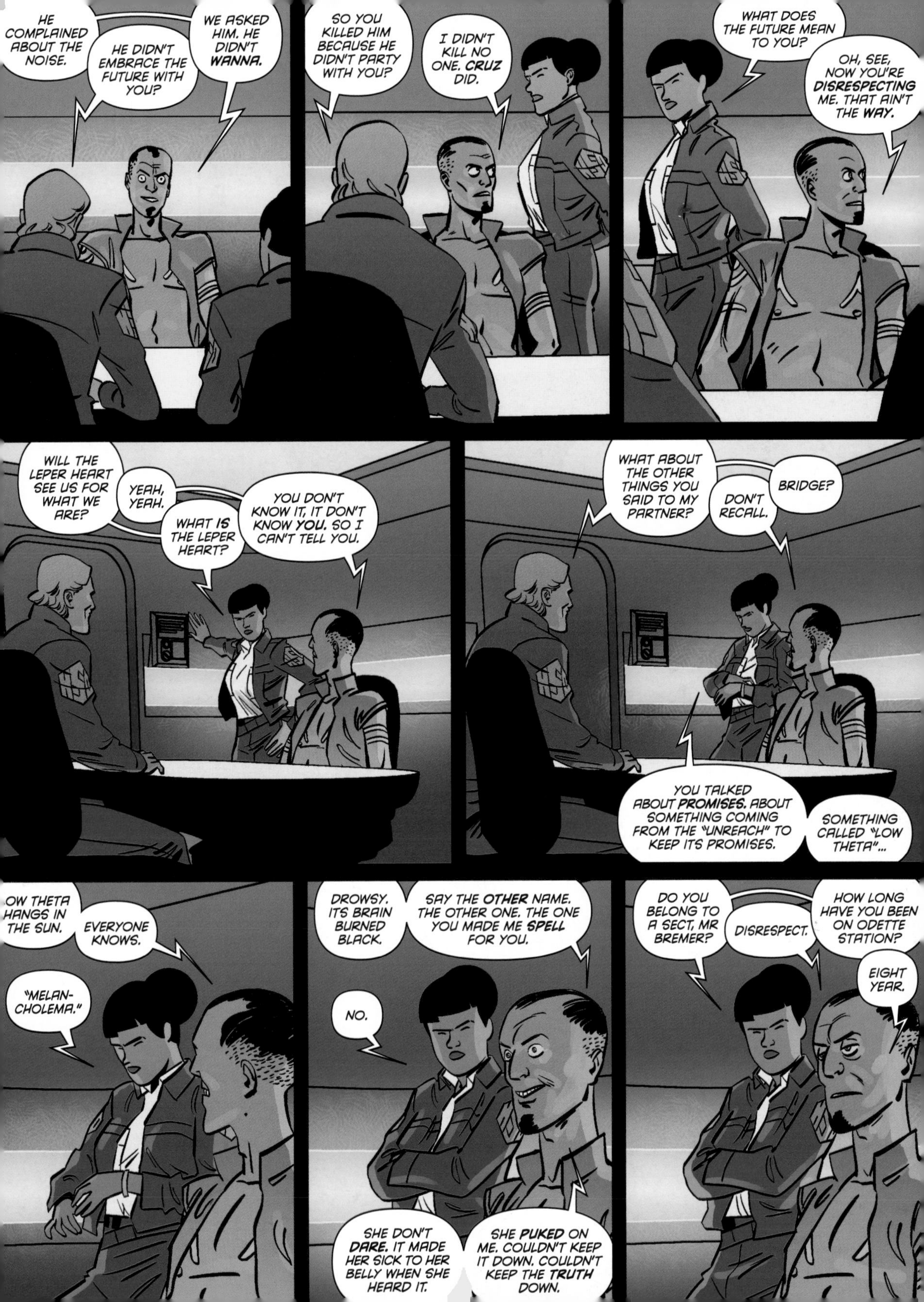

HE COMPLAINED ABOUT THE NOISE.
WE ASKED HIM. HE DIDN'T WANNA.
HE DIDN'T EMBRACE THE FUTURE WITH YOU?
SO YOU KILLED HIM BECAUSE HE DIDN'T PARTY WITH YOU?
I DIDN'T KILL NO ONE. CRUZ DID.
WHAT DOES THE FUTURE MEAN TO YOU?
OH, SEE, NOW YOU'RE DISRESPECTING ME. THAT AIN'T THE WAY.
WILL THE LEPER HEART SEE US FOR WHAT WE ARE?
YEAH, YEAH.
WHAT IS THE LEPER HEART?
YOU DON'T KNOW IT, IT DON'T KNOW YOU. SO I CAN'T TELL YOU.
WHAT ABOUT THE OTHER THINGS YOU SAID TO MY PARTNER?
BRIDGE?
DON'T RECALL.
YOU TALKED ABOUT PROMISES. ABOUT SOMETHING COMING FROM THE "UNREACH" TO KEEP ITS PROMISES.
SOMETHING CALLED "LOW THETA"...
OW THETA HANGS IN THE SUN.
EVERYONE KNOWS.
"MELAN-CHOLEMA."
DROWSY. ITS BRAIN BURNED BLACK.
SAY THE OTHER NAME. THE OTHER ONE. THE ONE YOU MADE ME SPELL FOR YOU.
NO.
SHE DON'T DARE. IT MADE HER SICK TO HER BELLY WHEN SHE HEARD IT.
SHE PUKED ON ME. COULDN'T KEEP IT DOWN. COULDN'T KEEP THE TRUTH DOWN.
DO YOU BELONG TO A SECT, MR BREMER?
DISRESPECT.
HOW LONG HAVE YOU BEEN ON ODETTE STATION?
EIGHT YEAR.

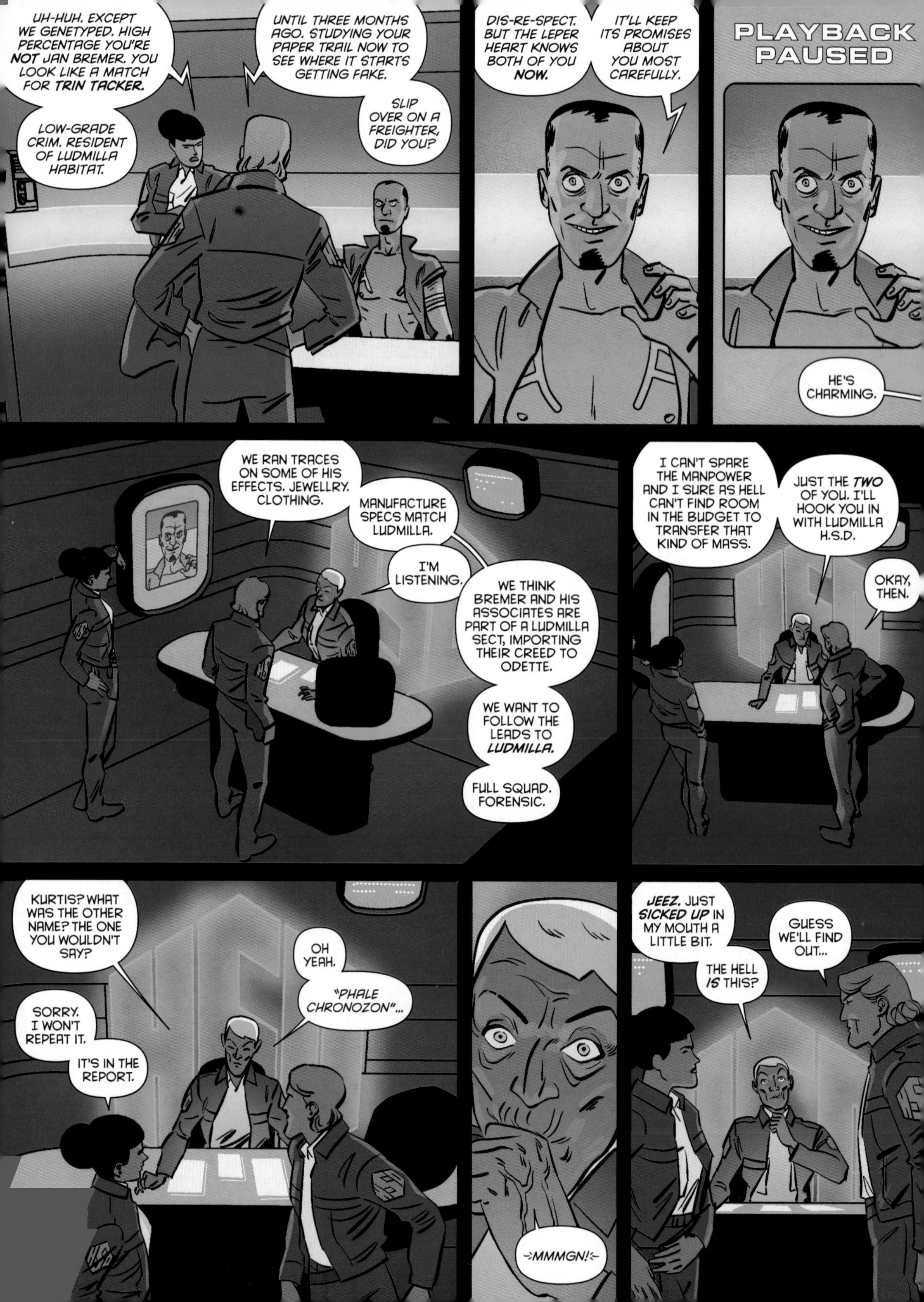
UH-HUH. EXCEPT WE GENETYPED. HIGH PERCENTAGE YOU'RE NOT JAN BREMER. YOU LOOK LIKE A MATCH FOR TRIN TACKER.
LOW-GRADE CRIM. RESIDENT OF LUDMILLA HABITAT.
UNTIL THREE MONTHS AGO. STUDYING YOUR PAPER TRAIL NOW TO SEE WHERE IT STARTS GETTING FAKE.
SLIP OVER ON A FREIGHTER, DID YOU?
DIS-RE-SPECT. BUT THE LEPER HEART KNOWS BOTH OF YOU NOW.
IT'LL KEEP ITS PROMISES ABOUT YOU MOST CAREFULLY.
PLAYBACK PAUSED
HE'S CHARMING.
WE RAN TRACES ON SOME OF HIS EFFECTS. JEWELLRY. CLOTHING.
MANUFACTURE SPECS MATCH LUDMILLA.
I'M LISTENING.
WE THINK BREMER AND HIS ASSOCIATES ARE PART OF A LUDMILLA SECT, IMPORTING THEIR CREED TO ODETTE.
WE WANT TO FOLLOW THE LEADS TO LUDMILLA.
FULL SQUAD. FORENSIC.
I CAN'T SPARE THE MANPOWER AND I SURE AS HELL CAN'T FIND ROOM IN THE BUDGET TO TRANSFER THAT KIND OF MASS.
JUST THE TWO OF YOU. I'LL HOOK YOU IN WITH LUDMILLA H.S.D.
OKAY, THEN.
KURTIS? WHAT WAS THE OTHER NAME? THE ONE YOU WOULDN'T SAY?
SORRY. I WON'T REPEAT IT.
IT'S IN THE REPORT.
OH YEAH.
"PHALE CHRONOZON"...
MMMGN!
JEEZ. JUST SICKED UP IN MY MOUTH A LITTLE BIT.
THE HELL IS THIS?
GUESS WE'LL FIND OUT...

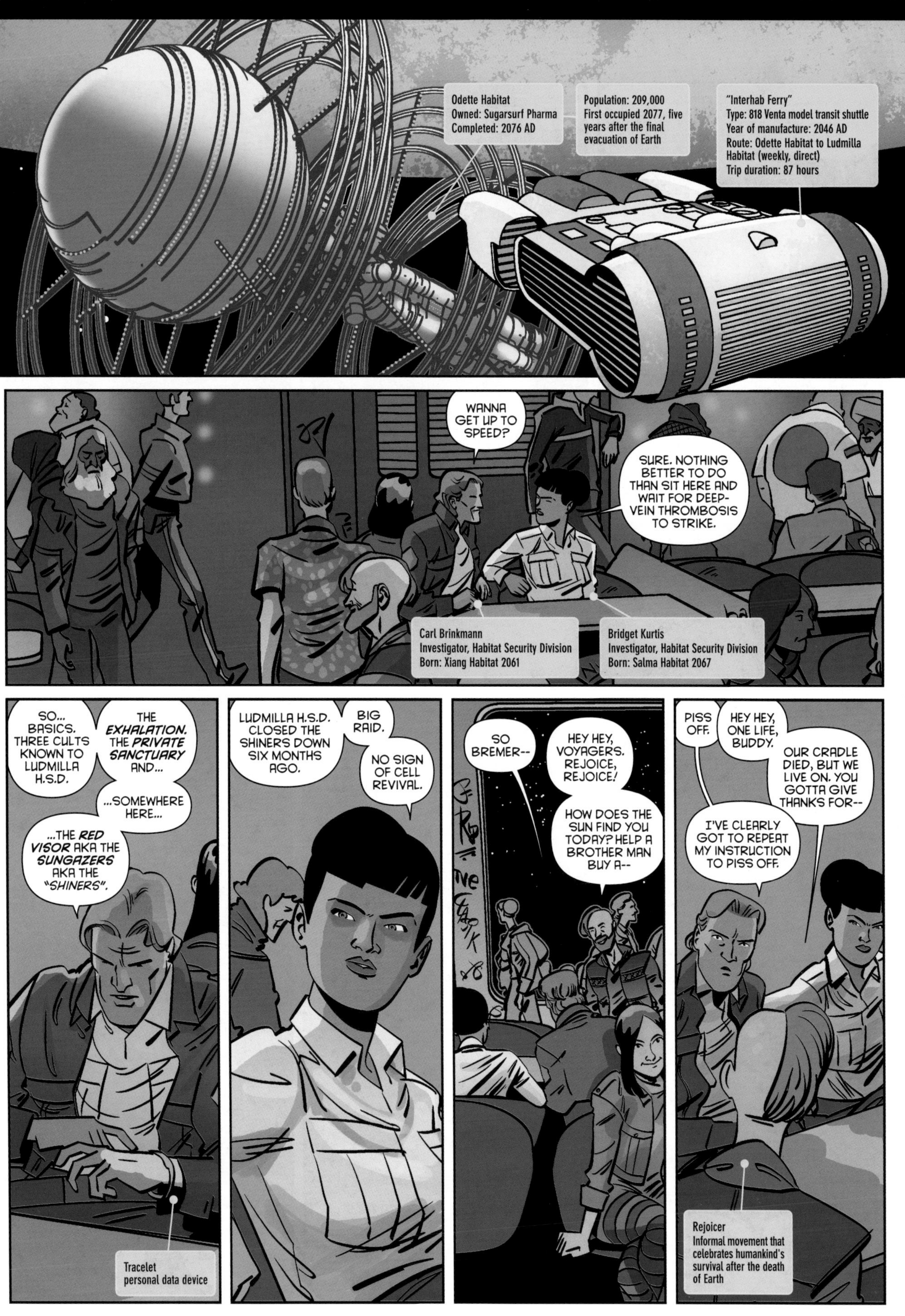

Odette Habitat
Owned: Sugarsurf Pharma
Completed: 2076 AD
Population: 209,000
First occupied 2077, five years after the final evacuation of Earth
"Interhab Ferry"
Type: 818 Venta model transit shuttle
Year of manufacture: 2046 AD
Route: Odette Habitat to Ludmilla Habitat (weekly, direct)
Trip duration: 87 hours
WANNA GET UP TO SPEED?
SURE. NOTHING BETTER TO DO THAN SIT HERE AND WAIT FOR DEEP-VEIN THROMBOSIS TO STRIKE.
Carl Brinkmann
Investigator, Habitat Security Division
Born: Xiang Habitat 2061
Bridget Kurtis
Investigator, Habitat Security Division
Born: Salma Habitat 2067
SO... BASICS. THREE CULTS KNOWN TO LUDMILLA H.S.D.
THE *EXHALATION*. THE *PRIVATE SANCTUARY* AND...
...SOMEWHERE HERE...
...THE *RED VISOR* AKA THE *SUNGAZERS* AKA THE "*SHINERS*".
Tracelet
personal data device
LUDMILLA H.S.D. CLOSED THE SHINERS DOWN SIX MONTHS AGO.
BIG RAID.
NO SIGN OF CELL REVIVAL.
SO BREMER--
HEY HEY, VOYAGERS. REJOICE, REJOICE!
HOW DOES THE SUN FIND YOU TODAY? HELP A BROTHER MAN BUY A--
PISS OFF.
HEY HEY, ONE LIFE, BUDDY.
OUR CRADLE DIED, BUT WE LIVE ON. YOU GOTTA GIVE THANKS FOR--
I'VE CLEARLY GOT TO REPEAT MY INSTRUCTION TO PISS OFF.
Rejoicer
Informal movement that celebrates humankind's survival after the death of Earth

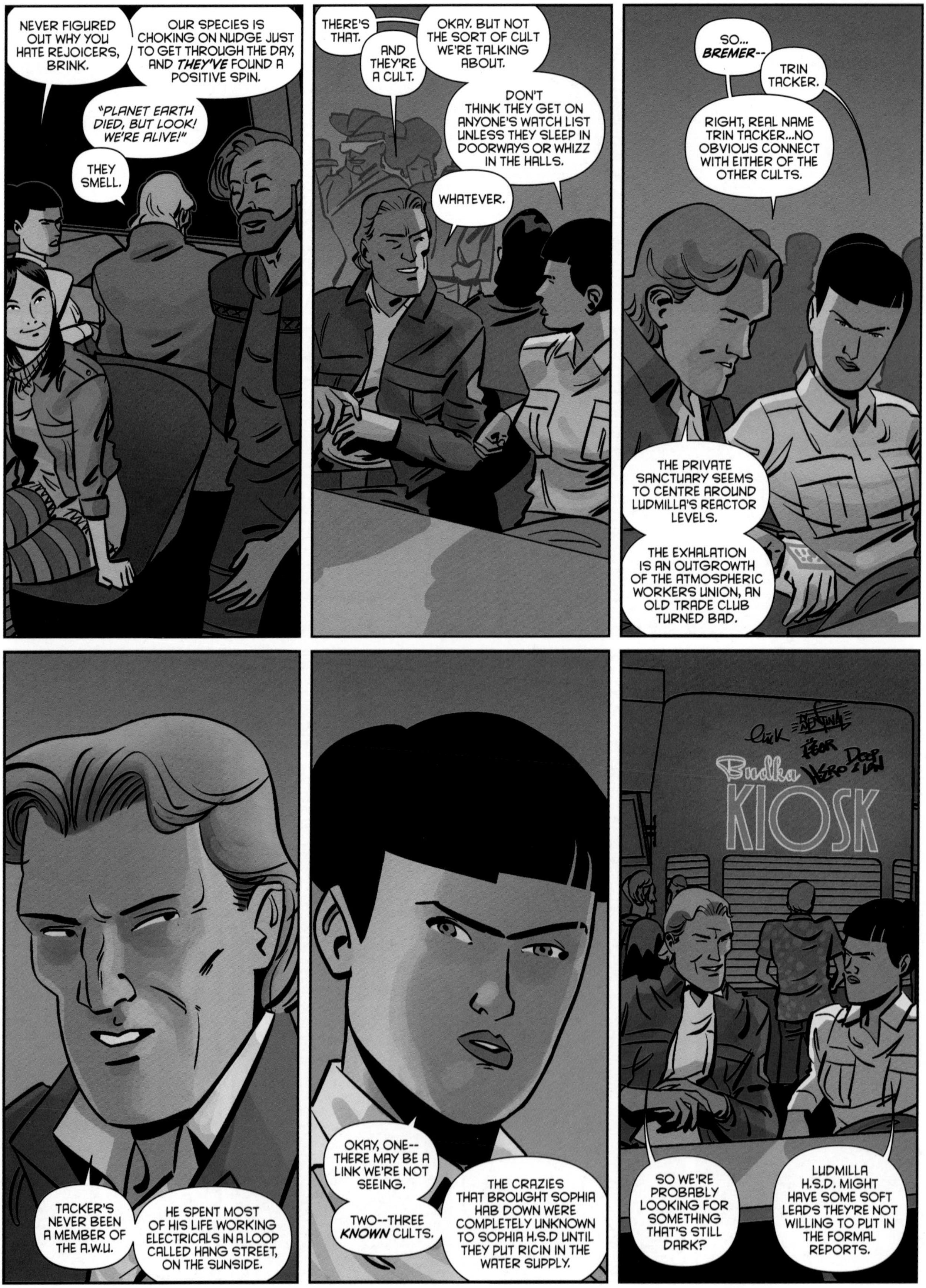
NEVER FIGURED OUT WHY YOU HATE REJOICERS, BRINK.
OUR SPECIES IS CHOKING ON NUDGE JUST TO GET THROUGH THE DAY, AND *THEY'VE* FOUND A POSITIVE SPIN.
"PLANET EARTH DIED, BUT LOOK! WE'RE ALIVE!"
THEY SMELL.
THERE'S THAT.
AND THEY'RE A CULT.
OKAY. BUT NOT THE SORT OF CULT WE'RE TALKING ABOUT.
DON'T THINK THEY GET ON ANYONE'S WATCH LIST UNLESS THEY SLEEP IN DOORWAYS OR WHIZZ IN THE HALLS.
WHATEVER.
SO... *BREMER--*
TRIN TACKER.
RIGHT, REAL NAME TRIN TACKER...NO OBVIOUS CONNECT WITH EITHER OF THE OTHER CULTS.
THE PRIVATE SANCTUARY SEEMS TO CENTRE AROUND LUDMILLA'S REACTOR LEVELS.
THE EXHALATION IS AN OUTGROWTH OF THE ATMOSPHERIC WORKERS UNION, AN OLD TRADE CLUB TURNED BAD.
TACKER'S NEVER BEEN A MEMBER OF THE A.W.U.
HE SPENT MOST OF HIS LIFE WORKING ELECTRICALS IN A LOOP CALLED HANG STREET, ON THE SUNSIDE.
OKAY, ONE-- THERE MAY BE A LINK WE'RE NOT SEEING.
TWO--THREE *KNOWN* CULTS.
THE CRAZIES THAT BROUGHT SOPHIA HAB DOWN WERE COMPLETELY UNKNOWN TO SOPHIA H.S.D UNTIL THEY PUT RICIN IN THE WATER SUPPLY.
Budka
KIOSK
SO WE'RE PROBABLY LOOKING FOR SOMETHING THAT'S STILL DARK?
LUDMILLA H.S.D. MIGHT HAVE SOME SOFT LEADS THEY'RE NOT WILLING TO PUT IN THE FORMAL REPORTS.

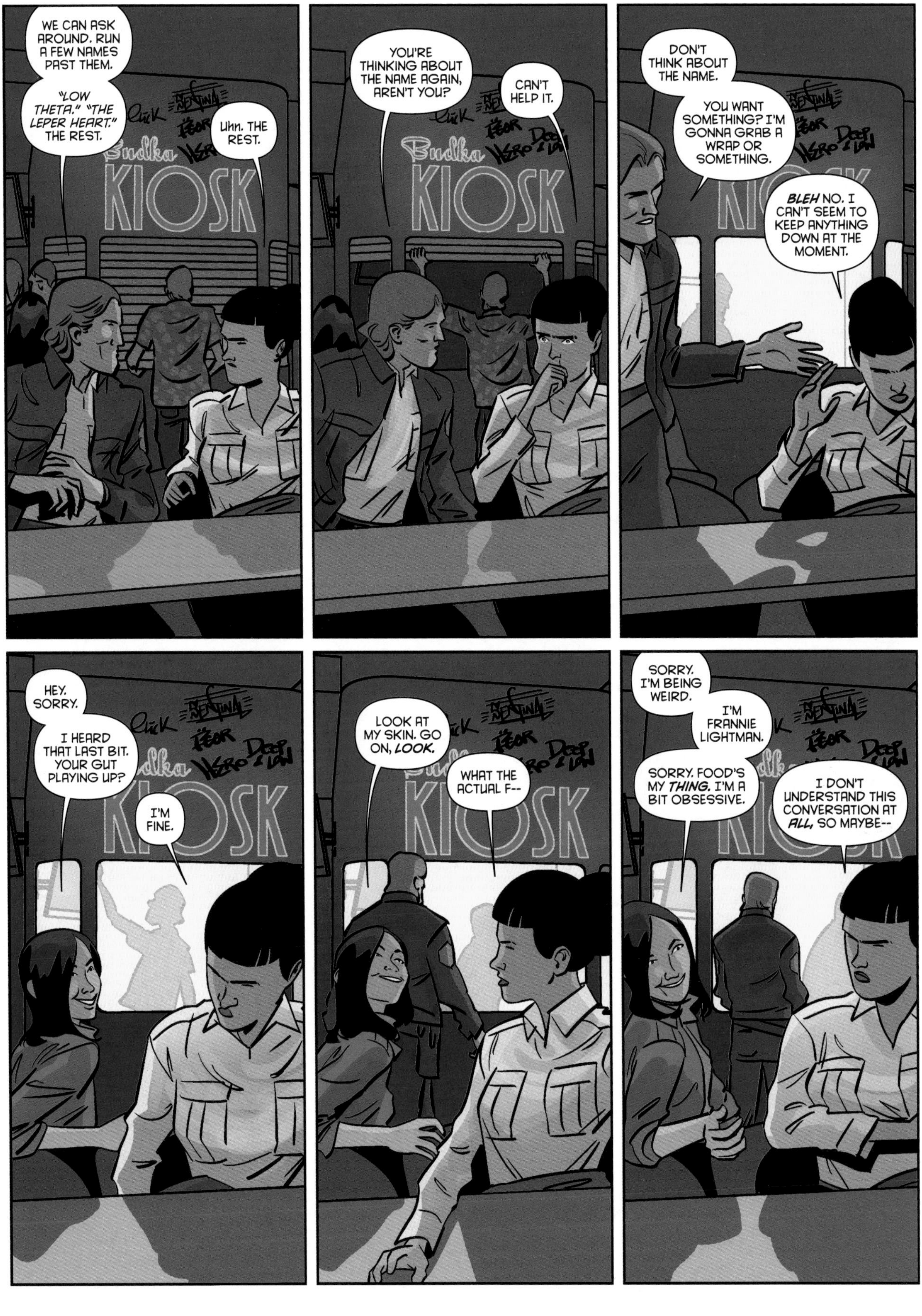
WE CAN ASK AROUND. RUN A FEW NAMES PAST THEM.
"LOW THETA." "THE LEPER HEART." THE REST.
Uhn. THE REST.
Budka KIOSK
YOU'RE THINKING ABOUT THE NAME AGAIN, AREN'T YOU?
CAN'T HELP IT.
DON'T THINK ABOUT THE NAME.
YOU WANT SOMETHING? I'M GONNA GRAB A WRAP OR SOMETHING.
BLEH NO. I CAN'T SEEM TO KEEP ANYTHING DOWN AT THE MOMENT.
HEY. SORRY.
I HEARD THAT LAST BIT. YOUR GUT PLAYING UP?
I'M FINE.
LOOK AT MY SKIN. GO ON, *LOOK.*
WHAT THE ACTUAL F--
SORRY. I'M BEING WEIRD.
I'M FRANNIE LIGHTMAN.
SORRY. FOOD'S MY *THING.* I'M A BIT OBSESSIVE.
I DON'T UNDERSTAND THIS CONVERSATION AT *ALL,* SO MAYBE--

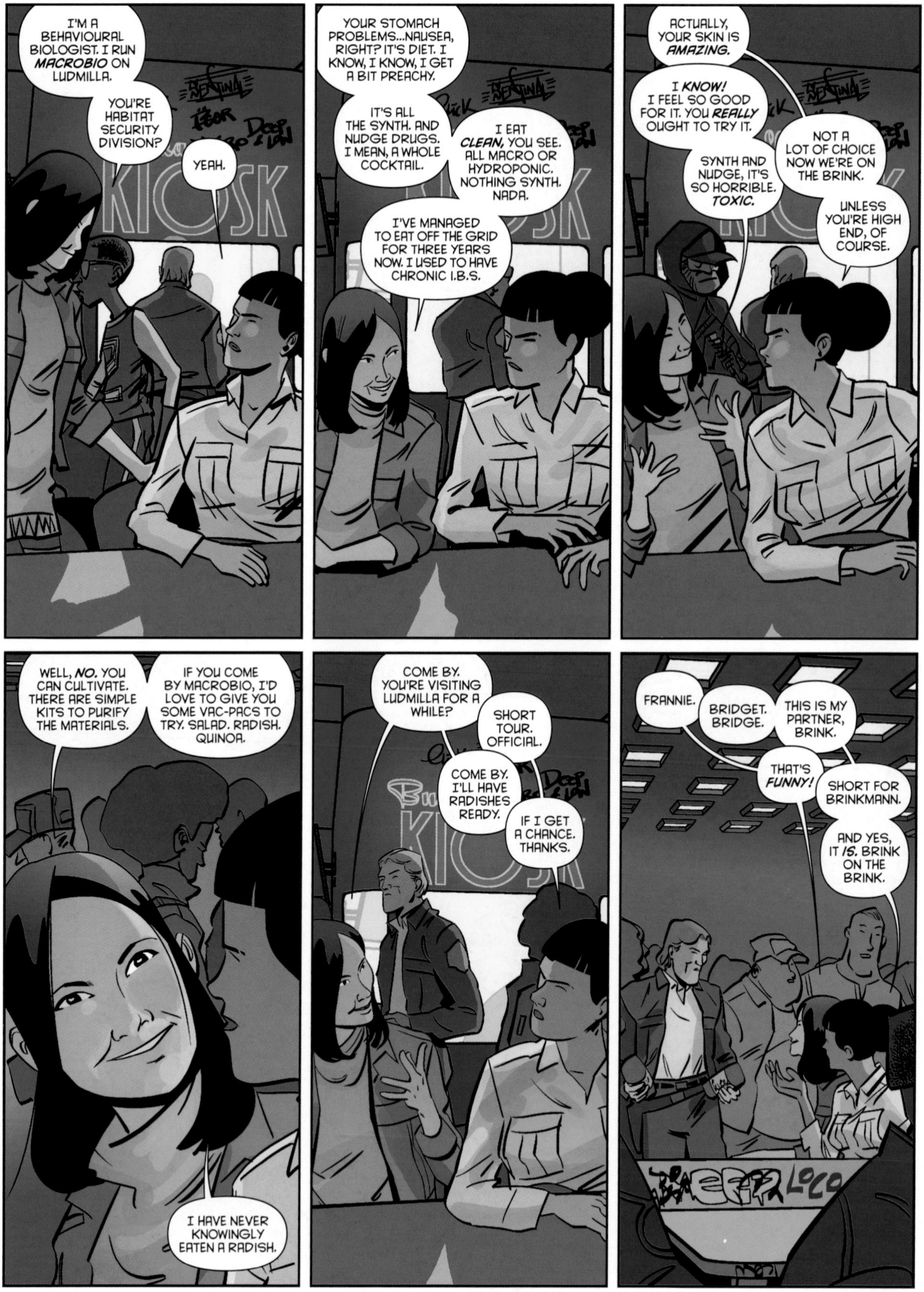
I'M A BEHAVIOURAL BIOLOGIST. I RUN *MACROBIO* ON LUDMILLA.
YOU'RE HABITAT SECURITY DIVISION?
YEAH.
KIOSK
YOUR STOMACH PROBLEMS...NAUSEA, RIGHT? IT'S DIET. I KNOW, I KNOW, I GET A BIT PREACHY.
IT'S ALL THE SYNTH. AND NUDGE DRUGS. I MEAN, A WHOLE COCKTAIL.
I EAT *CLEAN,* YOU SEE. ALL MACRO OR HYDROPONIC. NOTHING SYNTH. NADA.
I'VE MANAGED TO EAT OFF THE GRID FOR THREE YEARS NOW. I USED TO HAVE CHRONIC I.B.S.
ACTUALLY, YOUR SKIN IS *AMAZING.*
I *KNOW!* I FEEL SO GOOD FOR IT. YOU *REALLY* OUGHT TO TRY IT.
SYNTH AND NUDGE, IT'S SO HORRIBLE. *TOXIC.*
NOT A LOT OF CHOICE NOW WE'RE ON THE BRINK.
UNLESS YOU'RE HIGH END, OF COURSE.
WELL, *NO.* YOU CAN CULTIVATE. THERE ARE SIMPLE KITS TO PURIFY THE MATERIALS.
IF YOU COME BY MACROBIO, I'D LOVE TO GIVE YOU SOME VAC-PACS TO TRY. SALAD. RADISH. QUINOA.
I HAVE NEVER KNOWINGLY EATEN A RADISH.
COME BY. YOU'RE VISITING LUDMILLA FOR A WHILE?
SHORT TOUR. OFFICIAL.
COME BY. I'LL HAVE RADISHES READY.
IF I GET A CHANCE. THANKS.
KIOSK
FRANNIE.
BRIDGET. BRIDGE.
THIS IS MY PARTNER, BRINK.
THAT'S *FUNNY!*
SHORT FOR BRINKMANN.
AND YES, IT *IS.* BRINK ON THE BRINK.

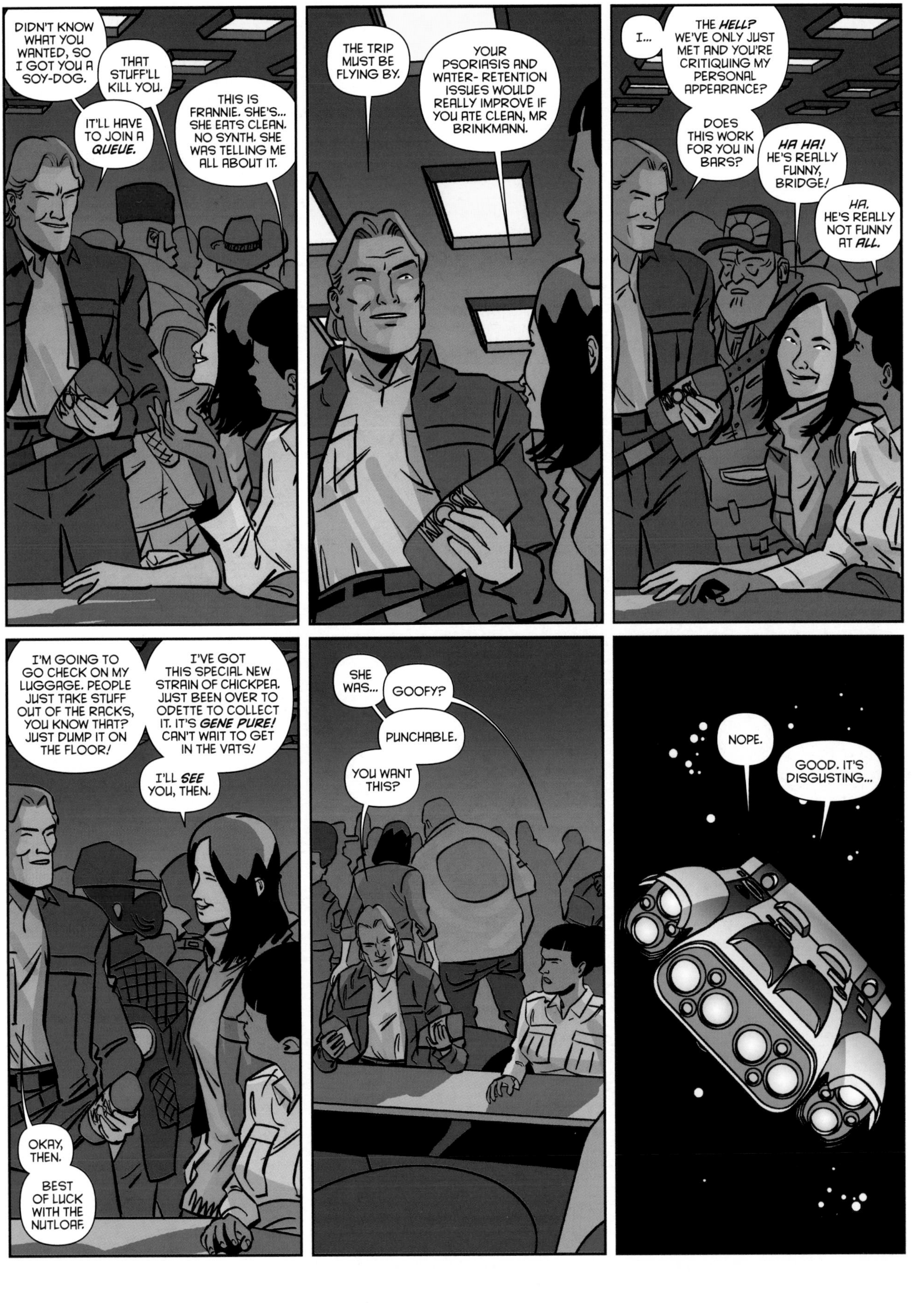
DIDN'T KNOW WHAT YOU WANTED, SO I GOT YOU A SOY-DOG.
THAT STUFF'LL KILL YOU.
IT'LL HAVE TO JOIN A *QUEUE.*
THIS IS FRANNIE. SHE'S... SHE EATS CLEAN. NO SYNTH. SHE WAS TELLING ME ALL ABOUT IT.
THE TRIP MUST BE FLYING BY.
YOUR PSORIASIS AND WATER- RETENTION ISSUES WOULD REALLY IMPROVE IF YOU ATE CLEAN, MR BRINKMANN.
I...
THE *HELL?* WE'VE ONLY JUST MET AND YOU'RE CRITIQUING MY PERSONAL APPEARANCE?
DOES THIS WORK FOR YOU IN BARS?
HA HA! HE'S REALLY FUNNY, BRIDGE!
HA. HE'S REALLY NOT FUNNY AT *ALL.*
I'M GOING TO GO CHECK ON MY LUGGAGE. PEOPLE JUST TAKE STUFF OUT OF THE RACKS, YOU KNOW THAT? JUST DUMP IT ON THE FLOOR!
I'VE GOT THIS SPECIAL NEW STRAIN OF CHICKPEA. JUST BEEN OVER TO ODETTE TO COLLECT IT. IT'S *GENE PURE!* CAN'T WAIT TO GET IN THE VATS!
I'LL *SEE* YOU, THEN.
OKAY, THEN.
BEST OF LUCK WITH THE NUTLOAF.
SHE WAS...
GOOFY?
PUNCHABLE.
YOU WANT THIS?
NOPE.
GOOD. IT'S DISGUSTING...

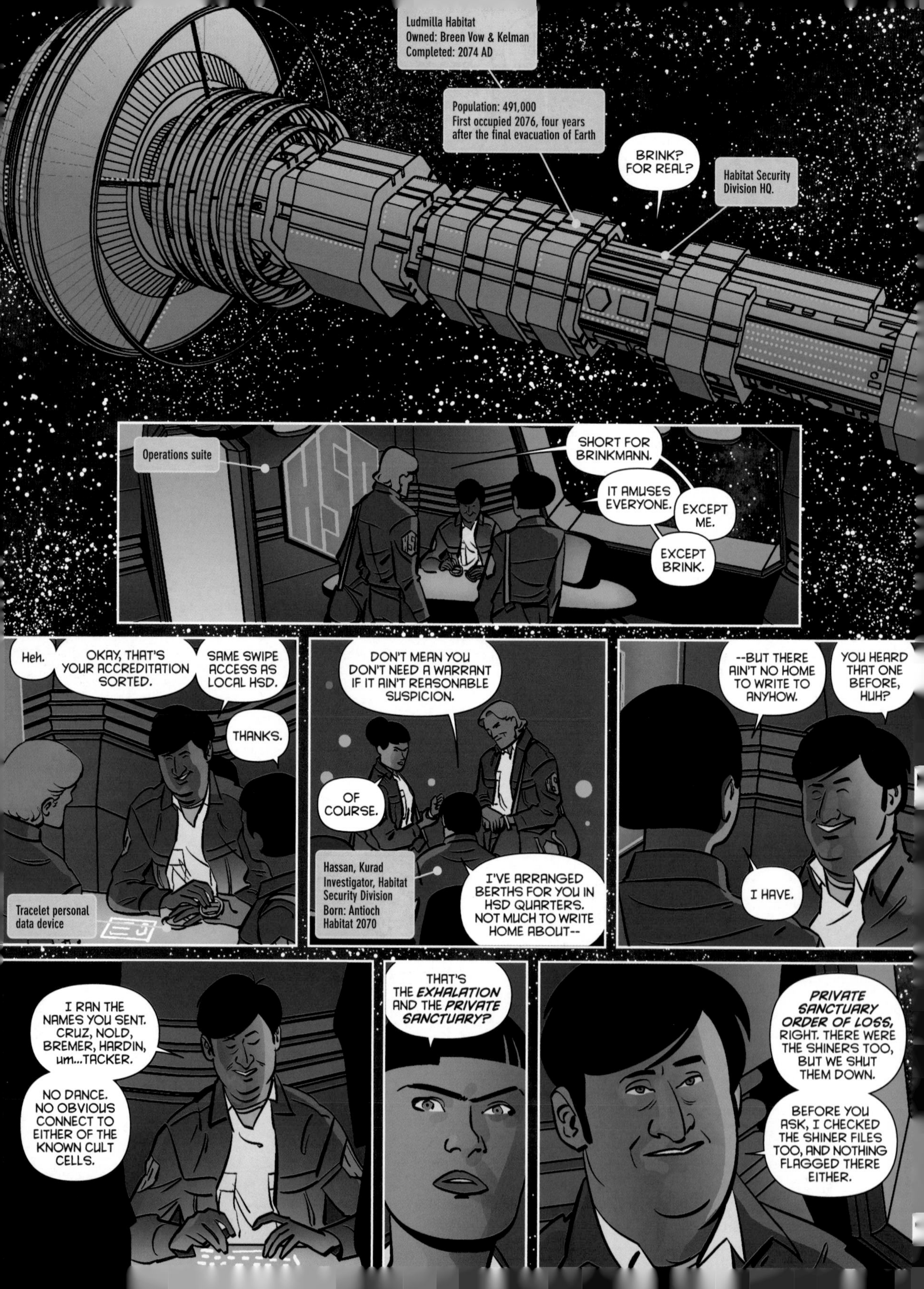
Ludmilla Habitat
Owned: Breen Vow & Kelman
Completed: 2074 AD
Population: 491,000
First occupied 2076, four years after the final evacuation of Earth
BRINK? FOR REAL?
Habitat Security Division HQ.
Operations suite
SHORT FOR BRINKMANN.
IT AMUSES EVERYONE.
EXCEPT ME.
EXCEPT BRINK.
Heh.
OKAY, THAT'S YOUR ACCREDITATION SORTED.
SAME SWIPE ACCESS AS LOCAL HSD.
THANKS.
Tracelet personal data device
DON'T MEAN YOU DON'T NEED A WARRANT IF IT AIN'T REASONABLE SUSPICION.
OF COURSE.
Hassan, Kurad
Investigator, Habitat Security Division
Born: Antioch Habitat 2070
I'VE ARRANGED BERTHS FOR YOU IN HSD QUARTERS. NOT MUCH TO WRITE HOME ABOUT--
--BUT THERE AIN'T NO HOME TO WRITE TO ANYHOW.
YOU HEARD THAT ONE BEFORE, HUH?
I HAVE.
I RAN THE NAMES YOU SENT. CRUZ, NOLD, BREMER, HARDIN, um...TACKER.
NO DANCE. NO OBVIOUS CONNECT TO EITHER OF THE KNOWN CULT CELLS.
THAT'S THE *EXHALATION* AND THE *PRIVATE SANCTUARY*?
PRIVATE SANCTUARY ORDER OF LOSS, RIGHT. THERE WERE THE SHINERS TOO, BUT WE SHUT THEM DOWN.
BEFORE YOU ASK, I CHECKED THE SHINER FILES TOO, AND NOTHING FLAGGED THERE EITHER.

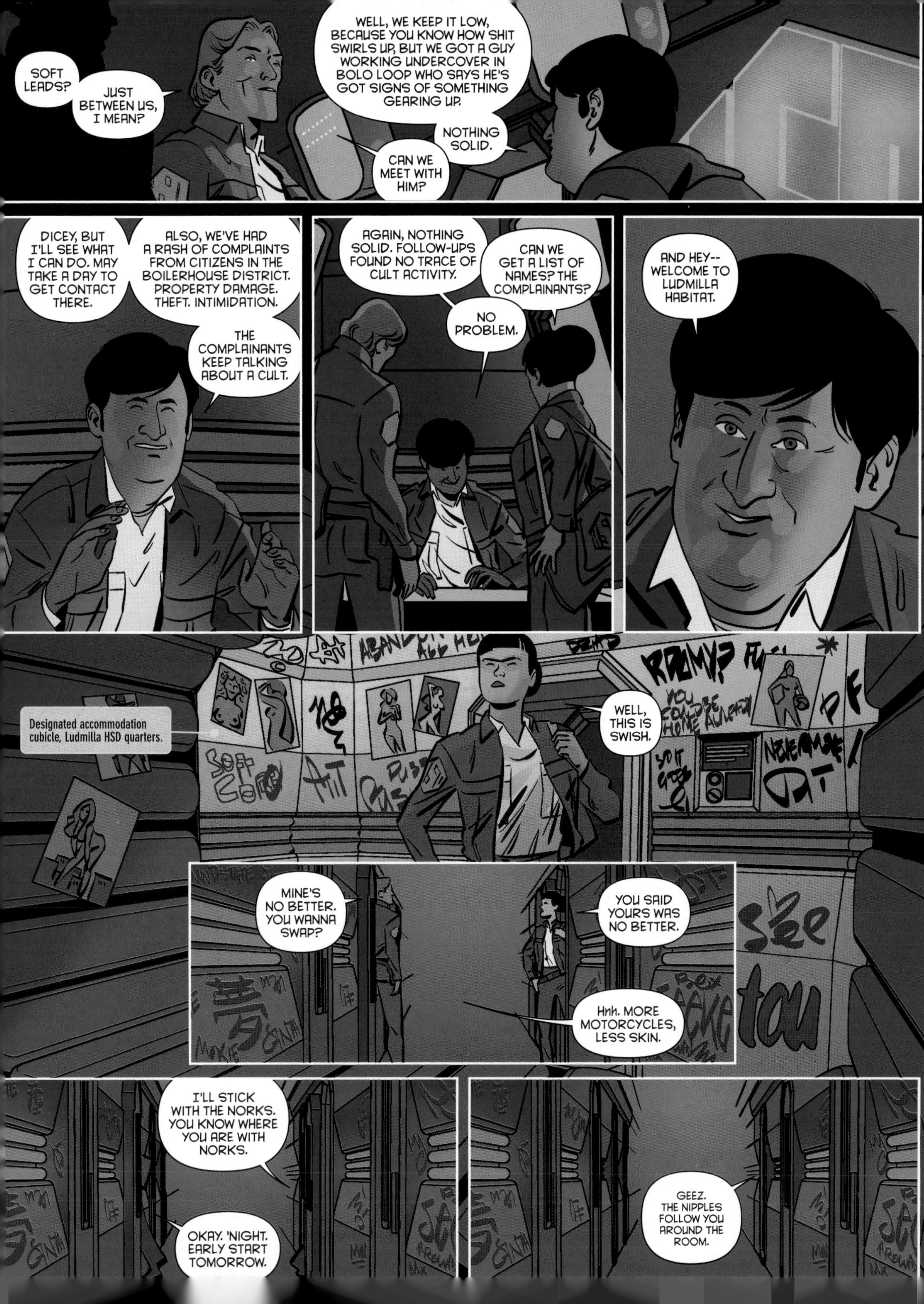
SOFT LEADS?
JUST BETWEEN US, I MEAN?
WELL, WE KEEP IT LOW, BECAUSE YOU KNOW HOW SHIT SWIRLS UP, BUT WE GOT A GUY WORKING UNDERCOVER IN BOLO LOOP WHO SAYS HE'S GOT SIGNS OF SOMETHING GEARING UP.
NOTHING SOLID.
CAN WE MEET WITH HIM?
DICEY, BUT I'LL SEE WHAT I CAN DO. MAY TAKE A DAY TO GET CONTACT THERE.
ALSO, WE'VE HAD A RASH OF COMPLAINTS FROM CITIZENS IN THE BOILERHOUSE DISTRICT. PROPERTY DAMAGE. THEFT. INTIMIDATION.
THE COMPLAINANTS KEEP TALKING ABOUT A CULT.
AGAIN, NOTHING SOLID. FOLLOW-UPS FOUND NO TRACE OF CULT ACTIVITY.
CAN WE GET A LIST OF NAMES? THE COMPLAINANTS?
NO PROBLEM.
AND HEY-- WELCOME TO LUDMILLA HABITAT.
Designated accommodation cubicle, Ludmilla HSD quarters.
WELL, THIS IS SWISH.
MINE'S NO BETTER. YOU WANNA SWAP?
YOU SAID YOURS WAS NO BETTER.
Hnh. MORE MOTORCYCLES, LESS SKIN.
I'LL STICK WITH THE NORKS. YOU KNOW WHERE YOU ARE WITH NORKS.
OKAY. 'NIGHT. EARLY START TOMORROW.
GEEZ. THE NIPPLES FOLLOW YOU AROUND THE ROOM.

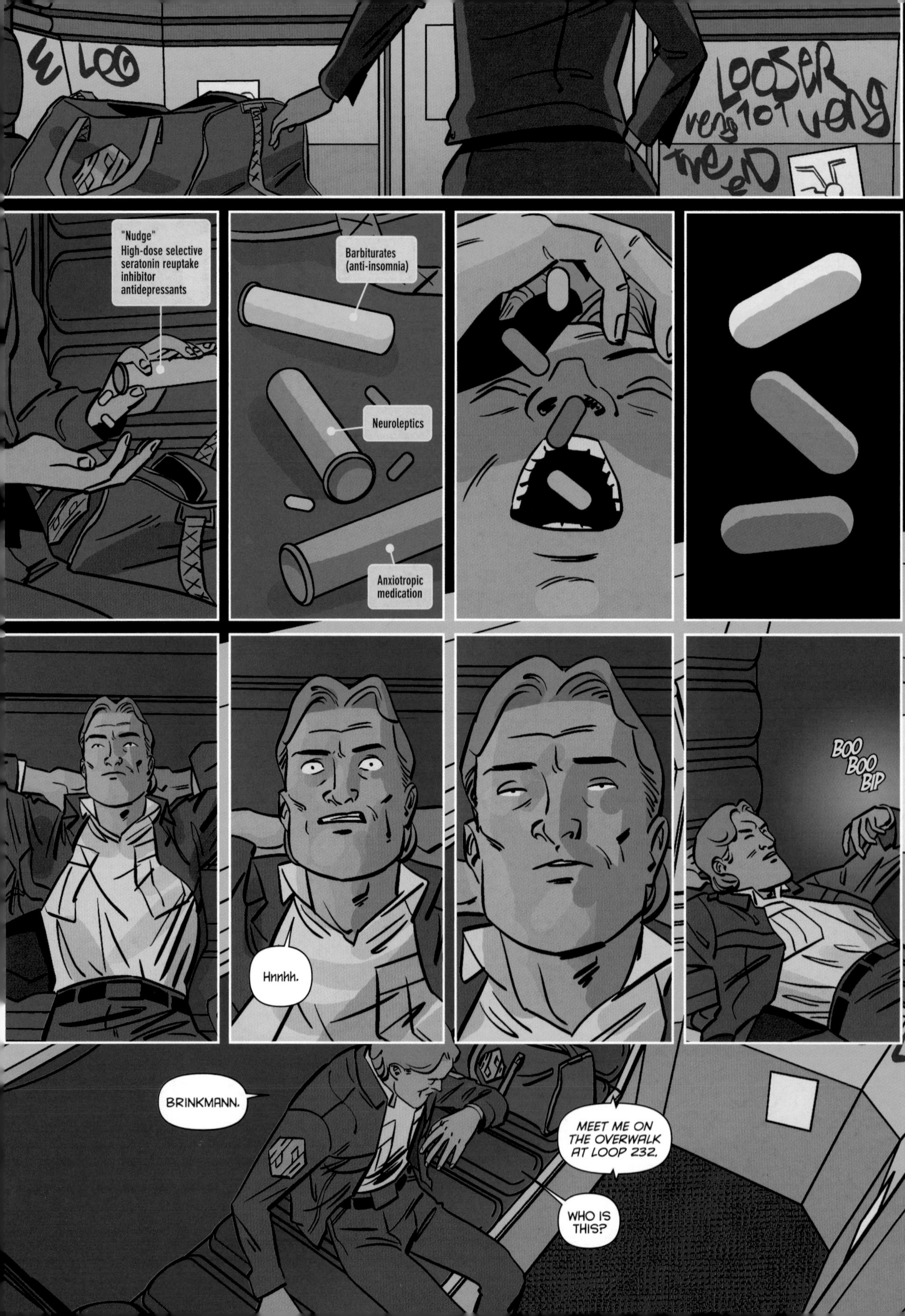
LOOSER
"Nudge" High-dose selective seratonin reuptake inhibitor antidepressants
Barbiturates (anti-insomnia)
Neuroleptics
Anxiotropic medication
Hnnhh.
BOO BOO BIP
BRINKMANN.
MEET ME ON THE OVERWALK AT LOOP 232.
WHO IS THIS?

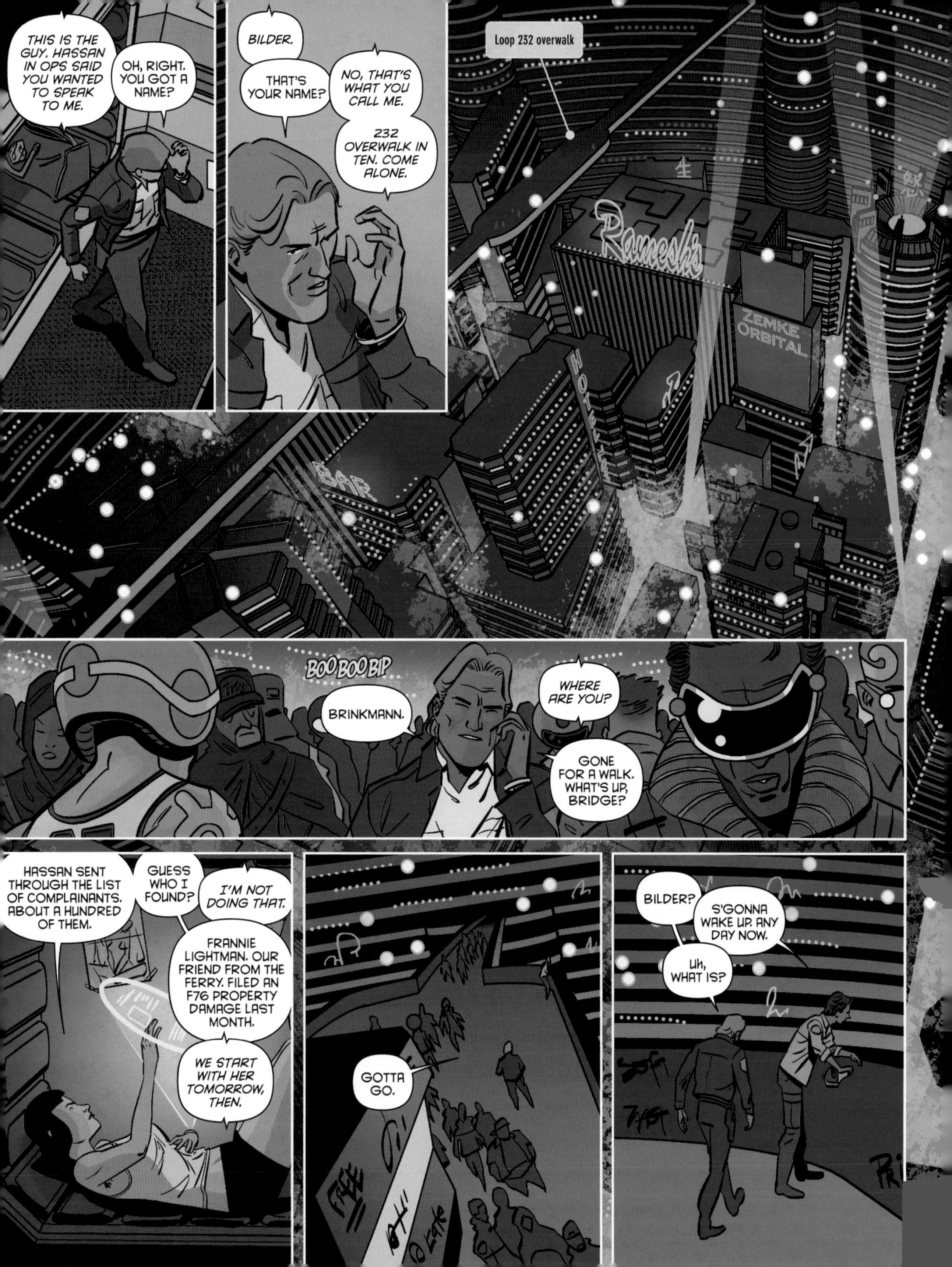
THIS IS THE GUY. HASSAN IN OPS SAID YOU WANTED TO SPEAK TO ME.
OH, RIGHT. YOU GOT A NAME?
BILDER.
THAT'S YOUR NAME?
NO, THAT'S WHAT YOU CALL ME.
232 OVERWALK IN TEN. COME ALONE.
Loop 232 overwalk
Ramesh's
ZEMKE ORBITAL
HOTEL
BAR
BOO BOO BIP
BRINKMANN.
WHERE ARE YOU?
GONE FOR A WALK. WHAT'S UP, BRIDGE?
HASSAN SENT THROUGH THE LIST OF COMPLAINANTS. ABOUT A HUNDRED OF THEM.
GUESS WHO I FOUND?
I'M NOT DOING THAT.
FRANNIE LIGHTMAN. OUR FRIEND FROM THE FERRY. FILED AN F76 PROPERTY DAMAGE LAST MONTH.
WE START WITH HER TOMORROW, THEN.
GOTTA GO.
BILDER?
S'GONNA WAKE UP. ANY DAY NOW.
UH, WHAT IS?

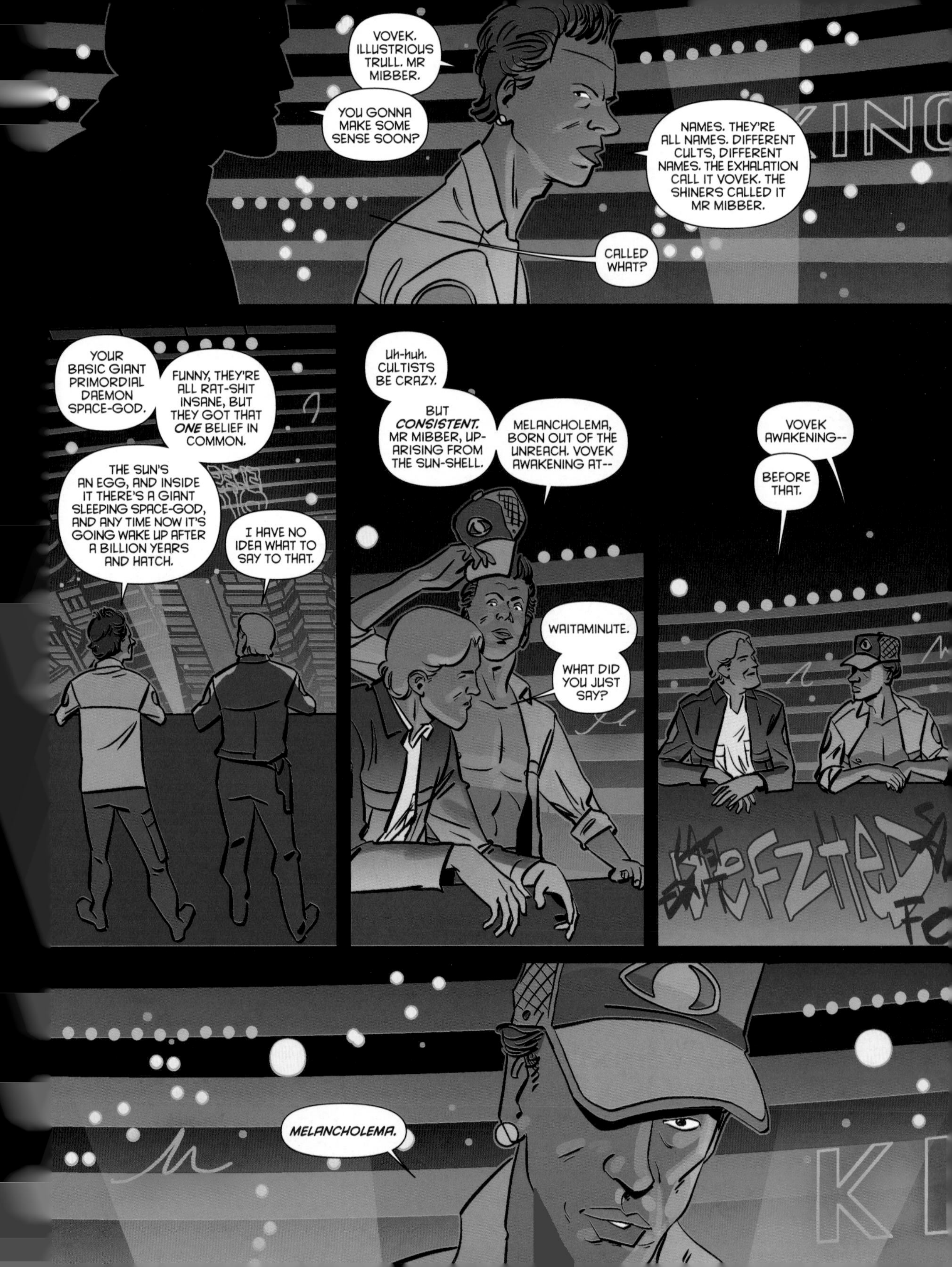

VOVEK. ILLUSTRIOUS TRULL. MR MIBBER.
YOU GONNA MAKE SOME SENSE SOON?
NAMES. THEY'RE ALL NAMES. DIFFERENT CULTS, DIFFERENT NAMES. THE EXHALATION CALL IT VOVEK. THE SHINERS CALLED IT MR MIBBER.
CALLED WHAT?
YOUR BASIC GIANT PRIMORDIAL DAEMON SPACE-GOD.
FUNNY, THEY'RE ALL RAT-SHIT INSANE, BUT THEY GOT THAT ONE BELIEF IN COMMON.
THE SUN'S AN EGG, AND INSIDE IT THERE'S A GIANT SLEEPING SPACE-GOD, AND ANY TIME NOW IT'S GOING WAKE UP AFTER A BILLION YEARS AND HATCH.
I HAVE NO IDEA WHAT TO SAY TO THAT.
Uh-huh. CULTISTS BE CRAZY.
BUT CONSISTENT. MR MIBBER, UP-ARISING FROM THE SUN-SHELL.
MELANCHOLEMA, BORN OUT OF THE UNREACH. VOVEK AWAKENING AT--
WAITAMINUTE.
WHAT DID YOU JUST SAY?
VOVEK AWAKENING--
BEFORE THAT.
MELANCHOLEMA.

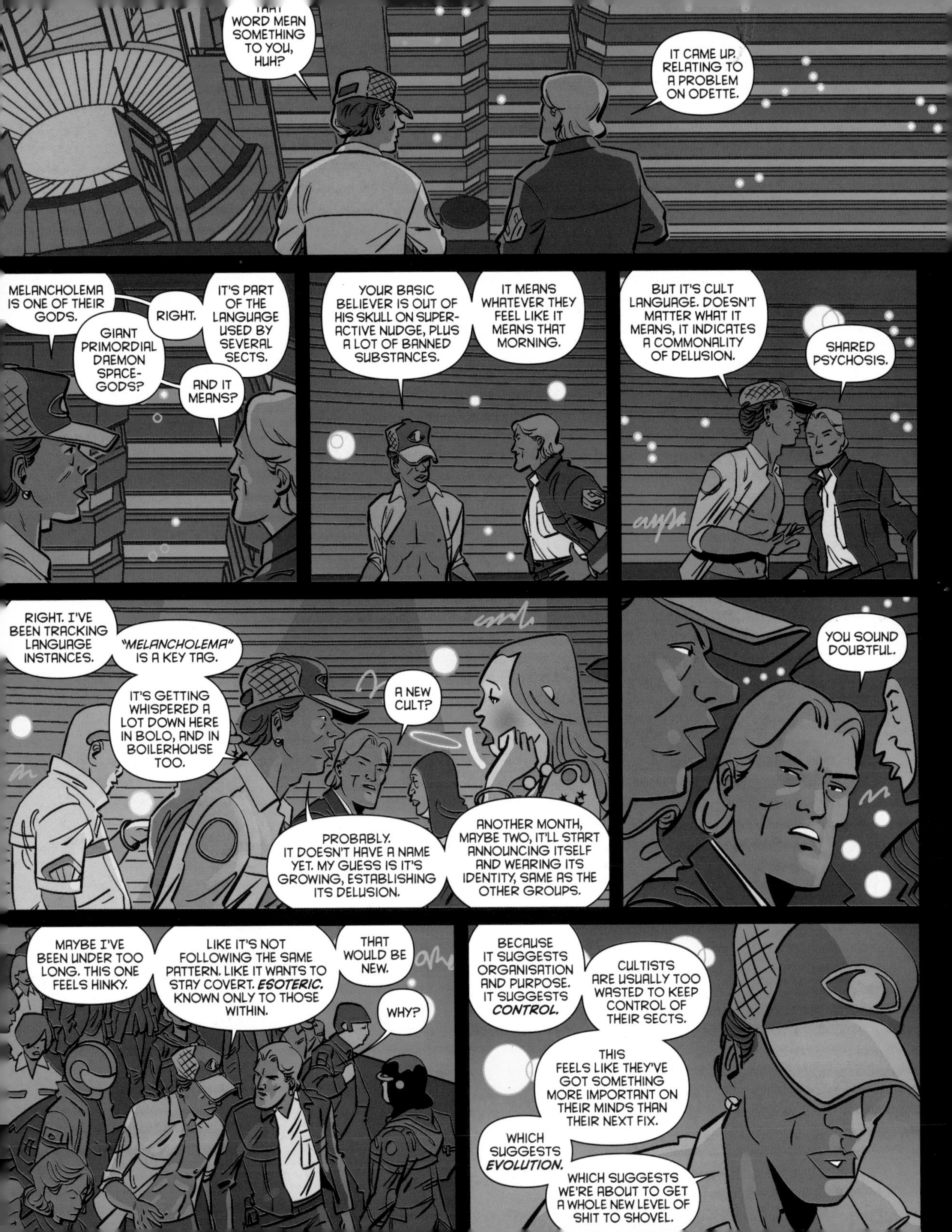

WORD MEAN SOMETHING TO YOU, HUH?
IT CAME UP. RELATING TO A PROBLEM ON ODETTE.
MELANCHOLEMA IS ONE OF THEIR GODS.
GIANT PRIMORDIAL DAEMON SPACE-GODS?
RIGHT.
IT'S PART OF THE LANGUAGE USED BY SEVERAL SECTS.
AND IT MEANS?
YOUR BASIC BELIEVER IS OUT OF HIS SKULL ON SUPER-ACTIVE NUDGE, PLUS A LOT OF BANNED SUBSTANCES.
IT MEANS WHATEVER THEY FEEL LIKE IT MEANS THAT MORNING.
BUT IT'S CULT LANGUAGE. DOESN'T MATTER WHAT IT MEANS, IT INDICATES A COMMONALITY OF DELUSION.
SHARED PSYCHOSIS.
RIGHT. I'VE BEEN TRACKING LANGUAGE INSTANCES.
"MELANCHOLEMA" IS A KEY TAG.
IT'S GETTING WHISPERED A LOT DOWN HERE IN BOLO, AND IN BOILERHOUSE TOO.
A NEW CULT?
PROBABLY. IT DOESN'T HAVE A NAME YET. MY GUESS IS IT'S GROWING, ESTABLISHING ITS DELUSION.
ANOTHER MONTH, MAYBE TWO, IT'LL START ANNOUNCING ITSELF AND WEARING ITS IDENTITY, SAME AS THE OTHER GROUPS.
YOU SOUND DOUBTFUL.
MAYBE I'VE BEEN UNDER TOO LONG. THIS ONE FEELS HINKY.
LIKE IT'S NOT FOLLOWING THE SAME PATTERN. LIKE IT WANTS TO STAY COVERT. ***ESOTERIC.*** KNOWN ONLY TO THOSE WITHIN.
THAT WOULD BE NEW.
WHY?
BECAUSE IT SUGGESTS ORGANISATION AND PURPOSE. IT SUGGESTS ***CONTROL.***
CULTISTS ARE USUALLY TOO WASTED TO KEEP CONTROL OF THEIR SECTS.
THIS FEELS LIKE THEY'VE GOT SOMETHING MORE IMPORTANT ON THEIR MINDS THAN THEIR NEXT FIX.
WHICH SUGGESTS ***EVOLUTION.***
WHICH SUGGESTS WE'RE ABOUT TO GET A WHOLE NEW LEVEL OF SHIT TO SHOVEL.

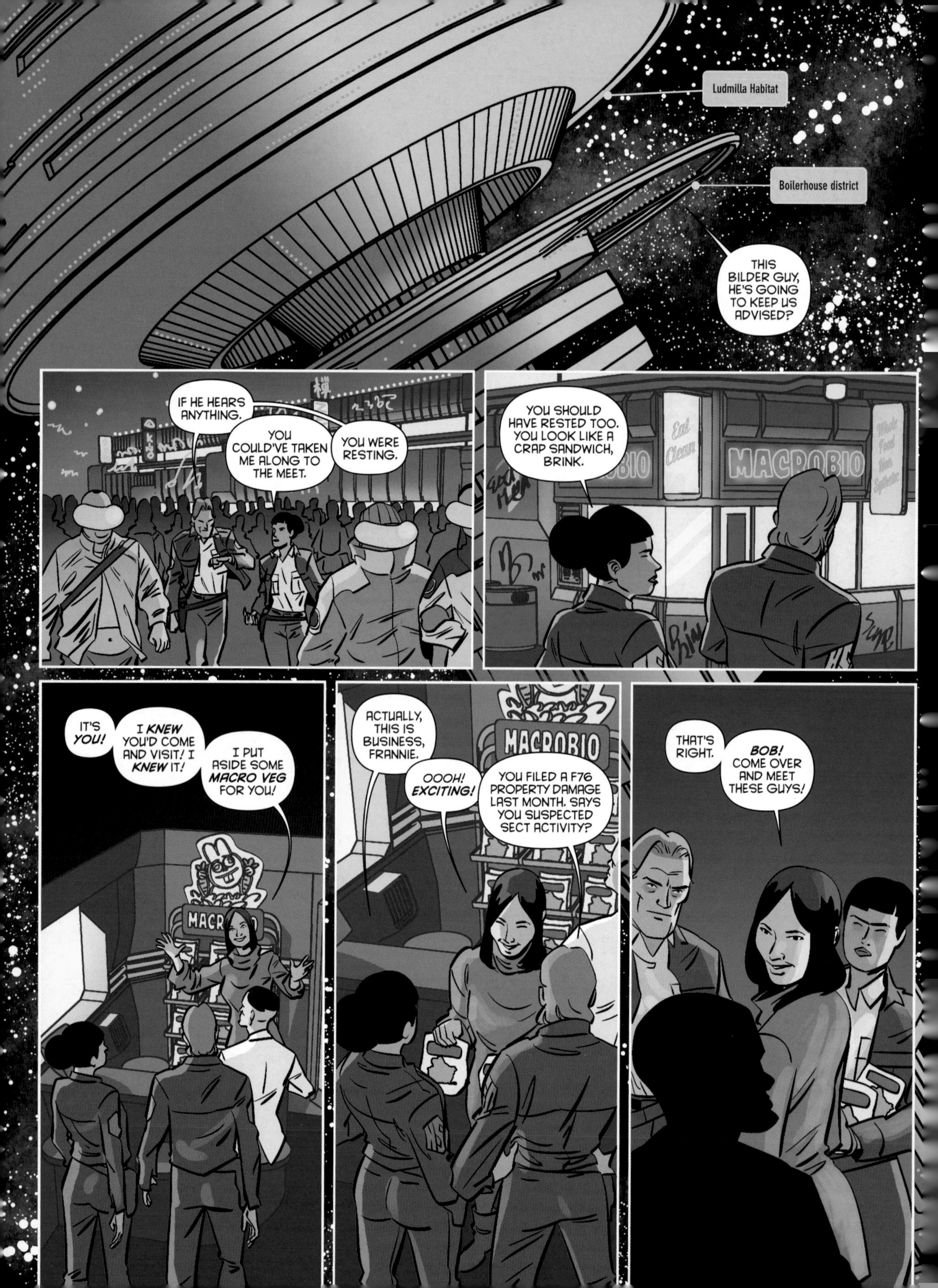

Ludmilla Habitat
Boilerhouse district
THIS BILDER GUY, HE'S GOING TO KEEP US ADVISED?
IF HE HEARS ANYTHING.
YOU COULD'VE TAKEN ME ALONG TO THE MEET.
YOU WERE RESTING.
YOU SHOULD HAVE RESTED TOO. YOU LOOK LIKE A CRAP SANDWICH, BRINK.
MACROBIO
Eat Clean
IT'S *YOU!*
I ***KNEW*** YOU'D COME AND VISIT! I ***KNEW*** IT!
I PUT ASIDE SOME ***MACRO VEG*** FOR YOU!
MACROBIO
ACTUALLY, THIS IS BUSINESS, FRANNIE.
OOOH! ***EXCITING!***
YOU FILED A F76 PROPERTY DAMAGE LAST MONTH. SAYS YOU SUSPECTED SECT ACTIVITY?
THAT'S RIGHT.
BOB! COME OVER AND MEET THESE GUYS!

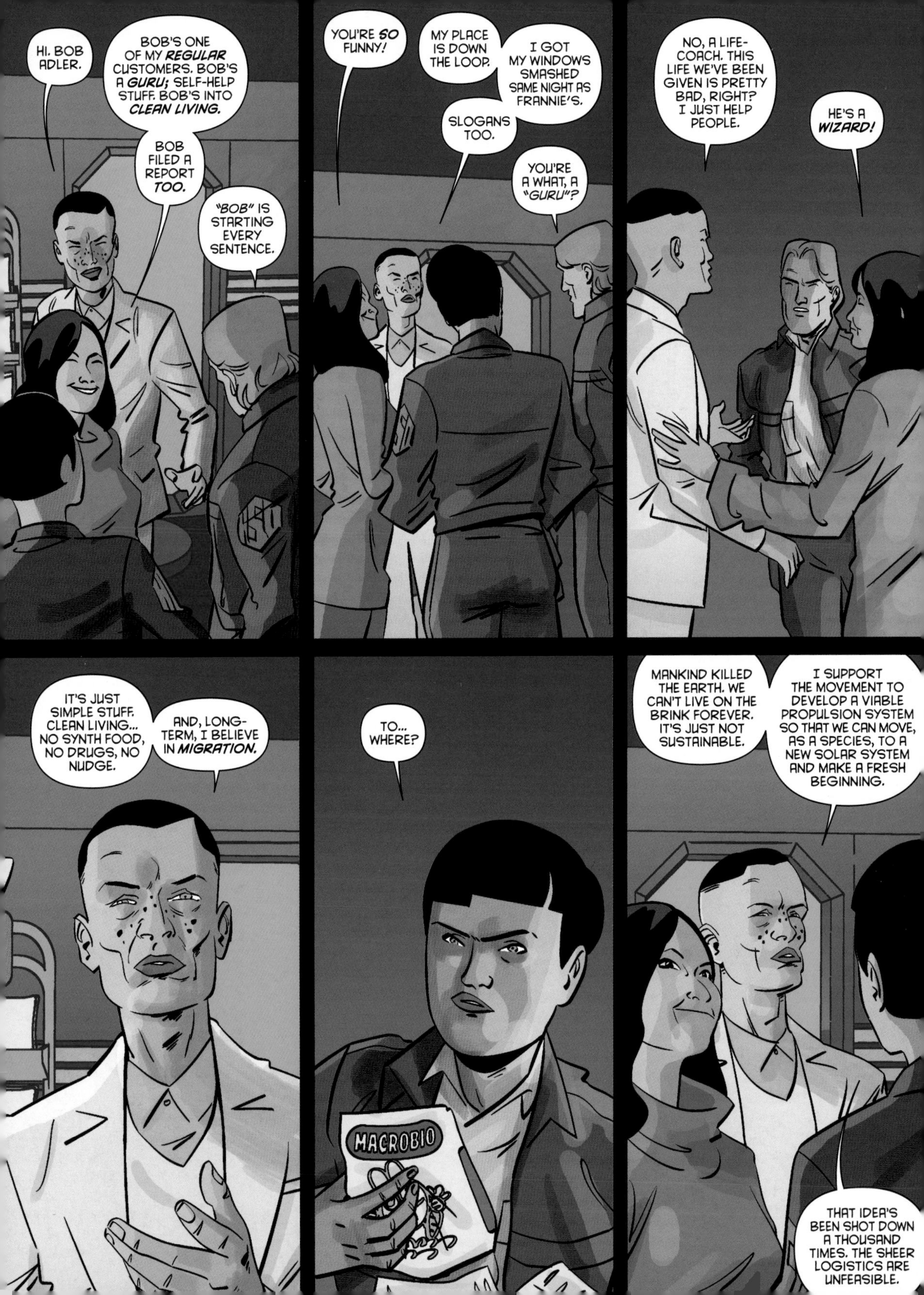
HI. BOB ADLER.
BOB'S ONE OF MY *REGULAR* CUSTOMERS. BOB'S A *GURU*; SELF-HELP STUFF. BOB'S INTO *CLEAN LIVING.*
BOB FILED A REPORT *TOO.*
"BOB" IS STARTING EVERY SENTENCE.
YOU'RE *SO* FUNNY!
MY PLACE IS DOWN THE LOOP.
I GOT MY WINDOWS SMASHED SAME NIGHT AS FRANNIE'S.
SLOGANS TOO.
YOU'RE A WHAT, A *"GURU"*?
NO, A LIFE-COACH. THIS LIFE WE'VE BEEN GIVEN IS PRETTY BAD, RIGHT? I JUST HELP PEOPLE.
HE'S A *WIZARD!*
IT'S JUST SIMPLE STUFF. CLEAN LIVING... NO SYNTH FOOD, NO DRUGS, NO NUDGE.
AND, LONG-TERM, I BELIEVE IN *MIGRATION.*
TO... WHERE?
MACROBIO
MANKIND KILLED THE EARTH. WE CAN'T LIVE ON THE BRINK FOREVER. IT'S JUST NOT SUSTAINABLE.
I SUPPORT THE MOVEMENT TO DEVELOP A VIABLE PROPULSION SYSTEM SO THAT WE CAN MOVE, AS A SPECIES, TO A NEW SOLAR SYSTEM AND MAKE A FRESH BEGINNING.
THAT IDEA'S BEEN SHOT DOWN A THOUSAND TIMES. THE SHEER LOGISTICS ARE UNFEASIBLE.

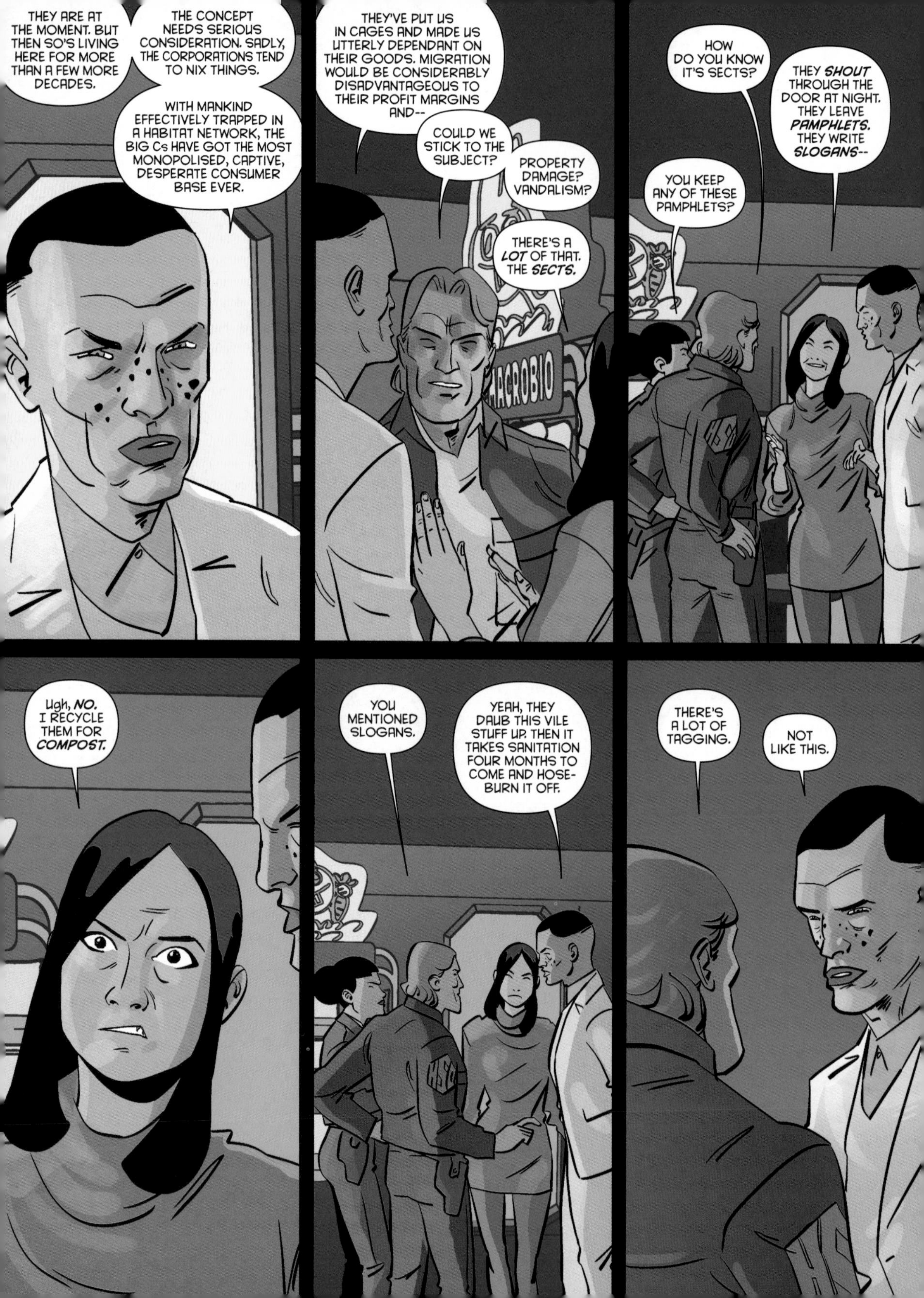
THEY ARE AT THE MOMENT. BUT THEN SO'S LIVING HERE FOR MORE THAN A FEW MORE DECADES.
THE CONCEPT NEEDS SERIOUS CONSIDERATION. SADLY, THE CORPORATIONS TEND TO NIX THINGS.
WITH MANKIND EFFECTIVELY TRAPPED IN A HABITAT NETWORK, THE BIG Cs HAVE GOT THE MOST MONOPOLISED, CAPTIVE, DESPERATE CONSUMER BASE EVER.
THEY'VE PUT US IN CAGES AND MADE US UTTERLY DEPENDANT ON THEIR GOODS. MIGRATION WOULD BE CONSIDERABLY DISADVANTAGEOUS TO THEIR PROFIT MARGINS AND--
COULD WE STICK TO THE SUBJECT?
PROPERTY DAMAGE? VANDALISM?
THERE'S A *LOT* OF THAT. THE *SECTS.*
MACROBIO
HOW DO YOU KNOW IT'S SECTS?
THEY *SHOUT* THROUGH THE DOOR AT NIGHT. THEY LEAVE *PAMPHLETS.* THEY WRITE *SLOGANS*--
YOU KEEP ANY OF THESE PAMPHLETS?
Ugh, *NO.* I RECYCLE THEM FOR *COMPOST.*
YOU MENTIONED SLOGANS.
YEAH, THEY DAUB THIS VILE STUFF UP. THEN IT TAKES SANITATION FOUR MONTHS TO COME AND HOSE-BURN IT OFF.
THERE'S A LOT OF TAGGING.
NOT LIKE THIS.

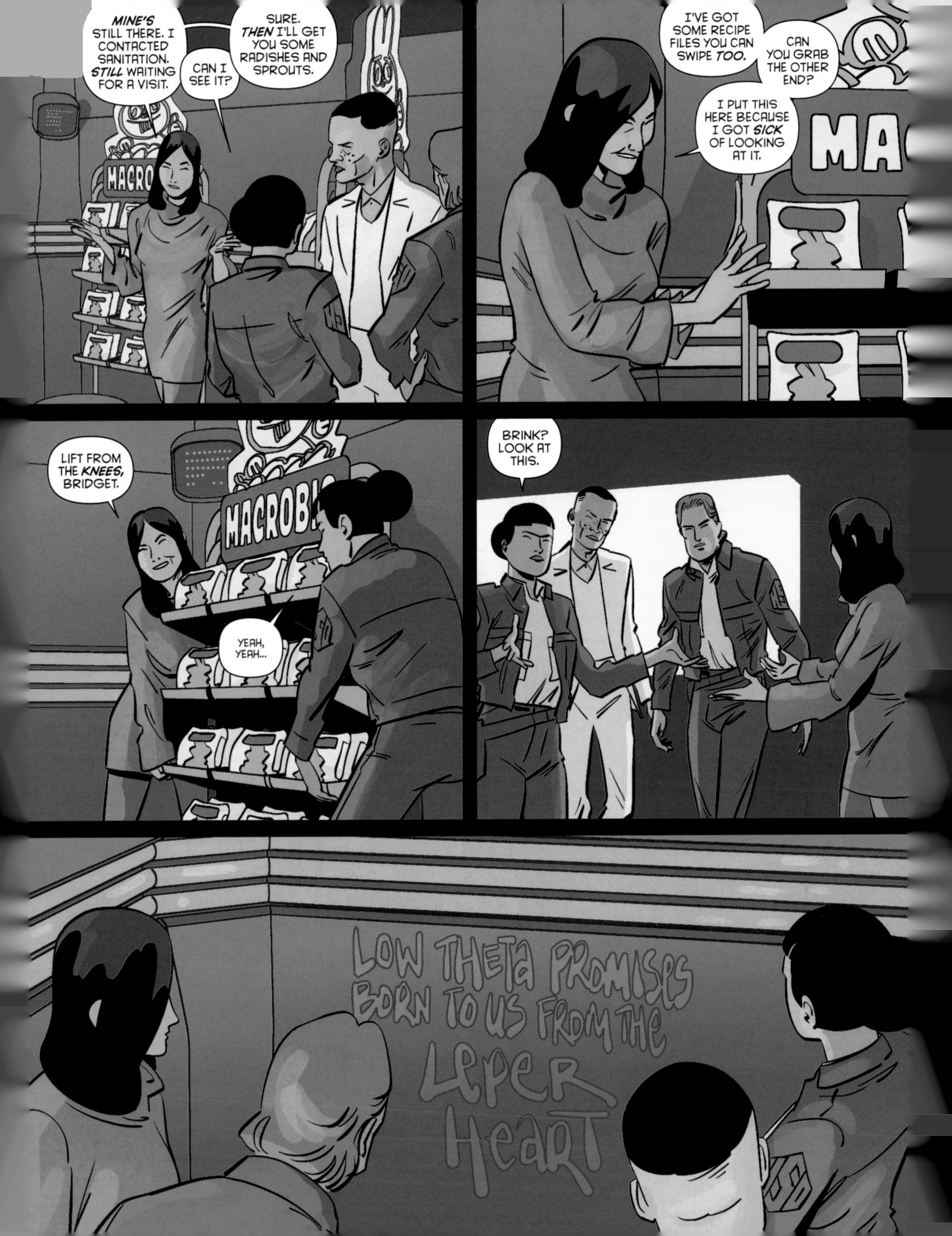
MINE'S STILL THERE. I CONTACTED SANITATION. STILL WAITING FOR A VISIT.
SURE. THEN I'LL GET YOU SOME RADISHES AND SPROUTS.
CAN I SEE IT?
MACROBI
I'VE GOT SOME RECIPE FILES YOU CAN SWIPE TOO.
CAN YOU GRAB THE OTHER END?
I PUT THIS HERE BECAUSE I GOT SICK OF LOOKING AT IT.
LIFT FROM THE KNEES, BRIDGET.
MACROBI
YEAH, YEAH...
BRINK? LOOK AT THIS.
LOW THETA PROMISES BORN TO US FROM THE LEPER HEART

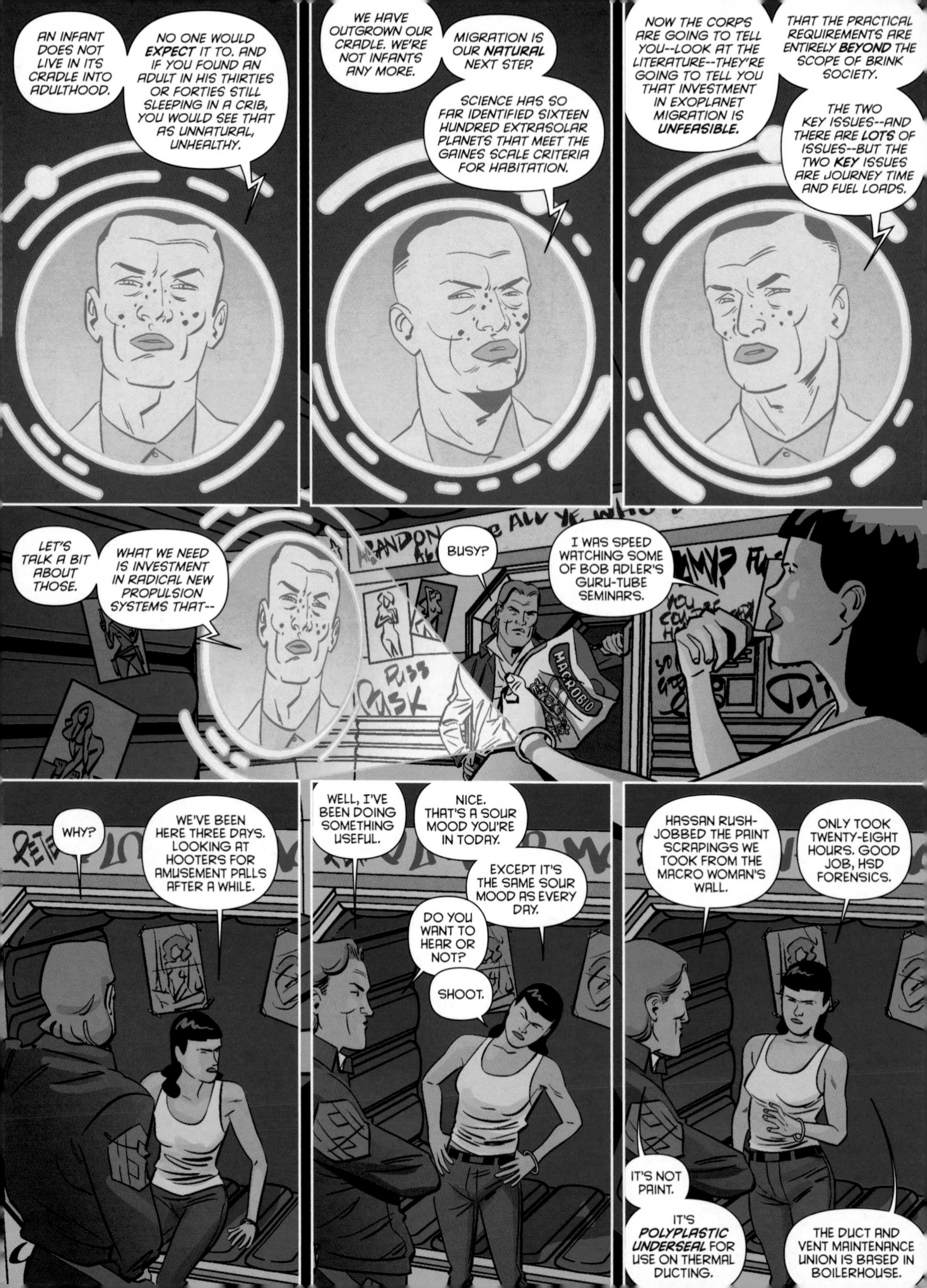
AN INFANT DOES NOT LIVE IN ITS CRADLE INTO ADULTHOOD.
NO ONE WOULD EXPECT IT TO. AND IF YOU FOUND AN ADULT IN HIS THIRTIES OR FORTIES STILL SLEEPING IN A CRIB, YOU WOULD SEE THAT AS UNNATURAL, UNHEALTHY.
WE HAVE OUTGROWN OUR CRADLE. WE'RE NOT INFANTS ANY MORE.
MIGRATION IS OUR NATURAL NEXT STEP.
SCIENCE HAS SO FAR IDENTIFIED SIXTEEN HUNDRED EXTRASOLAR PLANETS THAT MEET THE GAINES SCALE CRITERIA FOR HABITATION.
NOW THE CORPS ARE GOING TO TELL YOU--LOOK AT THE LITERATURE--THEY'RE GOING TO TELL YOU THAT INVESTMENT IN EXOPLANET MIGRATION IS UNFEASIBLE.
THAT THE PRACTICAL REQUIREMENTS ARE ENTIRELY BEYOND THE SCOPE OF BRINK SOCIETY.
THE TWO KEY ISSUES--AND THERE ARE LOTS OF ISSUES--BUT THE TWO KEY ISSUES ARE JOURNEY TIME AND FUEL LOADS.
LET'S TALK A BIT ABOUT THOSE.
WHAT WE NEED IS INVESTMENT IN RADICAL NEW PROPULSION SYSTEMS THAT--
BUSY?
I WAS SPEED WATCHING SOME OF BOB ADLER'S GURU-TUBE SEMINARS.
MACROBIO
WHY?
WE'VE BEEN HERE THREE DAYS. LOOKING AT HOOTERS FOR AMUSEMENT PALLS AFTER A WHILE.
WELL, I'VE BEEN DOING SOMETHING USEFUL.
NICE. THAT'S A SOUR MOOD YOU'RE IN TODAY.
EXCEPT IT'S THE SAME SOUR MOOD AS EVERY DAY.
DO YOU WANT TO HEAR OR NOT?
SHOOT.
HASSAN RUSH-JOBBED THE PAINT SCRAPINGS WE TOOK FROM THE MACRO WOMAN'S WALL.
ONLY TOOK TWENTY-EIGHT HOURS. GOOD JOB, HSD FORENSICS.
IT'S NOT PAINT.
IT'S POLYPLASTIC UNDERSEAL FOR USE ON THERMAL DUCTING.
THE DUCT AND VENT MAINTENANCE UNION IS BASED IN BOILERHOUSE.

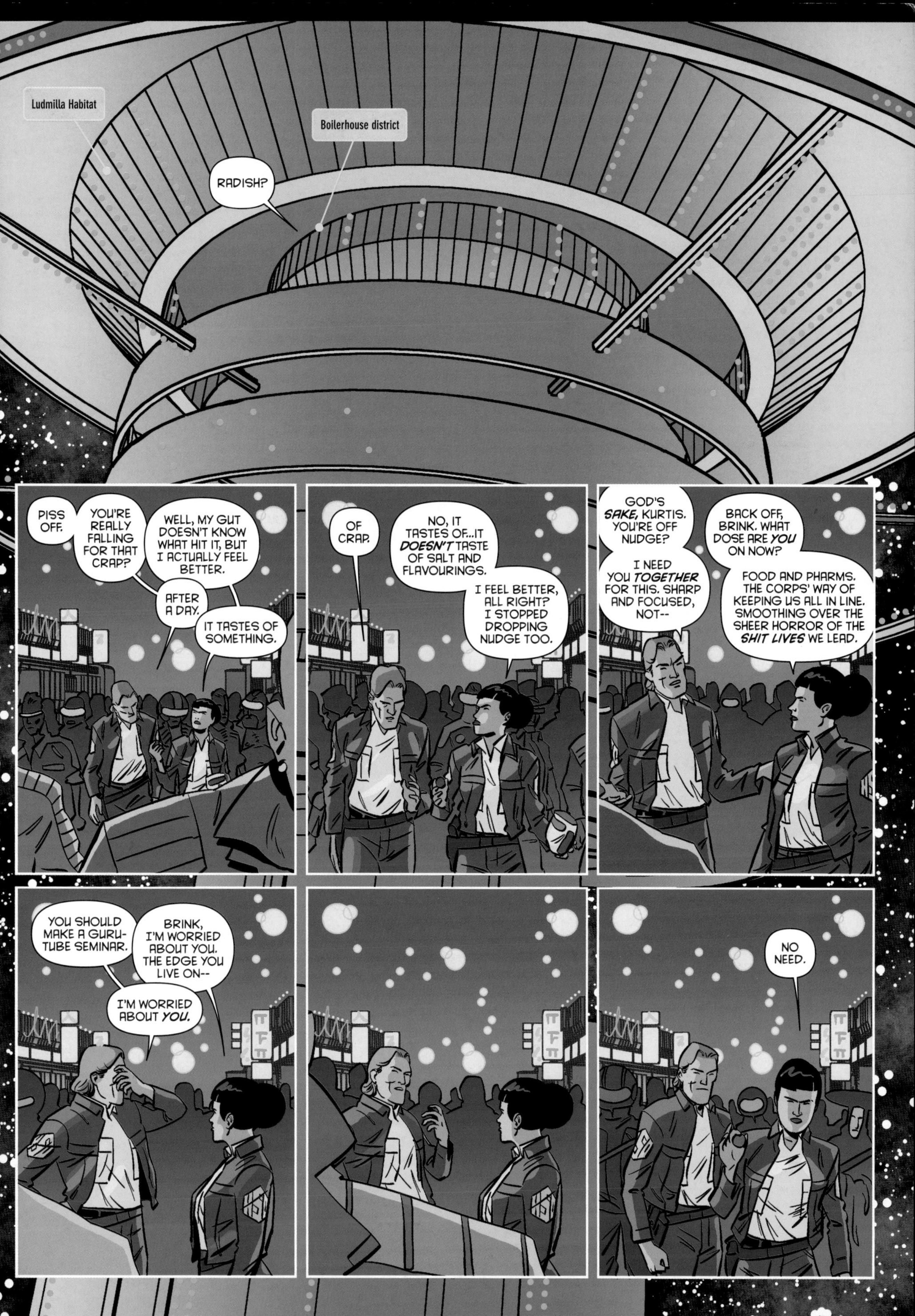
Ludmilla Habitat
Boilerhouse district
RADISH?
PISS OFF.
YOU'RE REALLY FALLING FOR THAT CRAP?
WELL, MY GUT DOESN'T KNOW WHAT HIT IT, BUT I ACTUALLY FEEL BETTER.
AFTER A DAY.
IT TASTES OF SOMETHING.
OF CRAP.
NO, IT TASTES OF...IT DOESN'T TASTE OF SALT AND FLAVOURINGS.
I FEEL BETTER, ALL RIGHT? I STOPPED DROPPING NUDGE TOO.
GOD'S SAKE, KURTIS. YOU'RE OFF NUDGE?
I NEED YOU TOGETHER FOR THIS. SHARP AND FOCUSED, NOT--
BACK OFF, BRINK. WHAT DOSE ARE YOU ON NOW?
FOOD AND PHARMS. THE CORPS' WAY OF KEEPING US ALL IN LINE. SMOOTHING OVER THE SHEER HORROR OF THE SHIT LIVES WE LEAD.
YOU SHOULD MAKE A GURU-TUBE SEMINAR.
BRINK, I'M WORRIED ABOUT YOU. THE EDGE YOU LIVE ON--
I'M WORRIED ABOUT YOU.
NO NEED.

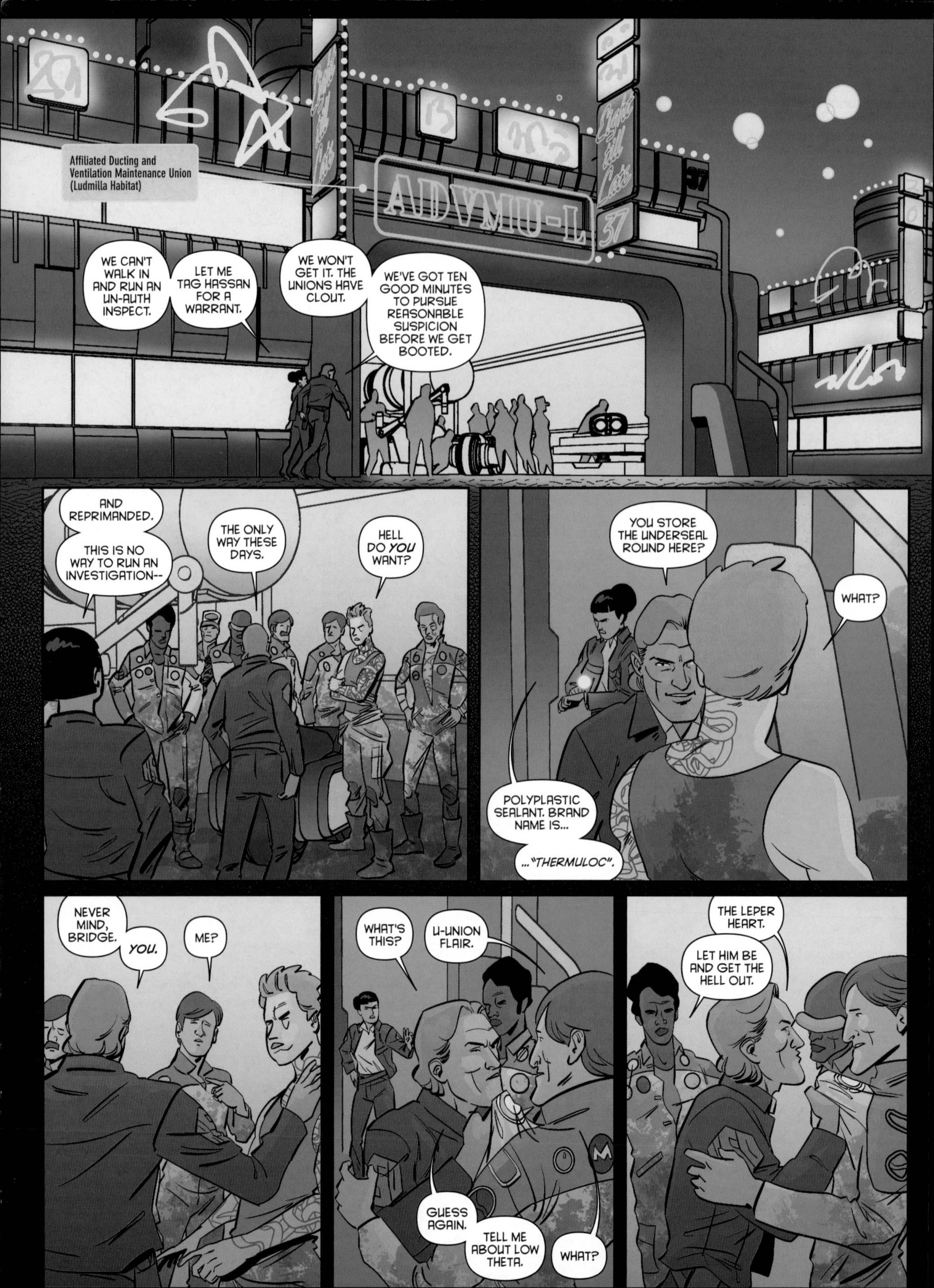
Affiliated Ducting and Ventilation Maintenance Union (Ludmilla Habitat)
ADVMU-L
37
WE CAN'T WALK IN AND RUN AN UN-AUTH INSPECT.
LET ME TAG HASSAN FOR A WARRANT.
WE WON'T GET IT. THE UNIONS HAVE CLOUT.
WE'VE GOT TEN GOOD MINUTES TO PURSUE REASONABLE SUSPICION BEFORE WE GET BOOTED.
AND REPRIMANDED.
THIS IS NO WAY TO RUN AN INVESTIGATION--
THE ONLY WAY THESE DAYS.
HELL DO *YOU* WANT?
YOU STORE THE UNDERSEAL ROUND HERE?
WHAT?
POLYPLASTIC SEALANT. BRAND NAME IS...
..."THERMULOC".
NEVER MIND, BRIDGE.
YOU.
ME?
WHAT'S THIS?
U-UNION FLAIR.
GUESS AGAIN.
TELL ME ABOUT LOW THETA.
WHAT?
THE LEPER HEART.
LET HIM BE AND GET THE HELL OUT.

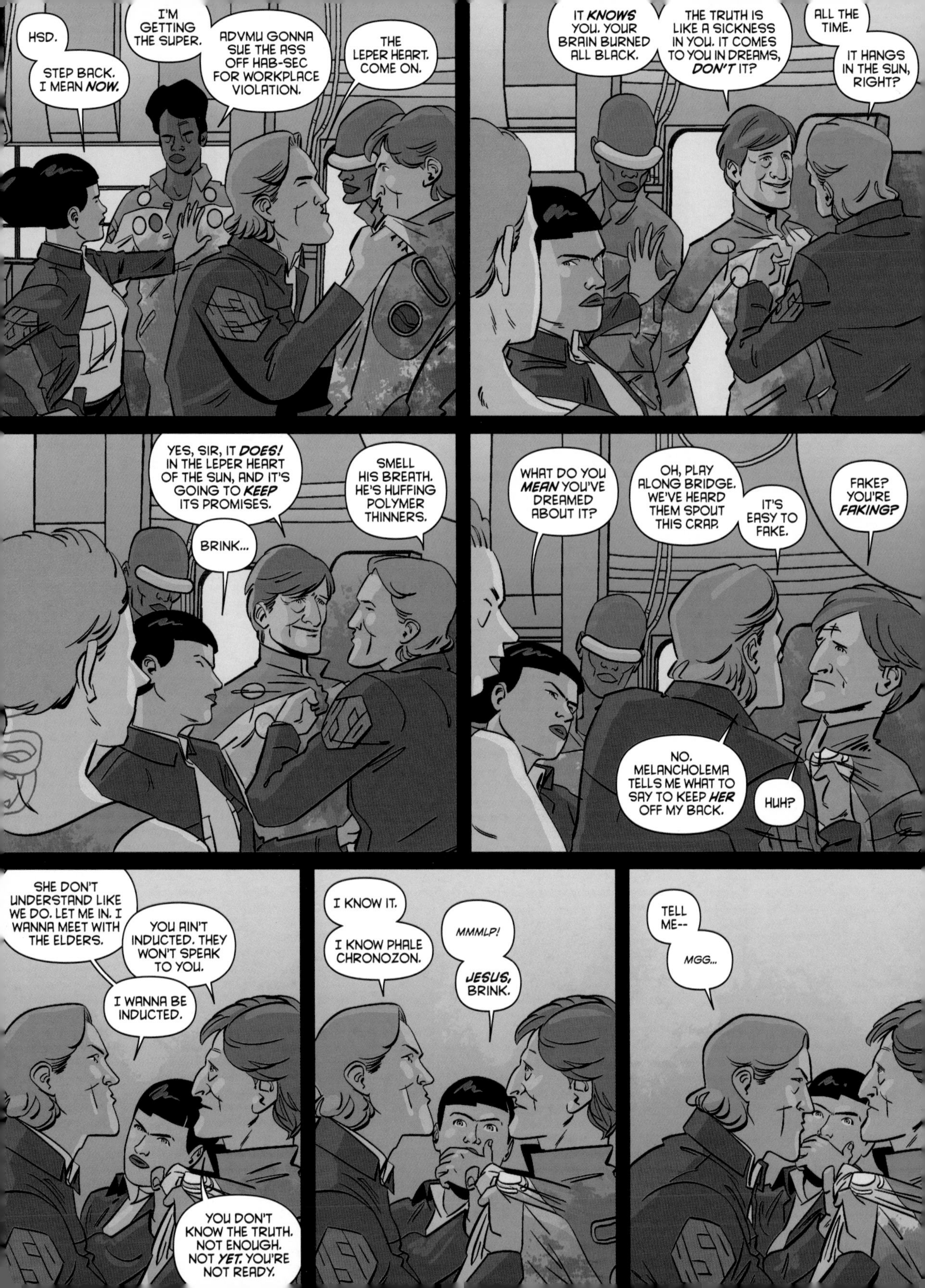
HSD.
STEP BACK. I MEAN NOW.
I'M GETTING THE SUPER.
ADVMU GONNA SUE THE ASS OFF HAB-SEC FOR WORKPLACE VIOLATION.
THE LEPER HEART. COME ON.
IT KNOWS YOU. YOUR BRAIN BURNED ALL BLACK.
THE TRUTH IS LIKE A SICKNESS IN YOU. IT COMES TO YOU IN DREAMS, DON'T IT?
ALL THE TIME.
IT HANGS IN THE SUN, RIGHT?
YES, SIR, IT DOES! IN THE LEPER HEART OF THE SUN, AND IT'S GOING TO KEEP ITS PROMISES.
BRINK...
SMELL HIS BREATH. HE'S HUFFING POLYMER THINNERS.
WHAT DO YOU MEAN YOU'VE DREAMED ABOUT IT?
OH, PLAY ALONG BRIDGE. WE'VE HEARD THEM SPOUT THIS CRAP.
IT'S EASY TO FAKE.
FAKE? YOU'RE FAKING?
NO. MELANCHOLEMA TELLS ME WHAT TO SAY TO KEEP HER OFF MY BACK.
HUH?
SHE DON'T UNDERSTAND LIKE WE DO. LET ME IN. I WANNA MEET WITH THE ELDERS.
YOU AIN'T INDUCTED. THEY WON'T SPEAK TO YOU.
I WANNA BE INDUCTED.
YOU DON'T KNOW THE TRUTH. NOT ENOUGH. NOT YET. YOU'RE NOT READY.
I KNOW IT.
I KNOW PHALE CHRONOZON.
MMMLP!
JESUS, BRINK.
TELL ME--
MGG...

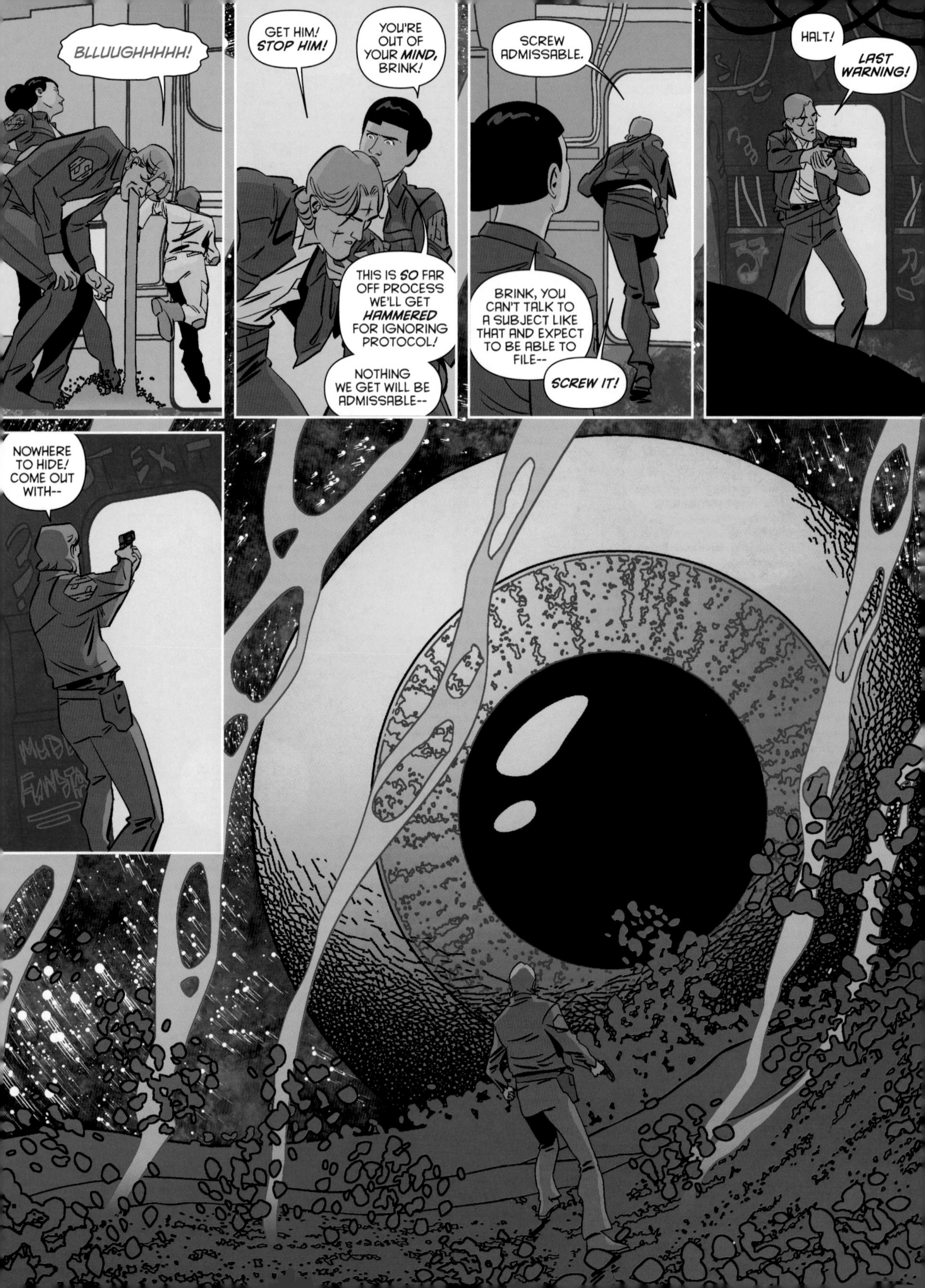

BLLUUGHHHHH!
GET HIM! STOP HIM!
YOU'RE OUT OF YOUR MIND, BRINK!
THIS IS SO FAR OFF PROCESS WE'LL GET HAMMERED FOR IGNORING PROTOCOL!
NOTHING WE GET WILL BE ADMISSABLE--
SCREW ADMISSABLE.
BRINK, YOU CAN'T TALK TO A SUBJECT LIKE THAT AND EXPECT TO BE ABLE TO FILE--
SCREW IT!
HALT!
LAST WARNING!
NOWHERE TO HIDE! COME OUT WITH--

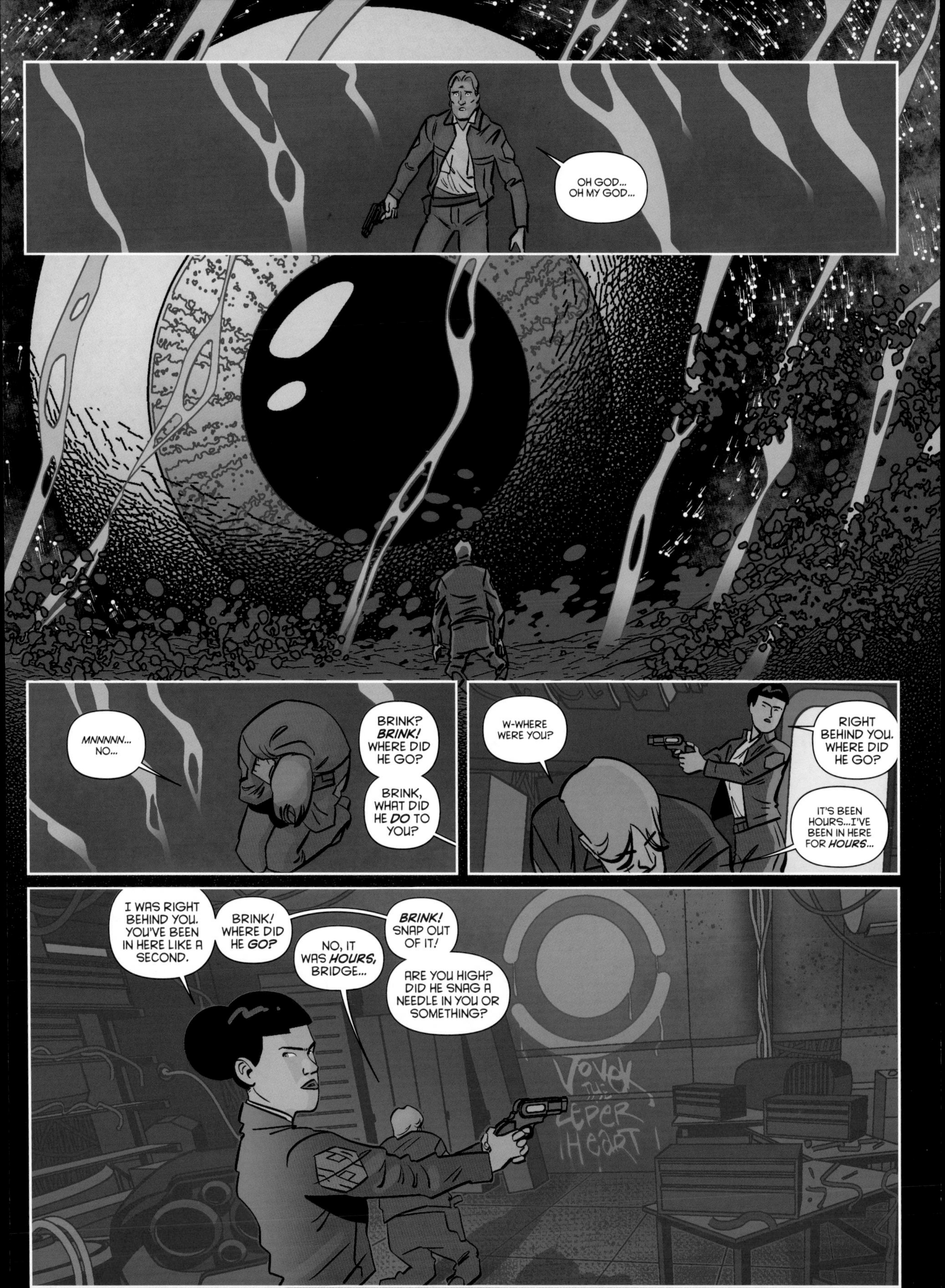
OH GOD... OH MY GOD...
MNNNNN... NO...
BRINK? ***BRINK!*** WHERE DID HE GO?
BRINK, WHAT DID HE ***DO*** TO YOU?
W-WHERE WERE YOU?
RIGHT BEHIND YOU. WHERE DID HE GO?
IT'S BEEN HOURS...I'VE BEEN IN HERE FOR ***HOURS***...
I WAS RIGHT BEHIND YOU. YOU'VE BEEN IN HERE LIKE A SECOND.
BRINK! WHERE DID HE ***GO?***
NO, IT WAS ***HOURS,*** BRIDGE...
BRINK! SNAP OUT OF IT!
ARE YOU HIGH? DID HE SNAG A NEEDLE IN YOU OR SOMETHING?

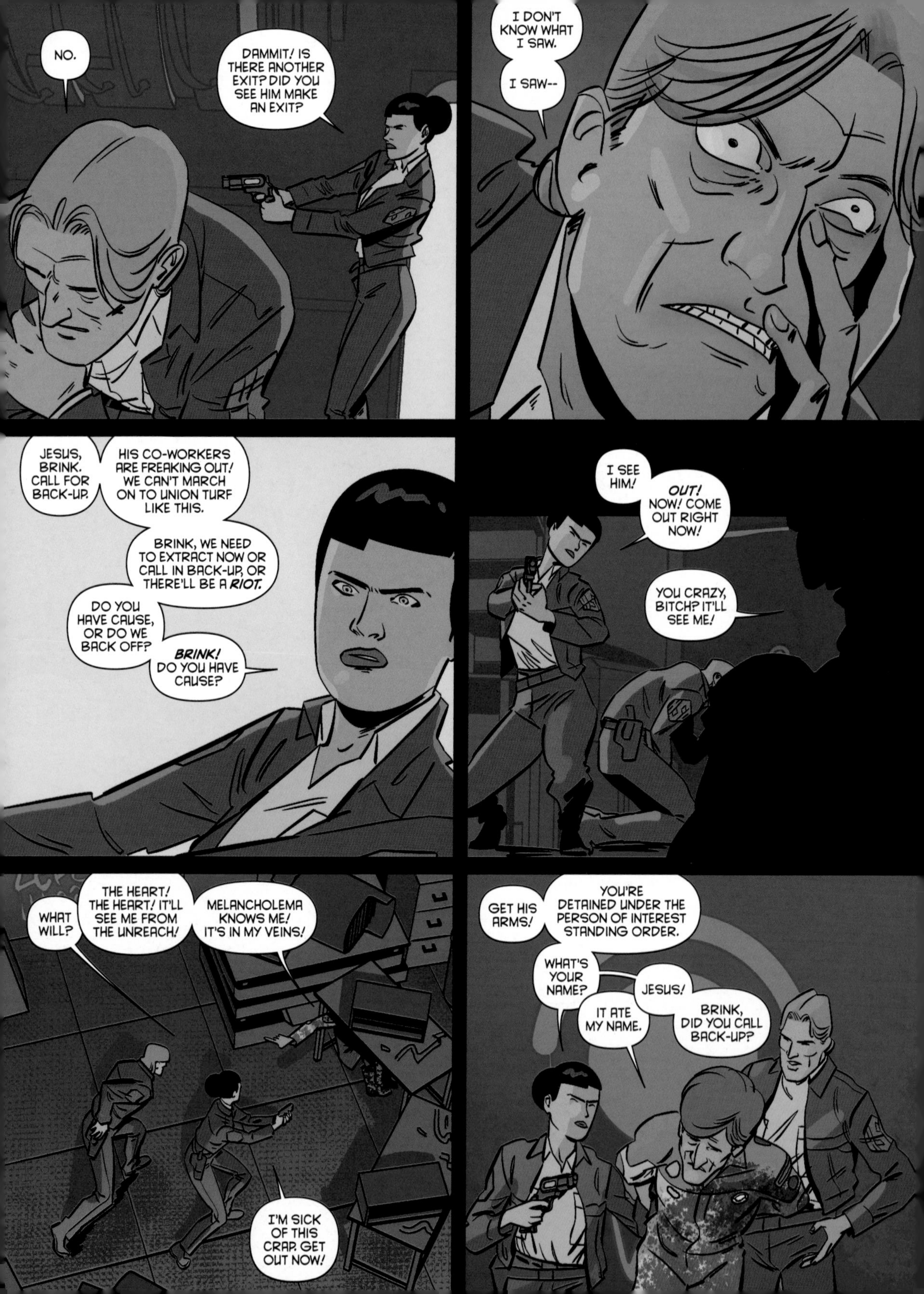
NO.
DAMMIT! IS THERE ANOTHER EXIT? DID YOU SEE HIM MAKE AN EXIT?
I DON'T KNOW WHAT I SAW.
I SAW--
JESUS, BRINK. CALL FOR BACK-UP.
HIS CO-WORKERS ARE FREAKING OUT! WE CAN'T MARCH ON TO UNION TURF LIKE THIS.
BRINK, WE NEED TO EXTRACT NOW OR CALL IN BACK-UP, OR THERE'LL BE A *RIOT.*
DO YOU HAVE CAUSE, OR DO WE BACK OFF?
BRINK! DO YOU HAVE CAUSE?
I SEE HIM!
OUT! NOW! COME OUT RIGHT NOW!
YOU CRAZY, BITCH? IT'LL SEE ME!
WHAT WILL?
THE HEART! THE HEART! IT'LL SEE ME FROM THE UNREACH!
MELANCHOLEMA KNOWS ME! IT'S IN MY VEINS!
I'M SICK OF THIS CRAP. GET OUT NOW!
GET HIS ARMS!
YOU'RE DETAINED UNDER THE PERSON OF INTEREST STANDING ORDER.
WHAT'S YOUR NAME?
JESUS!
IT ATE MY NAME.
BRINK, DID YOU CALL BACK-UP?

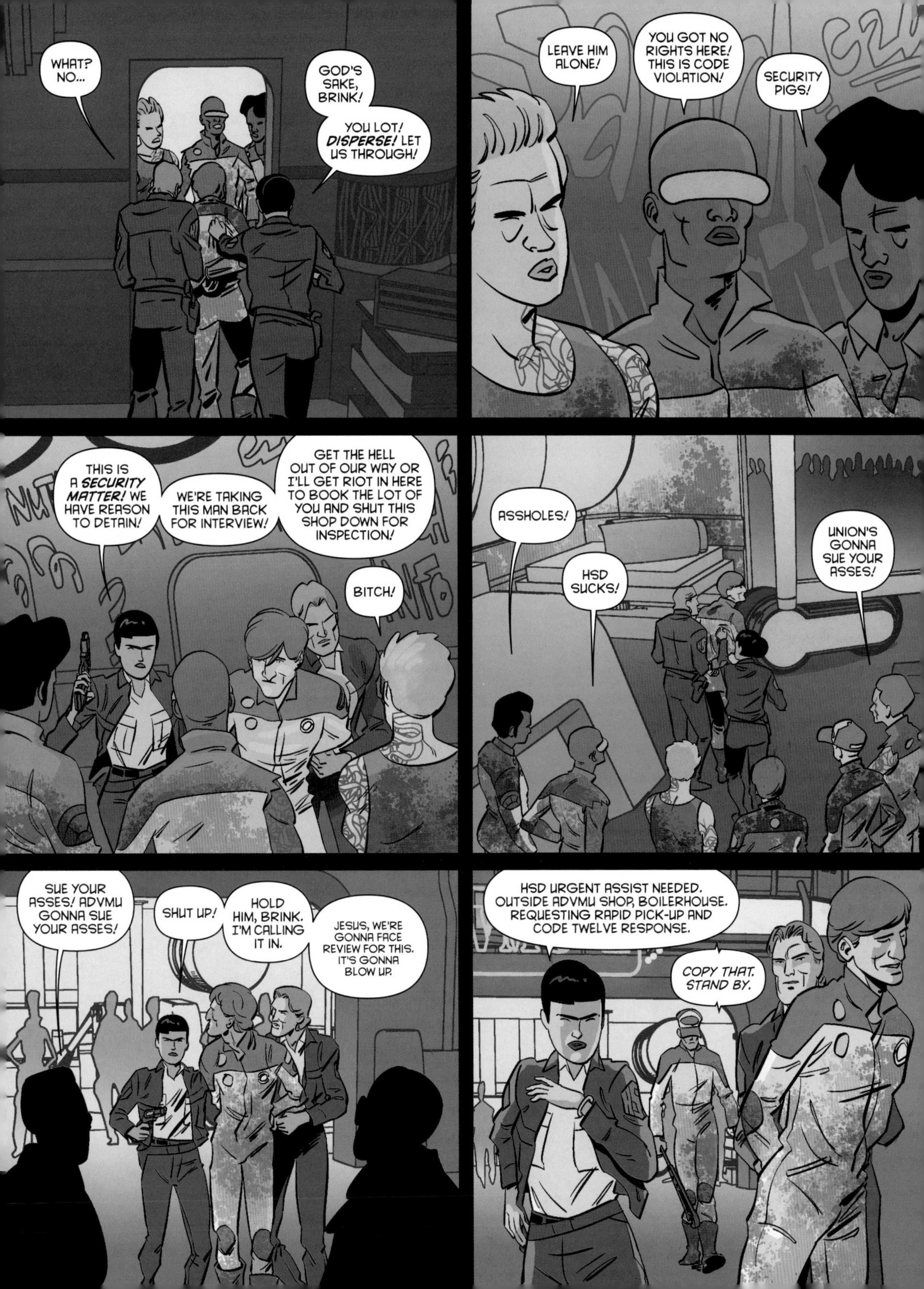

WHAT? NO...
GOD'S SAKE, BRINK!
YOU LOT! DISPERSE! LET US THROUGH!
LEAVE HIM ALONE!
YOU GOT NO RIGHTS HERE! THIS IS CODE VIOLATION!
SECURITY PIGS!
THIS IS A SECURITY MATTER! WE HAVE REASON TO DETAIN!
WE'RE TAKING THIS MAN BACK FOR INTERVIEW!
GET THE HELL OUT OF OUR WAY OR I'LL GET RIOT IN HERE TO BOOK THE LOT OF YOU AND SHUT THIS SHOP DOWN FOR INSPECTION!
BITCH!
ASSHOLES!
HSD SUCKS!
UNION'S GONNA SUE YOUR ASSES!
SUE YOUR ASSES! ADVMU GONNA SUE YOUR ASSES!
SHUT UP!
HOLD HIM, BRINK. I'M CALLING IT IN.
JESUS, WE'RE GONNA FACE REVIEW FOR THIS. IT'S GONNA BLOW UP.
HSD URGENT ASSIST NEEDED. OUTSIDE ADVMU SHOP, BOILERHOUSE. REQUESTING RAPID PICK-UP AND CODE TWELVE RESPONSE.
COPY THAT. STAND BY.

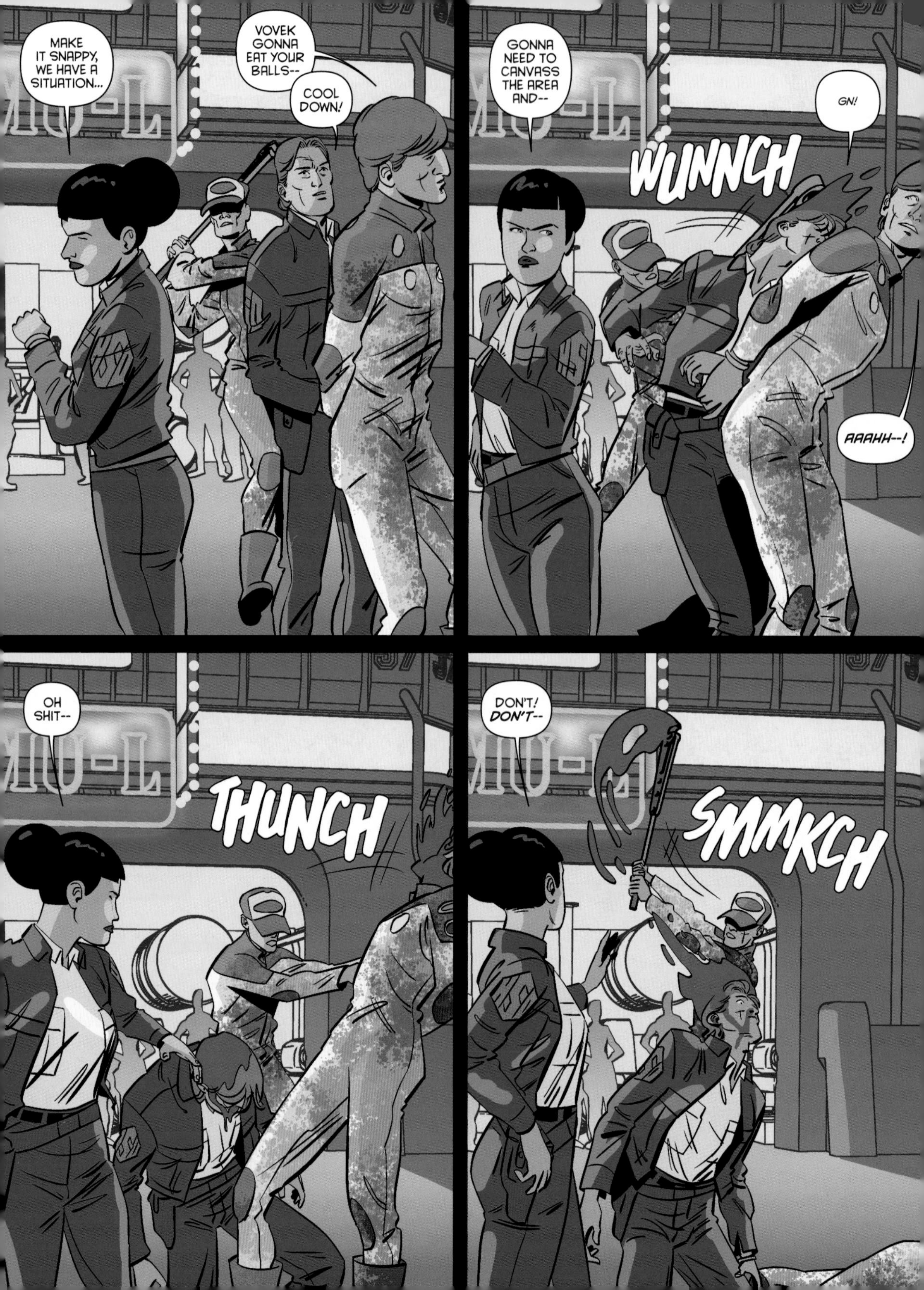

MAKE IT SNAPPY, WE HAVE A SITUATION...
VOVEK GONNA EAT YOUR BALLS--
COOL DOWN!
GONNA NEED TO CANVASS THE AREA AND--
GN!
WUNNCH
AAAHH--!
OH SHIT--
THUNCH
DON'T! DON'T--
SMMKCH

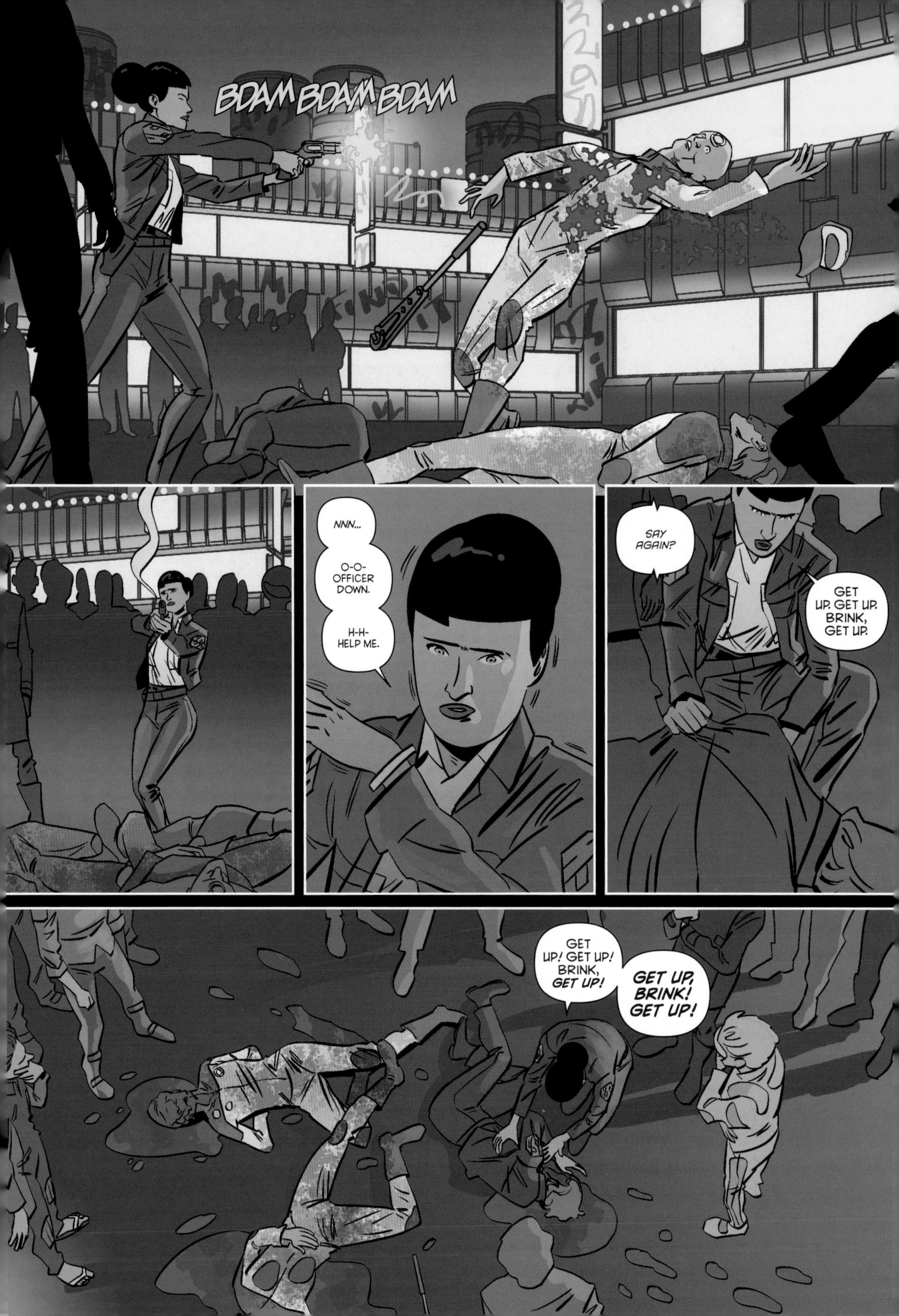
BDAM BDAM BDAM
NNN...
O-O-OFFICER DOWN.
H-H-HELP ME.
SAY AGAIN?
GET UP. GET UP. BRINK, GET UP.
GET UP! GET UP! BRINK, GET UP!
GET UP, BRINK! GET UP!

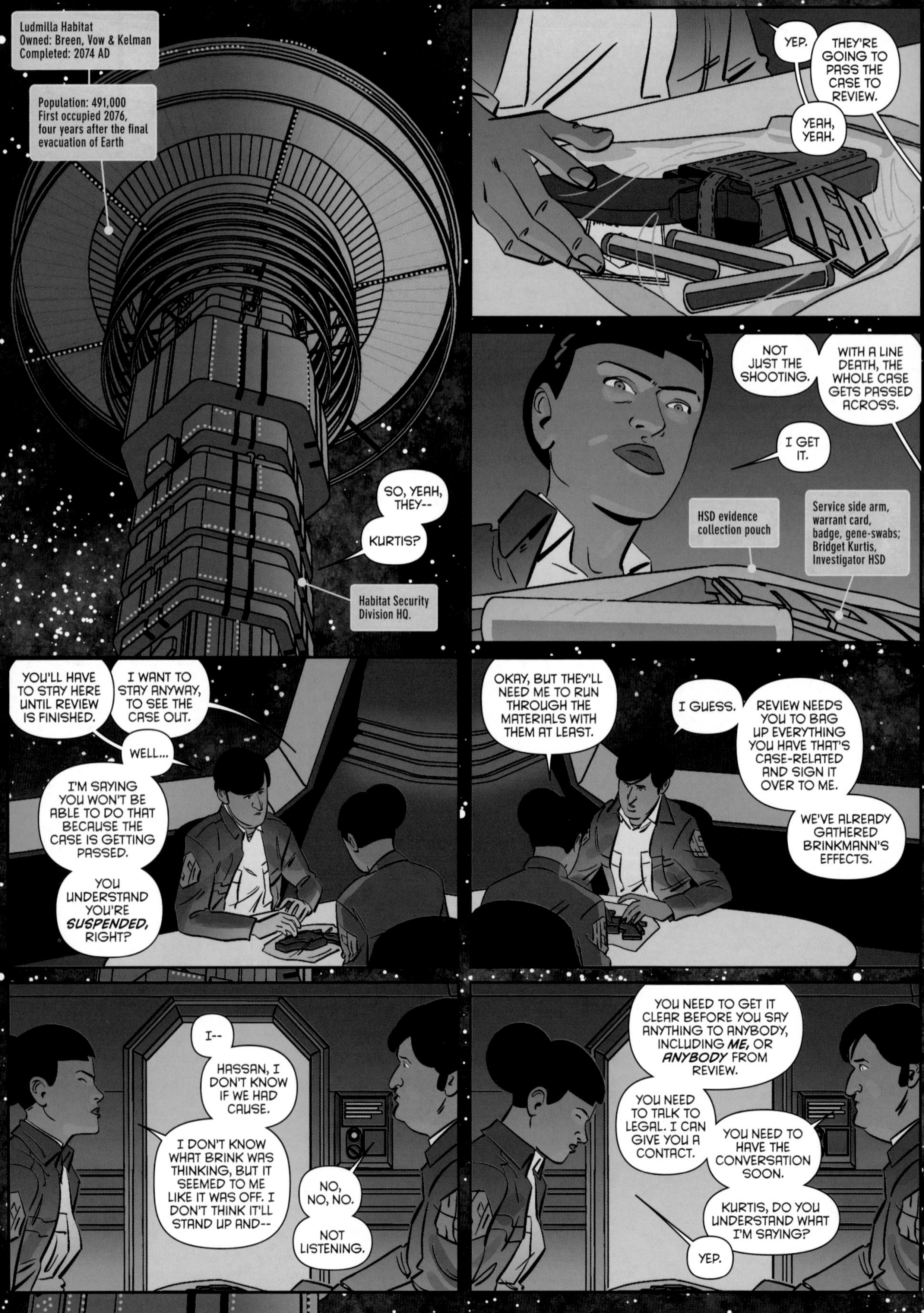

Ludmilla Habitat
Owned: Breen, Vow & Kelman
Completed: 2074 AD
Population: 491,000
First occupied 2076, four years after the final evacuation of Earth
SO, YEAH, THEY--
KURTIS?
Habitat Security Division HQ.
YEP.
THEY'RE GOING TO PASS THE CASE TO REVIEW.
YEAH, YEAH.
HSD
NOT JUST THE SHOOTING.
WITH A LINE DEATH, THE WHOLE CASE GETS PASSED ACROSS.
I GET IT.
HSD evidence collection pouch
Service side arm, warrant card, badge, gene-swabs; Bridget Kurtis, Investigator HSD
YOU'LL HAVE TO STAY HERE UNTIL REVIEW IS FINISHED.
I WANT TO STAY ANYWAY, TO SEE THE CASE OUT.
WELL...
I'M SAYING YOU WON'T BE ABLE TO DO THAT BECAUSE THE CASE IS GETTING PASSED.
YOU UNDERSTAND YOU'RE SUSPENDED, RIGHT?
OKAY, BUT THEY'LL NEED ME TO RUN THROUGH THE MATERIALS WITH THEM AT LEAST.
I GUESS.
REVIEW NEEDS YOU TO BAG UP EVERYTHING YOU HAVE THAT'S CASE-RELATED AND SIGN IT OVER TO ME.
WE'VE ALREADY GATHERED BRINKMANN'S EFFECTS.
I--
HASSAN, I DON'T KNOW IF WE HAD CAUSE.
I DON'T KNOW WHAT BRINK WAS THINKING, BUT IT SEEMED TO ME LIKE IT WAS OFF. I DON'T THINK IT'LL STAND UP AND--
NO, NO, NO.
NOT LISTENING.
YOU NEED TO GET IT CLEAR BEFORE YOU SAY ANYTHING TO ANYBODY, INCLUDING ME, OR ANYBODY FROM REVIEW.
YOU NEED TO TALK TO LEGAL. I CAN GIVE YOU A CONTACT.
YOU NEED TO HAVE THE CONVERSATION SOON.
KURTIS, DO YOU UNDERSTAND WHAT I'M SAYING?
YEP.

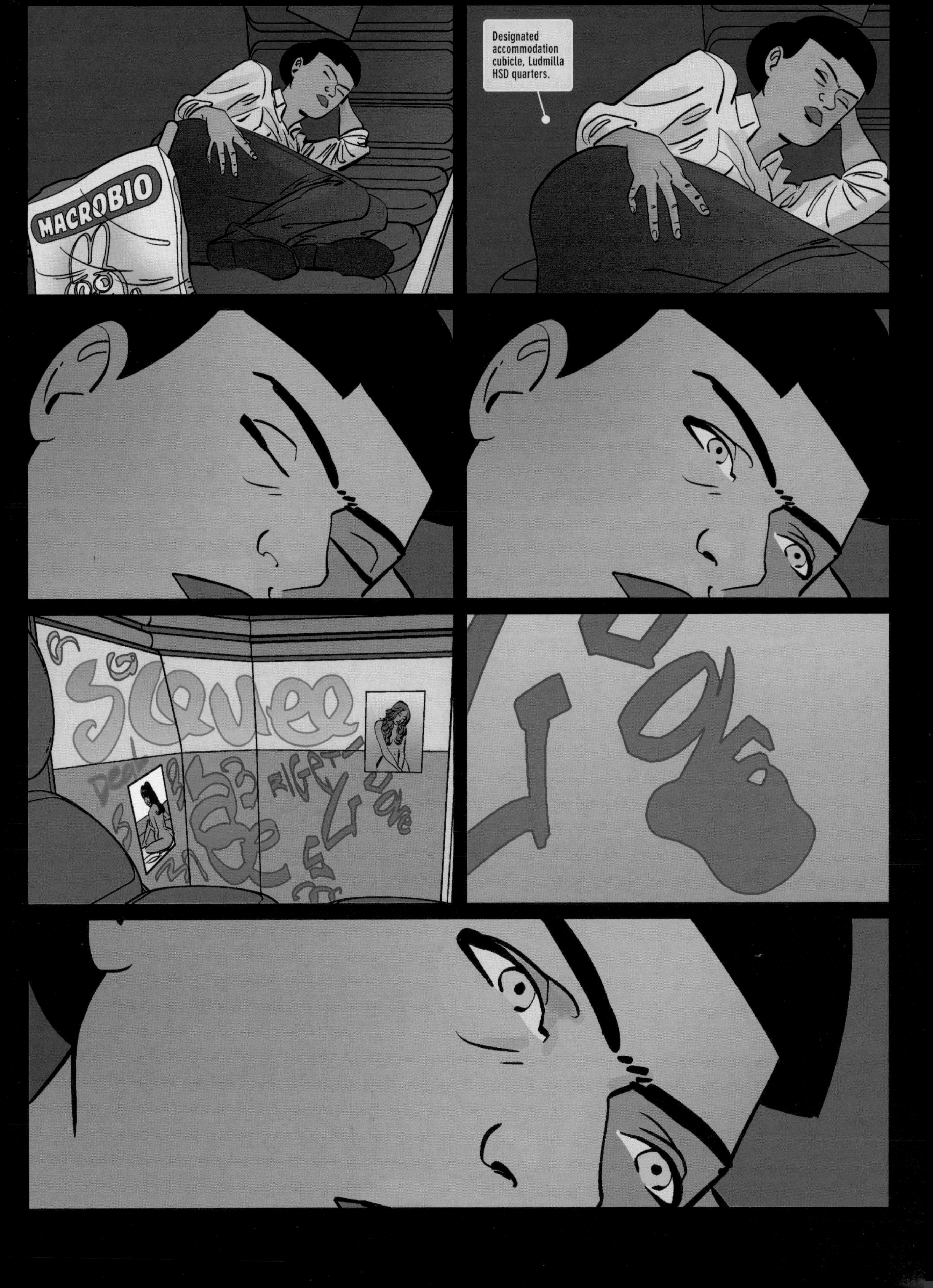
MACROBIO
Designated accommodation cubicle, Ludmilla HSD quarters.

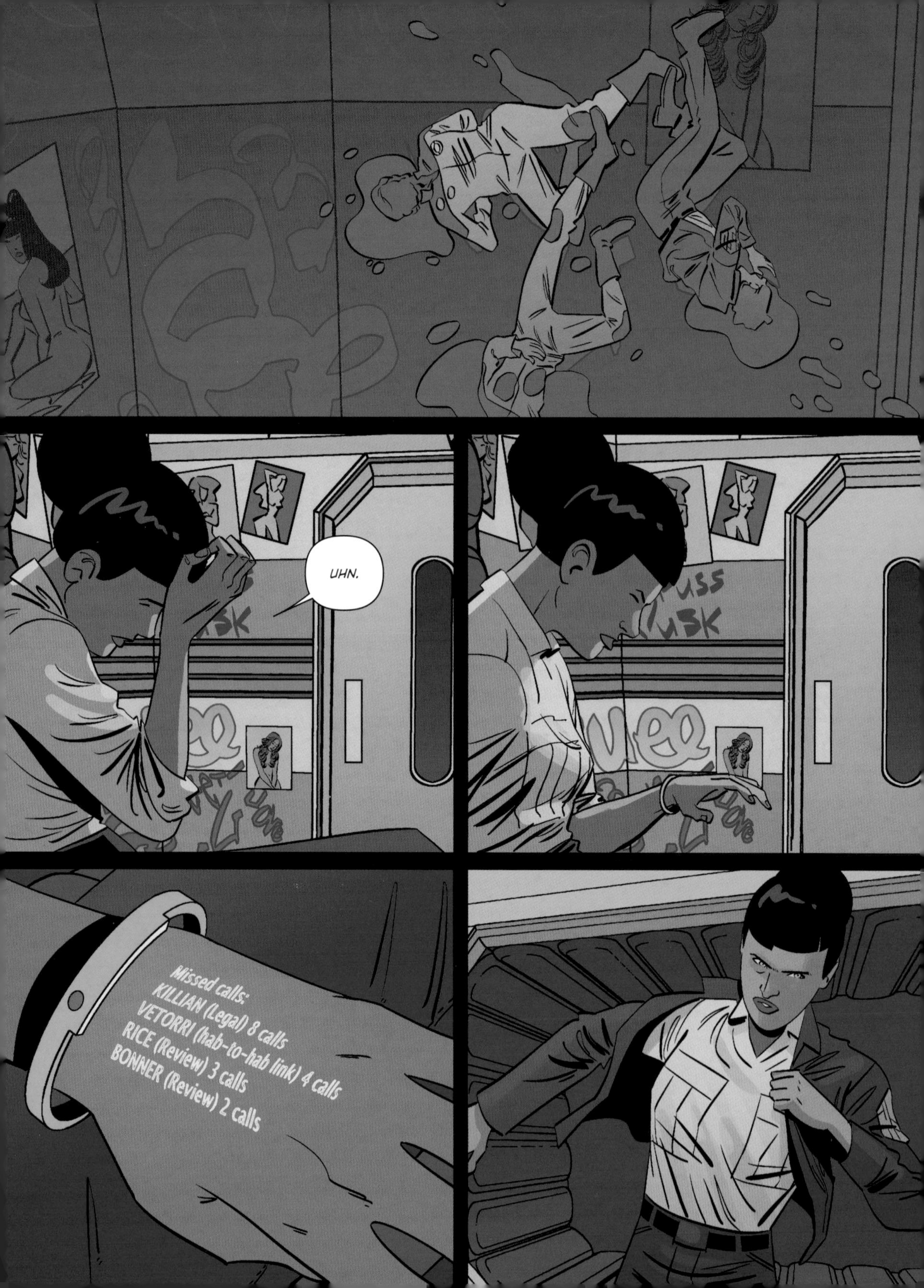
UHN.
Missed calls:
KILLIAN (Legal) 8 calls
VETORRI (hab-to-hab link) 4 calls
RICE (Review) 3 calls
BONNER (Review) 2 calls

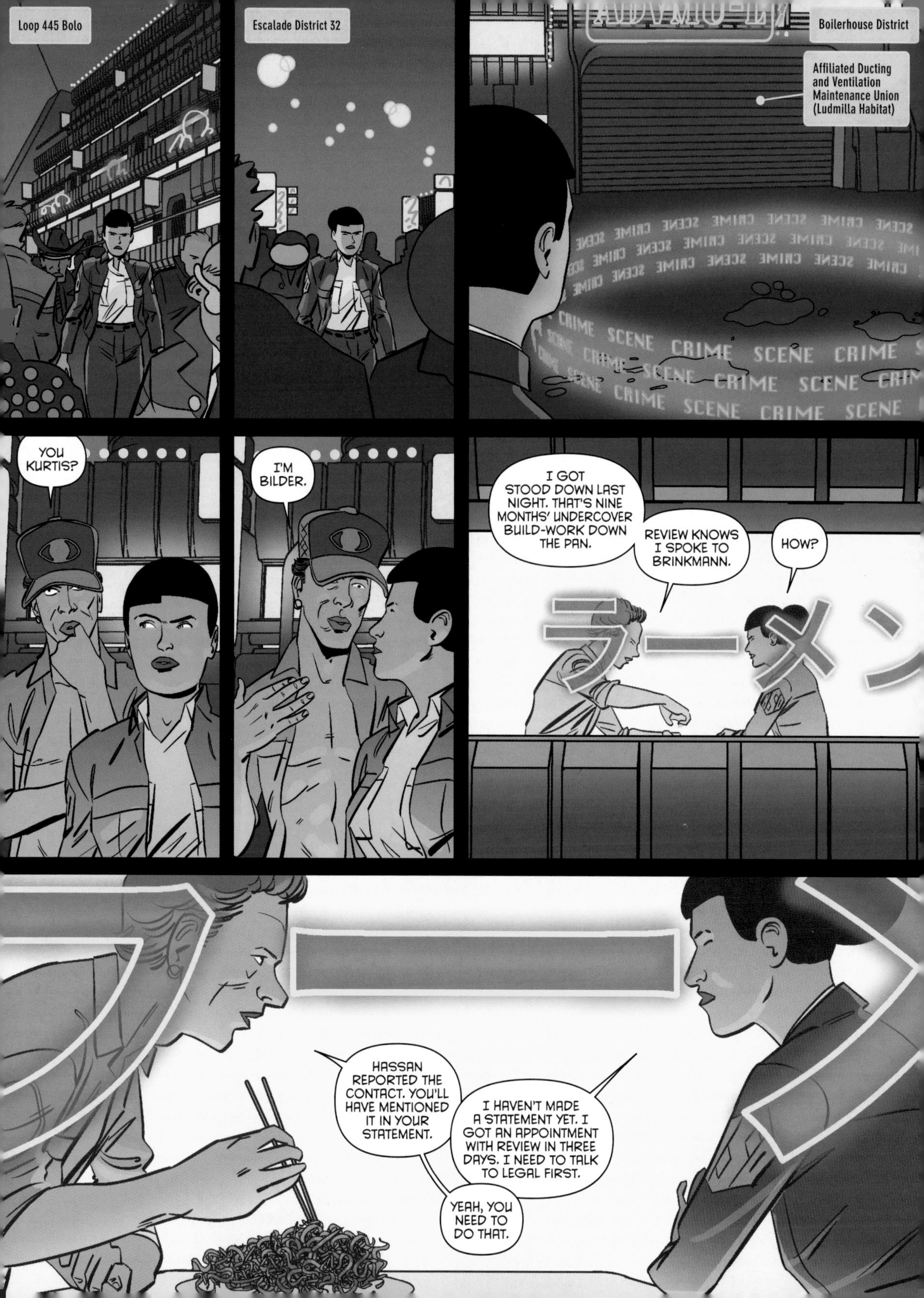
Loop 445 Bolo
Escalade District 32
Boilerhouse District
Affiliated Ducting and Ventilation Maintenance Union (Ludmilla Habitat)
CRIME SCENE CRIME SCENE CRIME SCENE
YOU KURTIS?
I'M BILDER.
I GOT STOOD DOWN LAST NIGHT. THAT'S NINE MONTHS' UNDERCOVER BUILD-WORK DOWN THE PAN.
REVIEW KNOWS I SPOKE TO BRINKMANN.
HOW?
ラーメン
HASSAN REPORTED THE CONTACT. YOU'LL HAVE MENTIONED IT IN YOUR STATEMENT.
I HAVEN'T MADE A STATEMENT YET. I GOT AN APPOINTMENT WITH REVIEW IN THREE DAYS. I NEED TO TALK TO LEGAL FIRST.
YEAH, YOU NEED TO DO THAT.

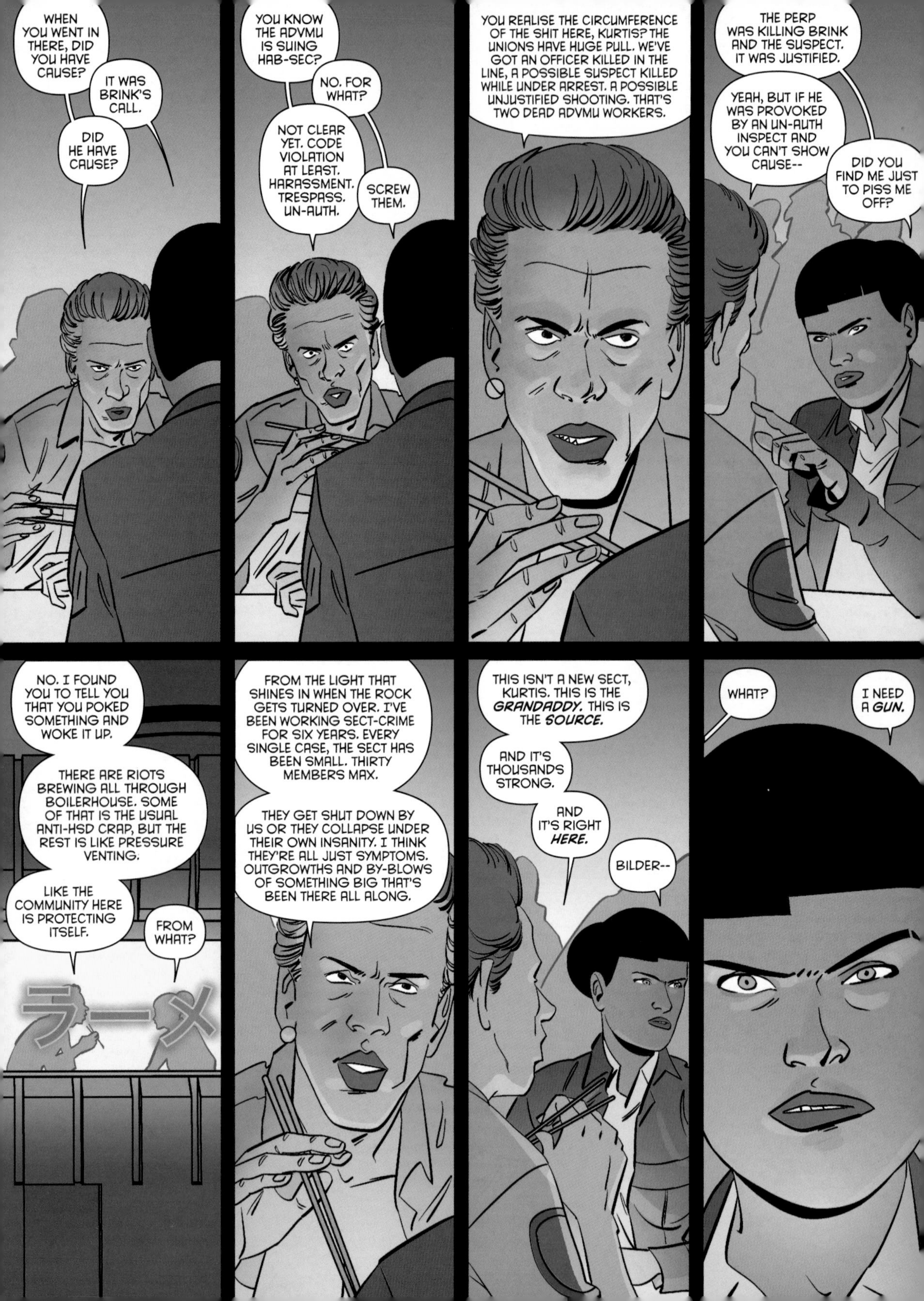
WHEN YOU WENT IN THERE, DID YOU HAVE CAUSE?
IT WAS BRINK'S CALL.
DID HE HAVE CAUSE?
YOU KNOW THE ADVMU IS SUING HAB-SEC?
NO. FOR WHAT?
NOT CLEAR YET. CODE VIOLATION AT LEAST. HARASSMENT. TRESPASS. UN-AUTH.
SCREW THEM.
YOU REALISE THE CIRCUMFERENCE OF THE SHIT HERE, KURTIS? THE UNIONS HAVE HUGE PULL. WE'VE GOT AN OFFICER KILLED IN THE LINE, A POSSIBLE SUSPECT KILLED WHILE UNDER ARREST. A POSSIBLE UNJUSTIFIED SHOOTING. THAT'S TWO DEAD ADVMU WORKERS.
THE PERP WAS KILLING BRINK AND THE SUSPECT. IT WAS JUSTIFIED.
YEAH, BUT IF HE WAS PROVOKED BY AN UN-AUTH INSPECT AND YOU CAN'T SHOW CAUSE--
DID YOU FIND ME JUST TO PISS ME OFF?
NO. I FOUND YOU TO TELL YOU THAT YOU POKED SOMETHING AND WOKE IT UP.
THERE ARE RIOTS BREWING ALL THROUGH BOILERHOUSE. SOME OF THAT IS THE USUAL ANTI-HSD CRAP, BUT THE REST IS LIKE PRESSURE VENTING.
LIKE THE COMMUNITY HERE IS PROTECTING ITSELF.
FROM WHAT?
ラーメ
FROM THE LIGHT THAT SHINES IN WHEN THE ROCK GETS TURNED OVER. I'VE BEEN WORKING SECT-CRIME FOR SIX YEARS. EVERY SINGLE CASE, THE SECT HAS BEEN SMALL. THIRTY MEMBERS MAX.
THEY GET SHUT DOWN BY US OR THEY COLLAPSE UNDER THEIR OWN INSANITY. I THINK THEY'RE ALL JUST SYMPTOMS. OUTGROWTHS AND BY-BLOWS OF SOMETHING BIG THAT'S BEEN THERE ALL ALONG.
THIS ISN'T A NEW SECT, KURTIS. THIS IS THE *GRANDADDY.* THIS IS THE *SOURCE.*
AND IT'S THOUSANDS STRONG.
AND IT'S RIGHT *HERE.*
BILDER--
WHAT?
I NEED A *GUN.*

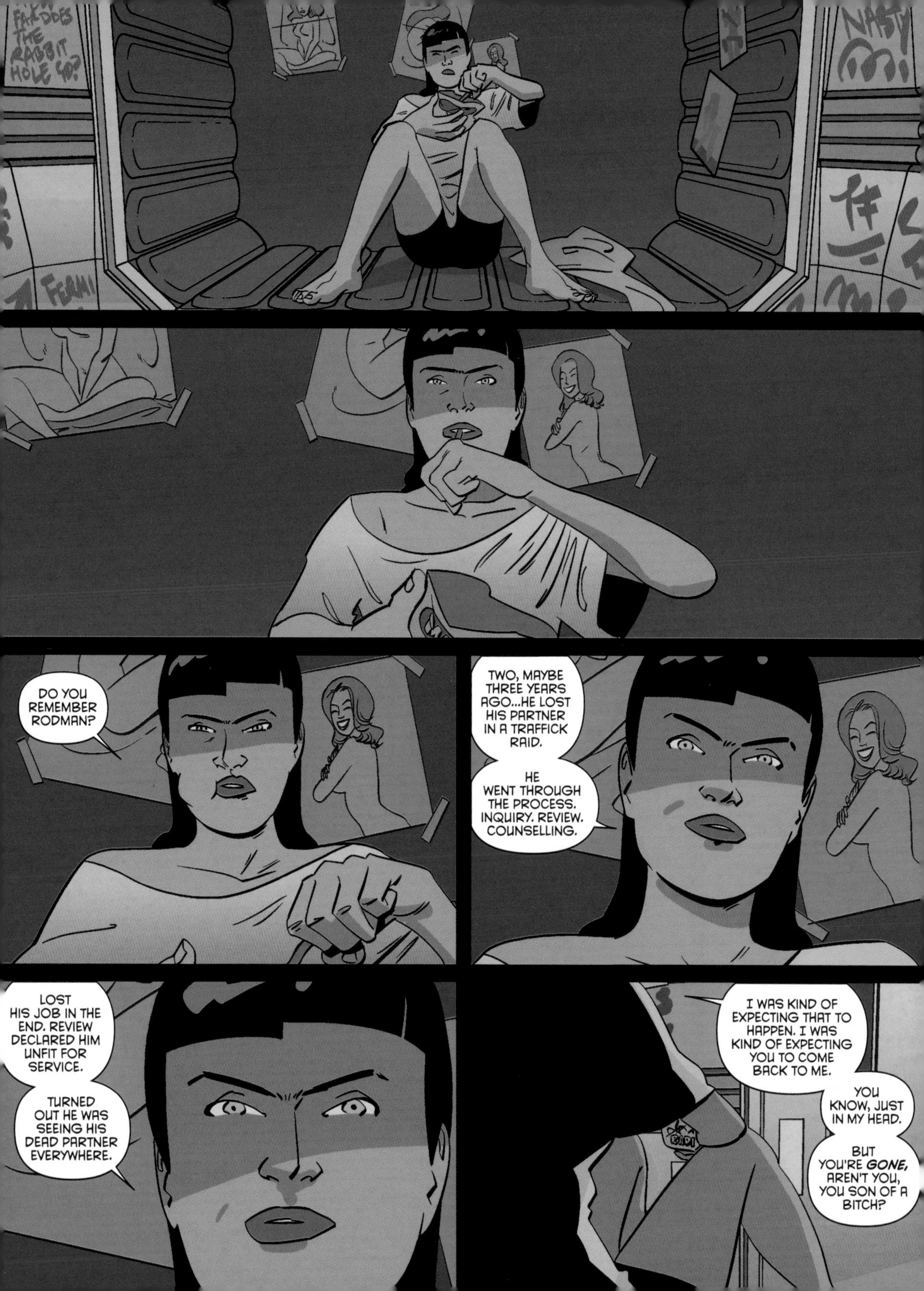
HOW FAR DOES THE RABBIT HOLE GO?
NASTY
FERMI
DO YOU REMEMBER RODMAN?
TWO, MAYBE THREE YEARS AGO...HE LOST HIS PARTNER IN A TRAFFICK RAID.
HE WENT THROUGH THE PROCESS. INQUIRY. REVIEW. COUNSELLING.
LOST HIS JOB IN THE END. REVIEW DECLARED HIM UNFIT FOR SERVICE.
TURNED OUT HE WAS SEEING HIS DEAD PARTNER EVERYWHERE.
I WAS KIND OF EXPECTING THAT TO HAPPEN. I WAS KIND OF EXPECTING YOU TO COME BACK TO ME.
YOU KNOW, JUST IN MY HEAD.
BUT YOU'RE ***GONE,*** AREN'T YOU, YOU SON OF A BITCH?

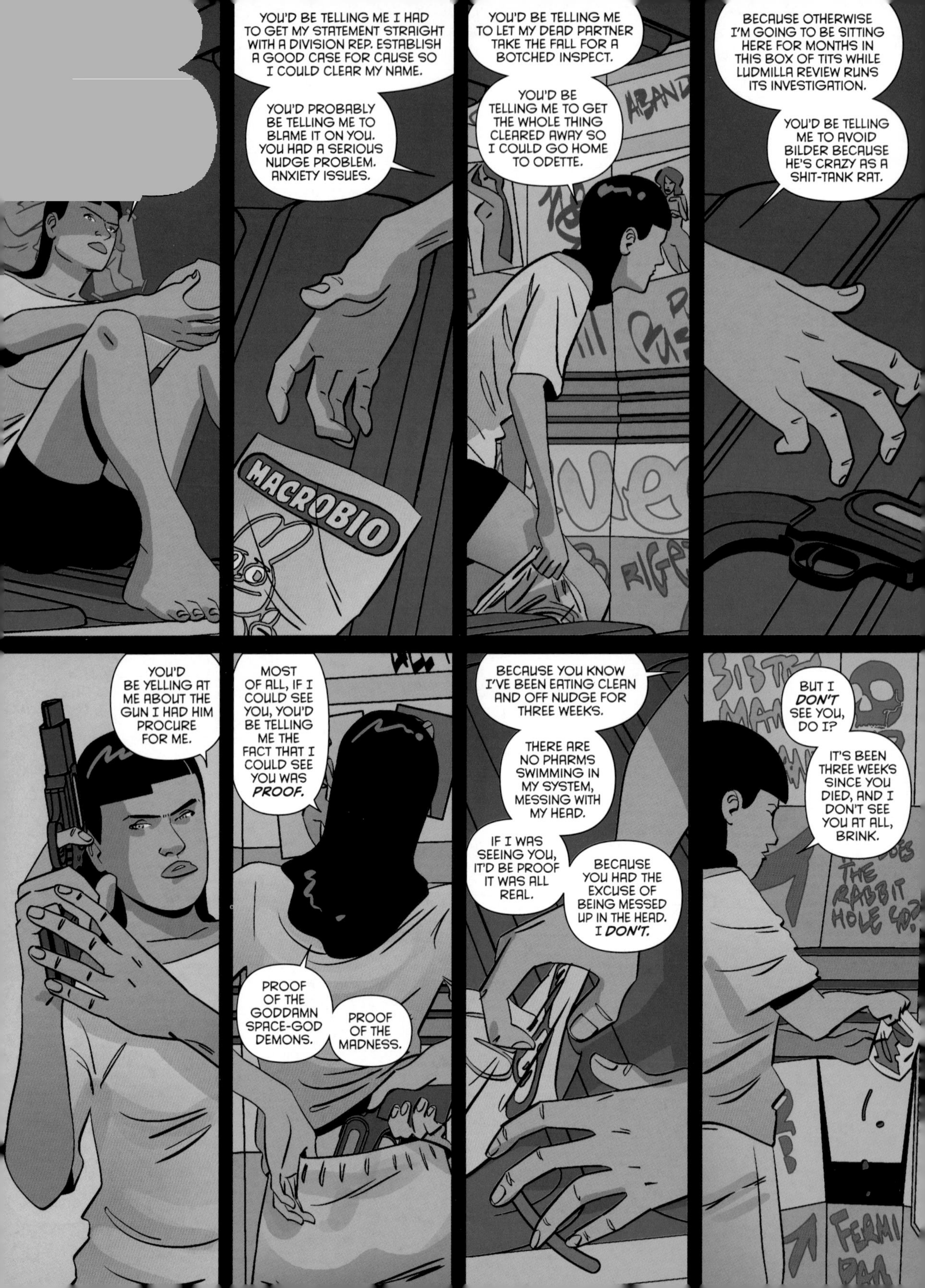

YOU'D BE TELLING ME I HAD TO GET MY STATEMENT STRAIGHT WITH A DIVISION REP. ESTABLISH A GOOD CASE FOR CAUSE SO I COULD CLEAR MY NAME.
YOU'D PROBABLY BE TELLING ME TO BLAME IT ON YOU. YOU HAD A SERIOUS NUDGE PROBLEM. ANXIETY ISSUES.
MACROBIO
YOU'D BE TELLING ME TO LET MY DEAD PARTNER TAKE THE FALL FOR A BOTCHED INSPECT.
YOU'D BE TELLING ME TO GET THE WHOLE THING CLEARED AWAY SO I COULD GO HOME TO ODETTE.
BECAUSE OTHERWISE I'M GOING TO BE SITTING HERE FOR MONTHS IN THIS BOX OF TITS WHILE LUDMILLA REVIEW RUNS ITS INVESTIGATION.
YOU'D BE TELLING ME TO AVOID BILDER BECAUSE HE'S CRAZY AS A SHIT-TANK RAT.
YOU'D BE YELLING AT ME ABOUT THE GUN I HAD HIM PROCURE FOR ME.
MOST OF ALL, IF I COULD SEE YOU, YOU'D BE TELLING ME THE FACT THAT I COULD SEE YOU WAS *PROOF.*
PROOF OF THE GODDAMN SPACE-GOD DEMONS.
PROOF OF THE MADNESS.
BECAUSE YOU KNOW I'VE BEEN EATING CLEAN AND OFF NUDGE FOR THREE WEEKS.
THERE ARE NO PHARMS SWIMMING IN MY SYSTEM, MESSING WITH MY HEAD.
IF I WAS SEEING YOU, IT'D BE PROOF IT WAS ALL REAL.
BECAUSE YOU HAD THE EXCUSE OF BEING MESSED UP IN THE HEAD. I *DON'T.*
BUT I *DON'T* SEE YOU, DO I?
IT'S BEEN THREE WEEKS SINCE YOU DIED, AND I DON'T SEE YOU AT ALL, BRINK.

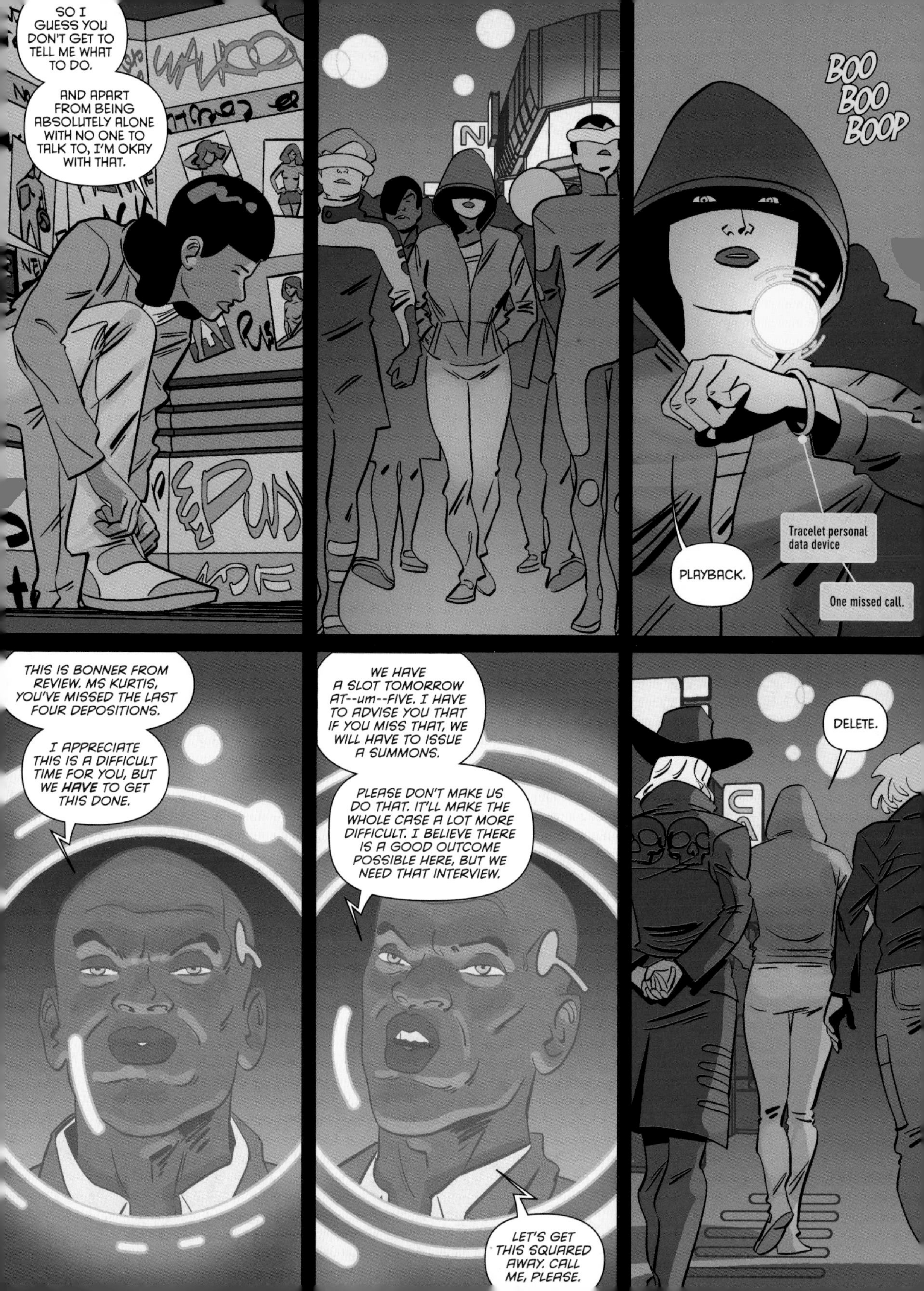

SO I GUESS YOU DON'T GET TO TELL ME WHAT TO DO.
AND APART FROM BEING ABSOLUTELY ALONE WITH NO ONE TO TALK TO, I'M OKAY WITH THAT.
BOO BOO BOOP
Tracelet personal data device
PLAYBACK.
One missed call.
THIS IS BONNER FROM REVIEW. MS KURTIS, YOU'VE MISSED THE LAST FOUR DEPOSITIONS.
I APPRECIATE THIS IS A DIFFICULT TIME FOR YOU, BUT WE HAVE TO GET THIS DONE.
WE HAVE A SLOT TOMORROW AT--um--FIVE. I HAVE TO ADVISE YOU THAT IF YOU MISS THAT, WE WILL HAVE TO ISSUE A SUMMONS.
PLEASE DON'T MAKE US DO THAT. IT'LL MAKE THE WHOLE CASE A LOT MORE DIFFICULT. I BELIEVE THERE IS A GOOD OUTCOME POSSIBLE HERE, BUT WE NEED THAT INTERVIEW.
LET'S GET THIS SQUARED AWAY. CALL ME, PLEASE.
DELETE.

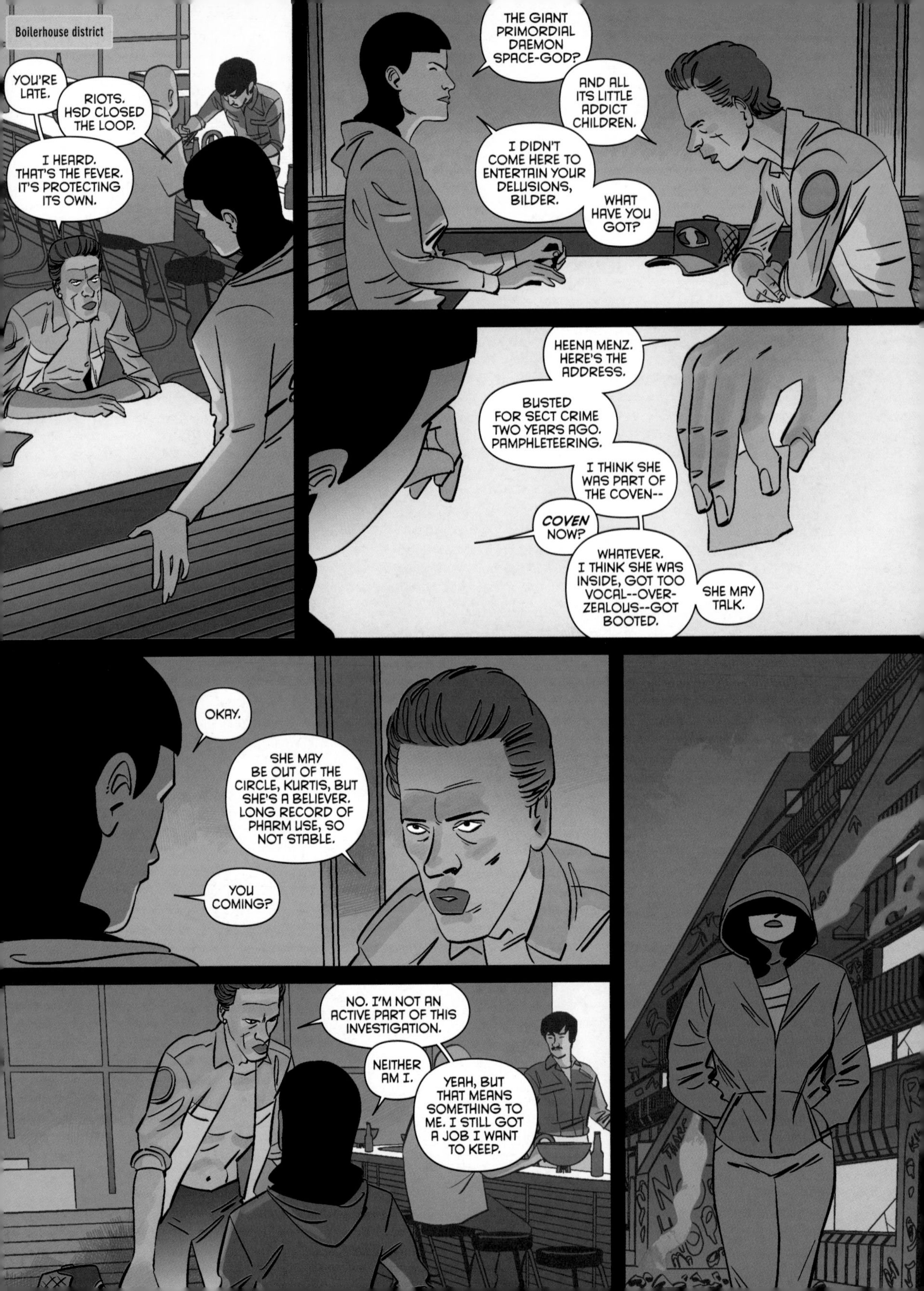
Boilerhouse district
YOU'RE LATE.
RIOTS. HSD CLOSED THE LOOP.
I HEARD. THAT'S THE FEVER. IT'S PROTECTING ITS OWN.
THE GIANT PRIMORDIAL DAEMON SPACE-GOD?
AND ALL ITS LITTLE ADDICT CHILDREN.
I DIDN'T COME HERE TO ENTERTAIN YOUR DELUSIONS, BILDER.
WHAT HAVE YOU GOT?
HEENA MENZ. HERE'S THE ADDRESS.
BUSTED FOR SECT CRIME TWO YEARS AGO. PAMPHLETEERING.
I THINK SHE WAS PART OF THE COVEN--
COVEN NOW?
WHATEVER. I THINK SHE WAS INSIDE, GOT TOO VOCAL--OVER-ZEALOUS--GOT BOOTED.
SHE MAY TALK.
OKAY.
SHE MAY BE OUT OF THE CIRCLE, KURTIS, BUT SHE'S A BELIEVER. LONG RECORD OF PHARM USE, SO NOT STABLE.
YOU COMING?
NO. I'M NOT AN ACTIVE PART OF THIS INVESTIGATION.
NEITHER AM I.
YEAH, BUT THAT MEANS SOMETHING TO ME. I STILL GOT A JOB I WANT TO KEEP.

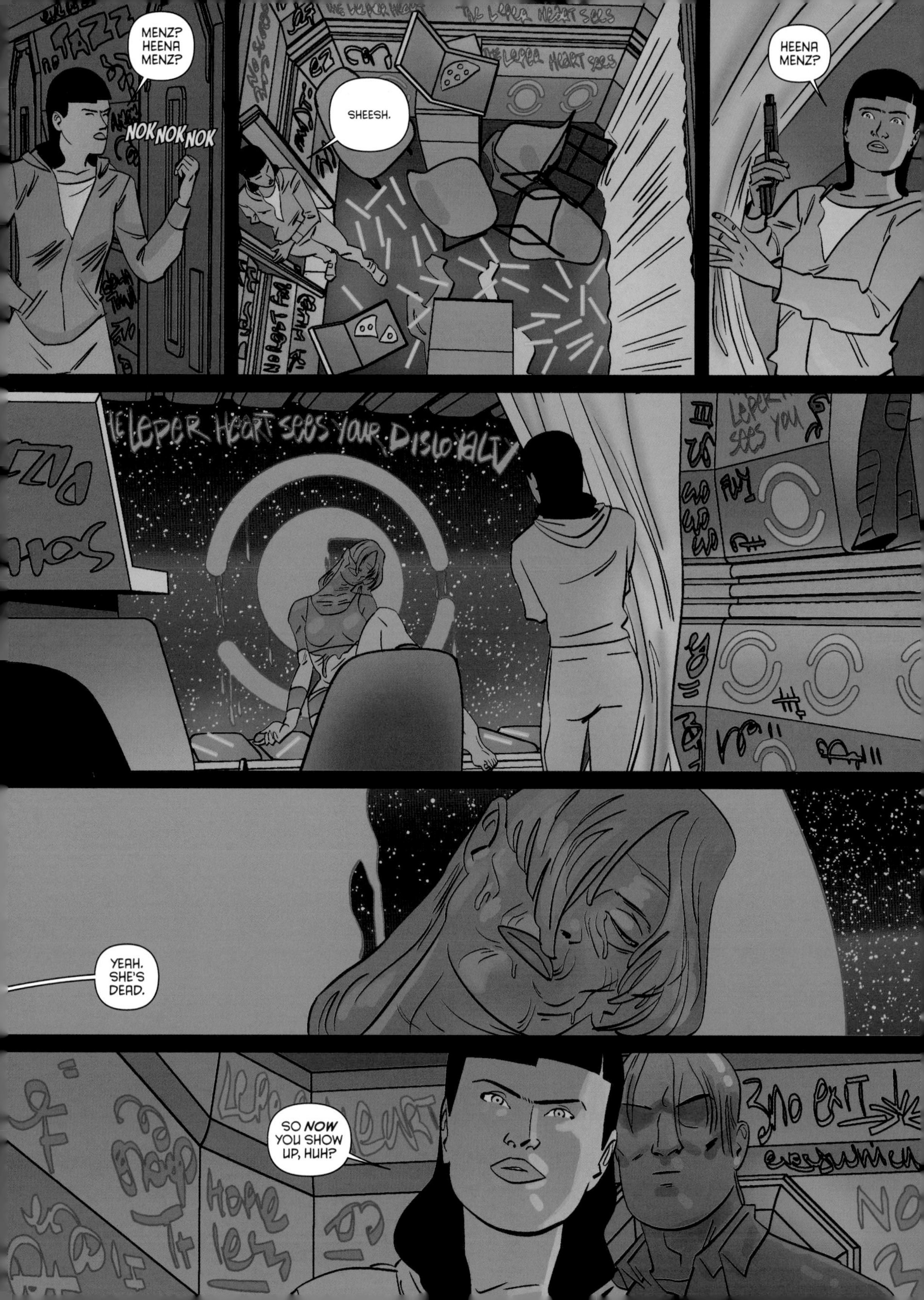
MENZ? HEENA MENZ?
NOK NOK NOK
SHEESH.
HEENA MENZ?
YEAH. SHE'S DEAD.
SO *NOW* YOU SHOW UP, HUH?

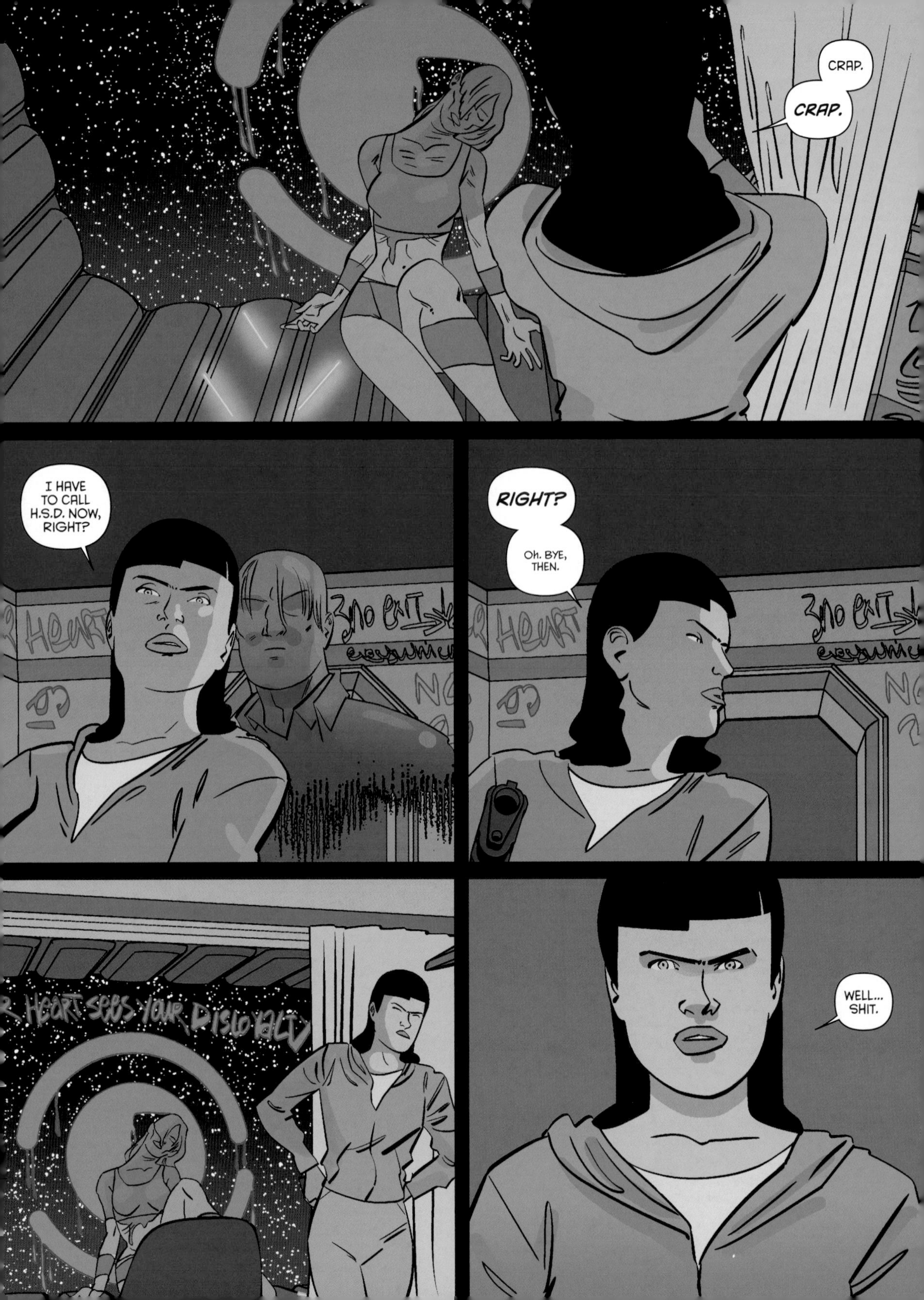
CRAP.
CRAP.
I HAVE TO CALL H.S.D. NOW, RIGHT?
RIGHT?
Oh. BYE, THEN.
HEART
NO EXIT
HEART SEES YOUR DISLOYALTY
WELL... SHIT.

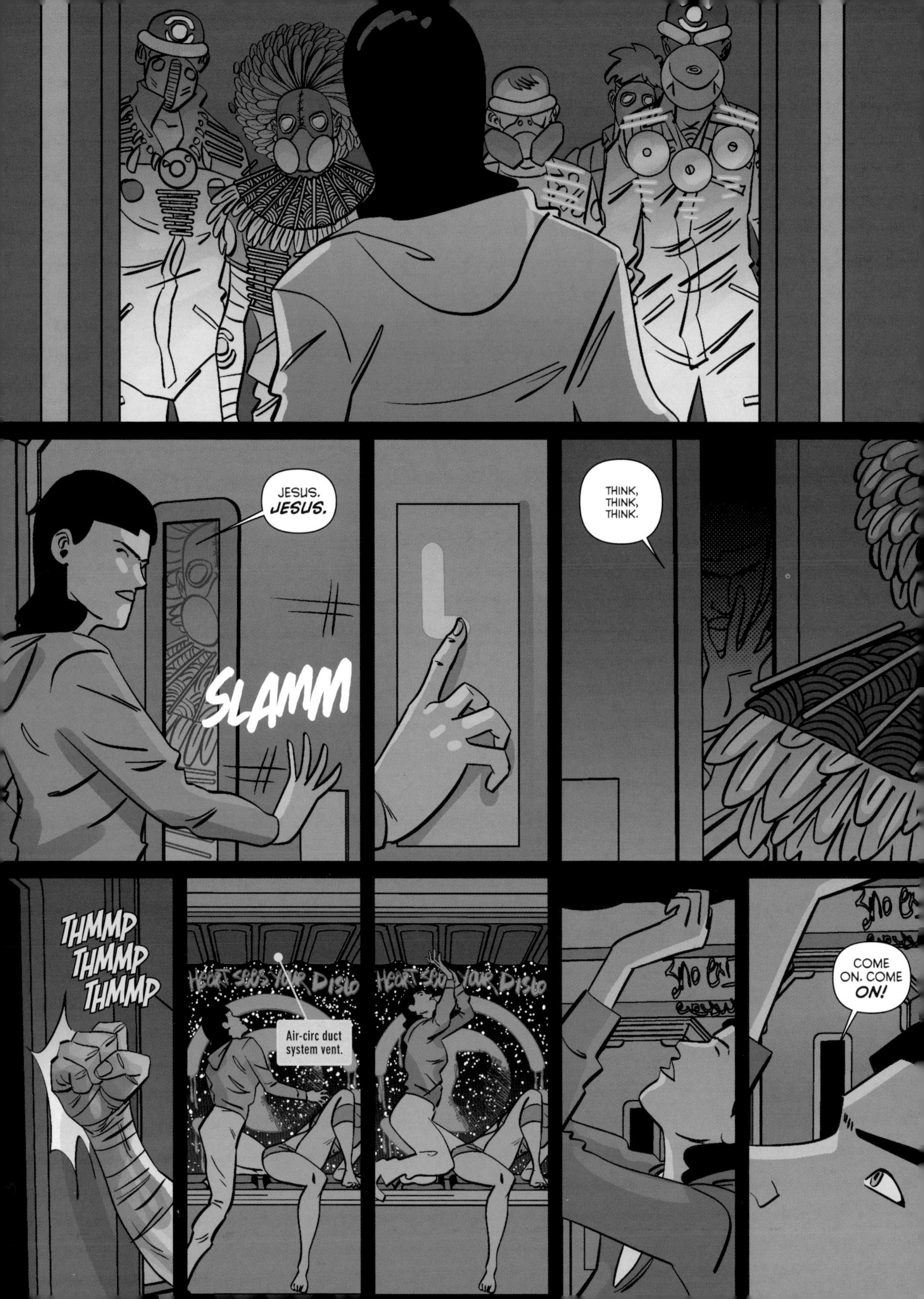
JESUS. JESUS.
SLAMM
THINK, THINK, THINK.
THMMP THMMP THMMP
Air-circ duct system vent.
COME ON. COME ON!

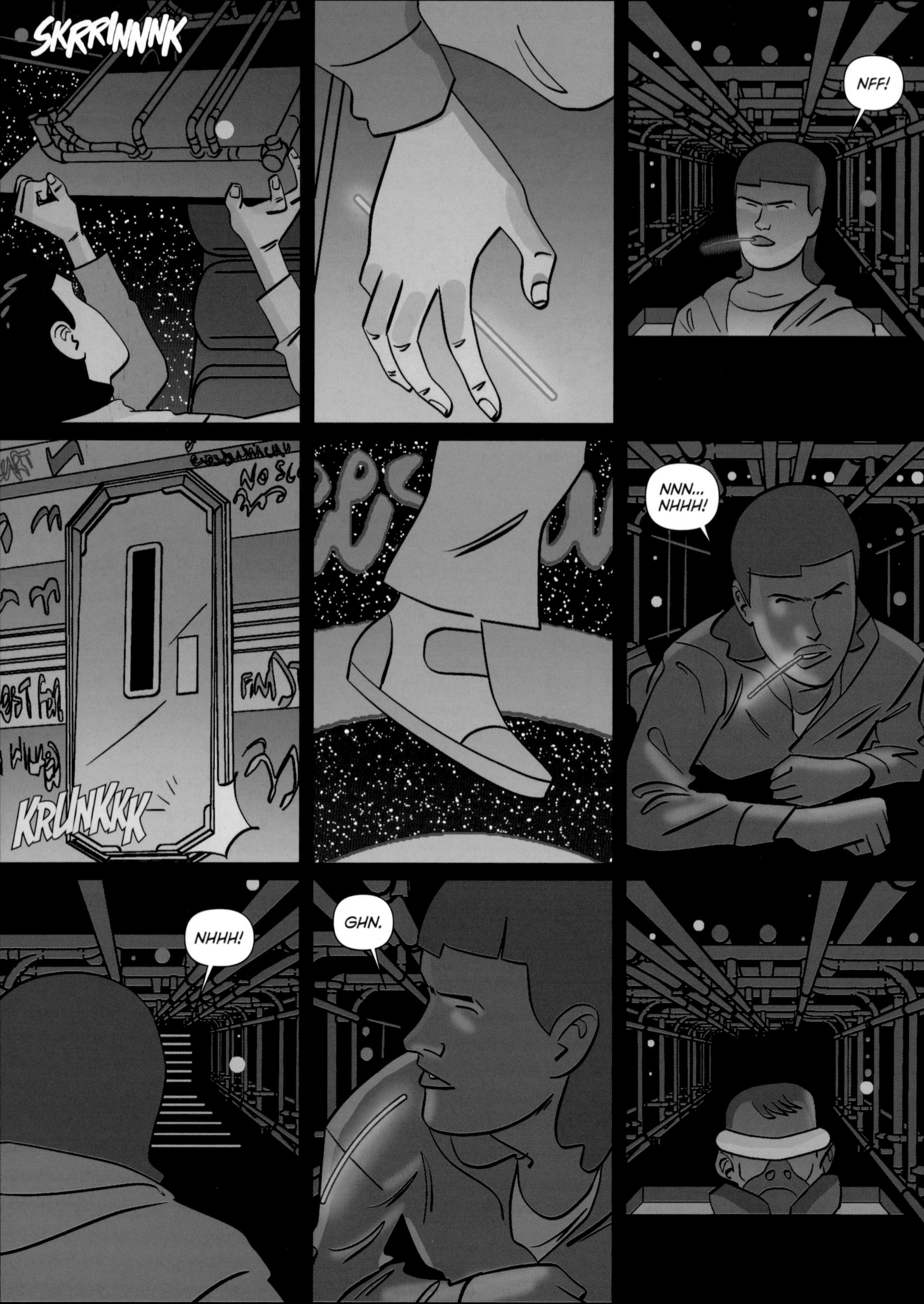
SKRRINNNK
NFF!
KRUNKKK
NNN... NHHH!
NHHH!
GHN.

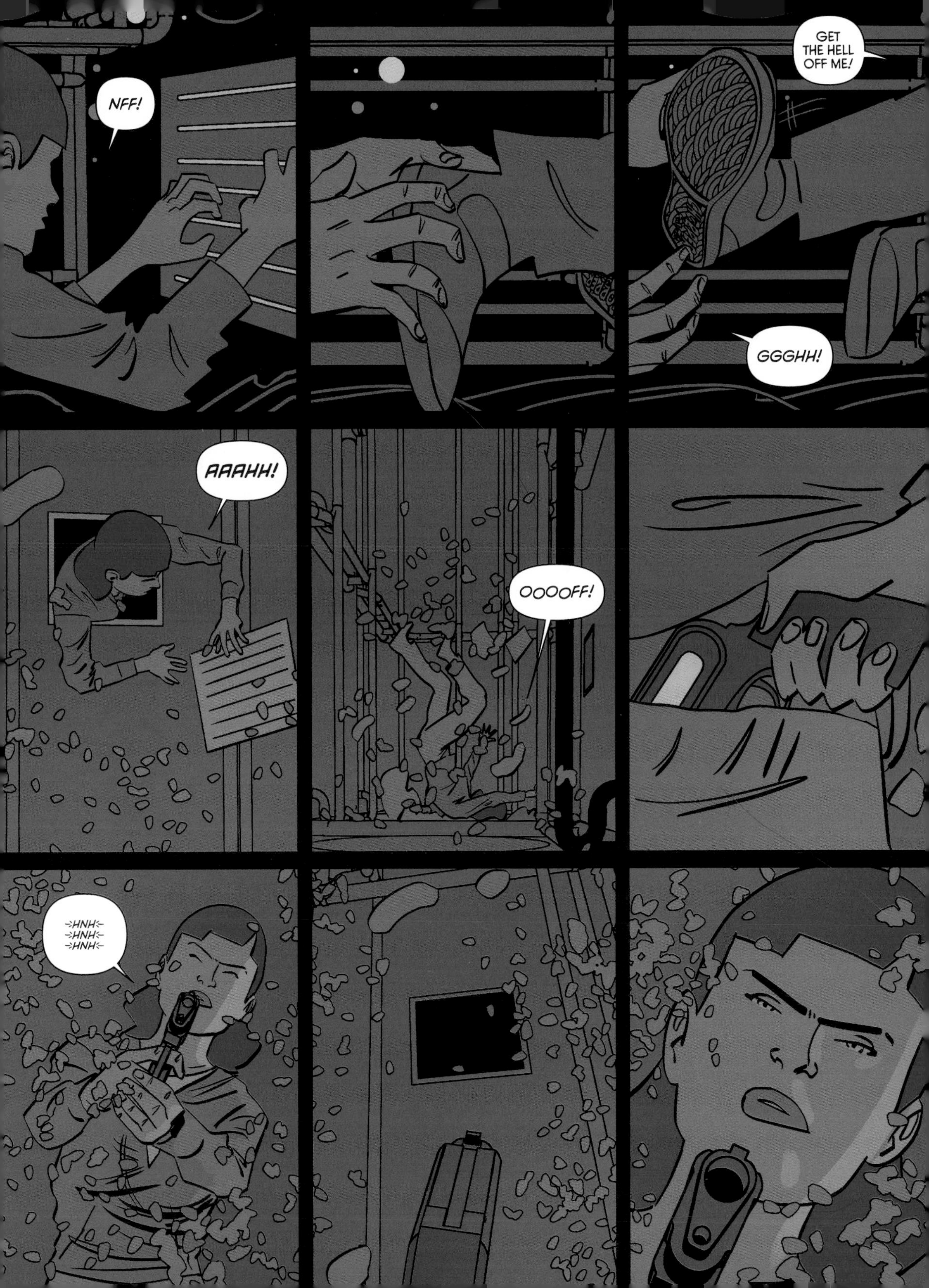
NFF!
GET THE HELL OFF ME!
GGGHH!
AAAHH!
OOOOFF!
HNH
HNH
HNH

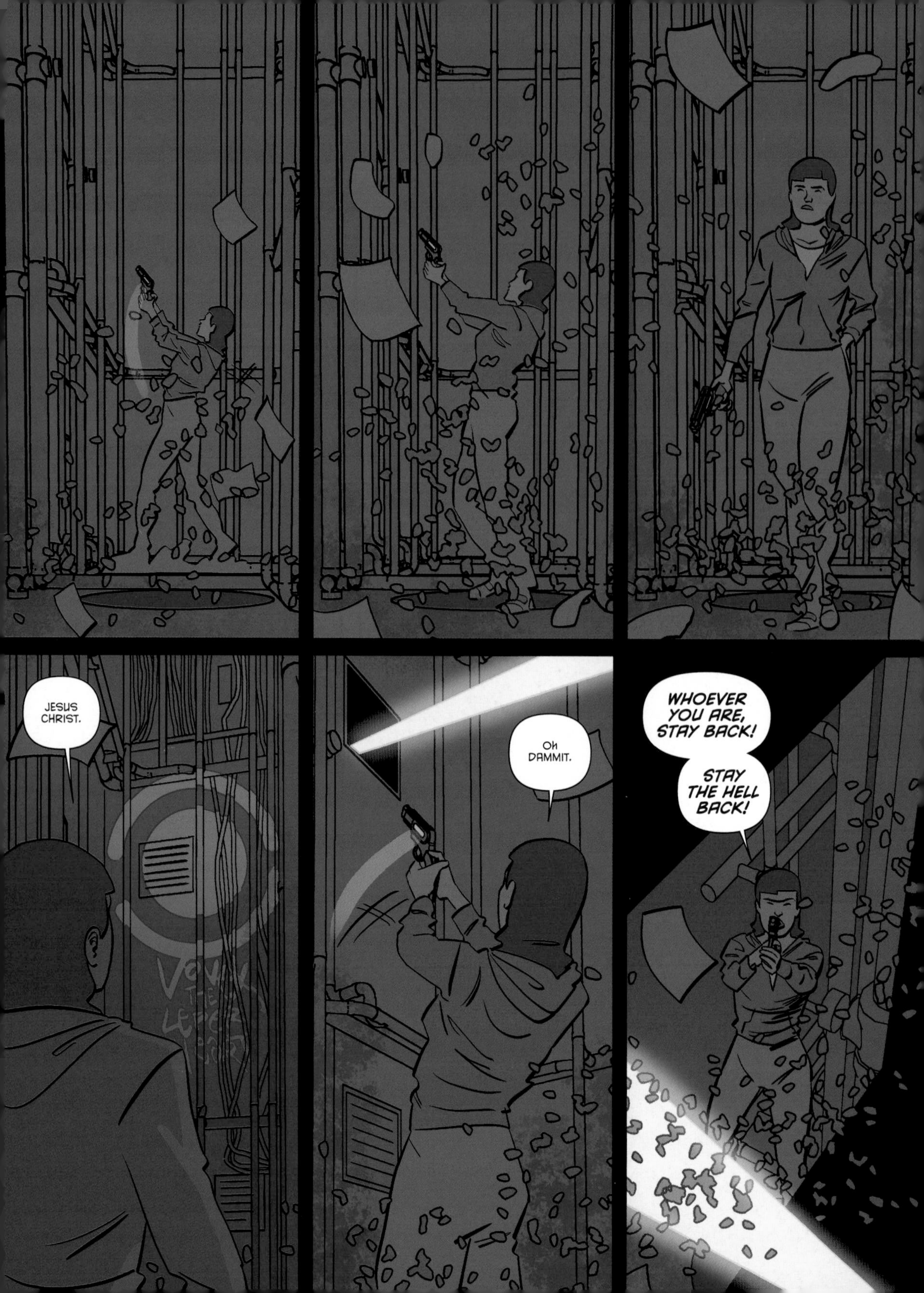
JESUS CHRIST.
Oh DAMMIT.
WHOEVER YOU ARE, STAY BACK!
STAY THE HELL BACK!

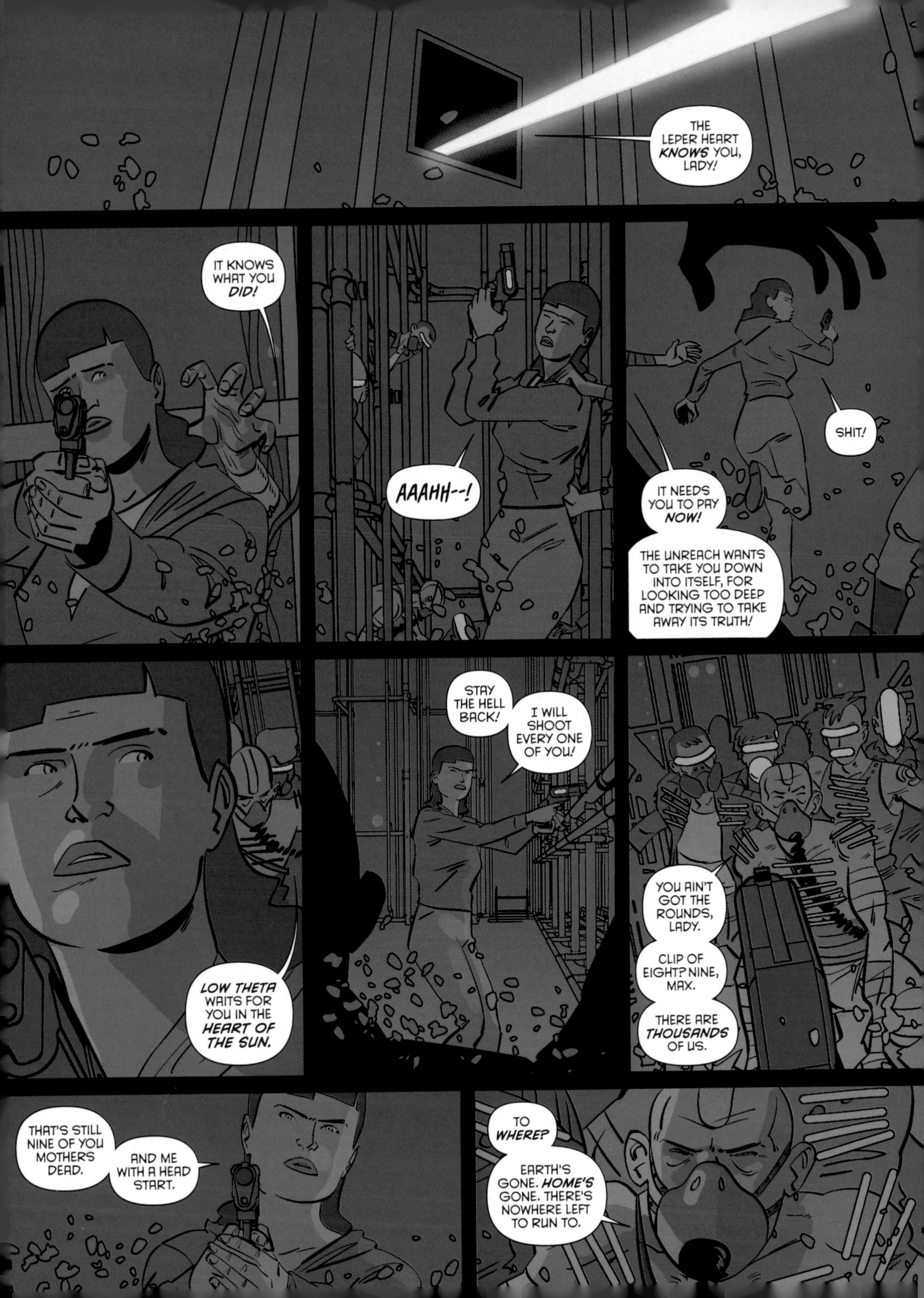
THE LEPER HEART KNOWS YOU, LADY!
IT KNOWS WHAT YOU DID!
AAAHH--!
SHIT!
IT NEEDS YOU TO PAY NOW!
THE UNREACH WANTS TO TAKE YOU DOWN INTO ITSELF, FOR LOOKING TOO DEEP AND TRYING TO TAKE AWAY ITS TRUTH!
LOW THETA WAITS FOR YOU IN THE HEART OF THE SUN.
STAY THE HELL BACK!
I WILL SHOOT EVERY ONE OF YOU!
YOU AIN'T GOT THE ROUNDS, LADY.
CLIP OF EIGHT? NINE, MAX.
THERE ARE THOUSANDS OF US.
THAT'S STILL NINE OF YOU MOTHERS DEAD.
AND ME WITH A HEAD START.
TO WHERE?
EARTH'S GONE. HOME'S GONE. THERE'S NOWHERE LEFT TO RUN TO.

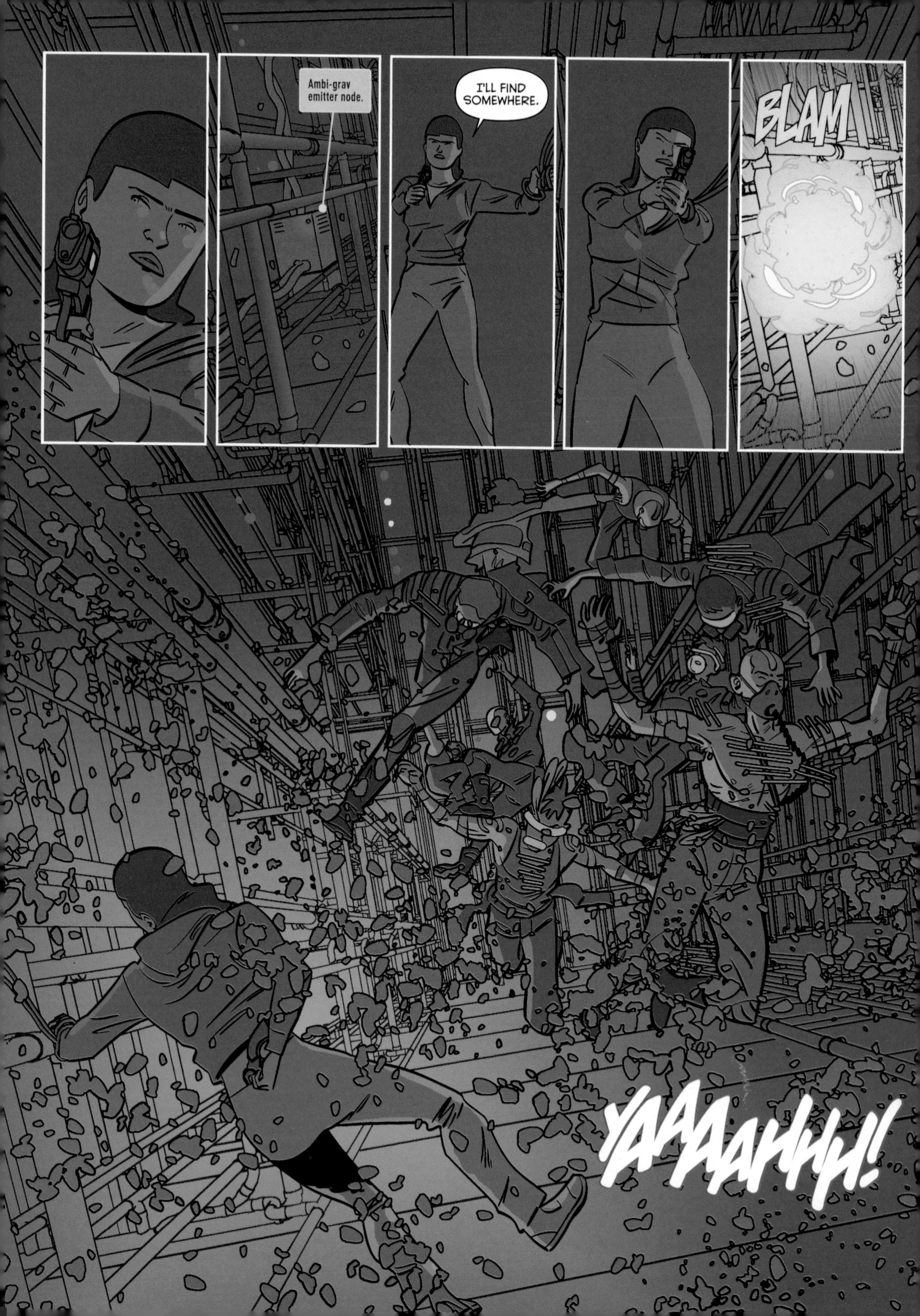
Ambi-grav emitter node.
I'LL FIND SOMEWHERE.
BLAM
YAAAAHHH!

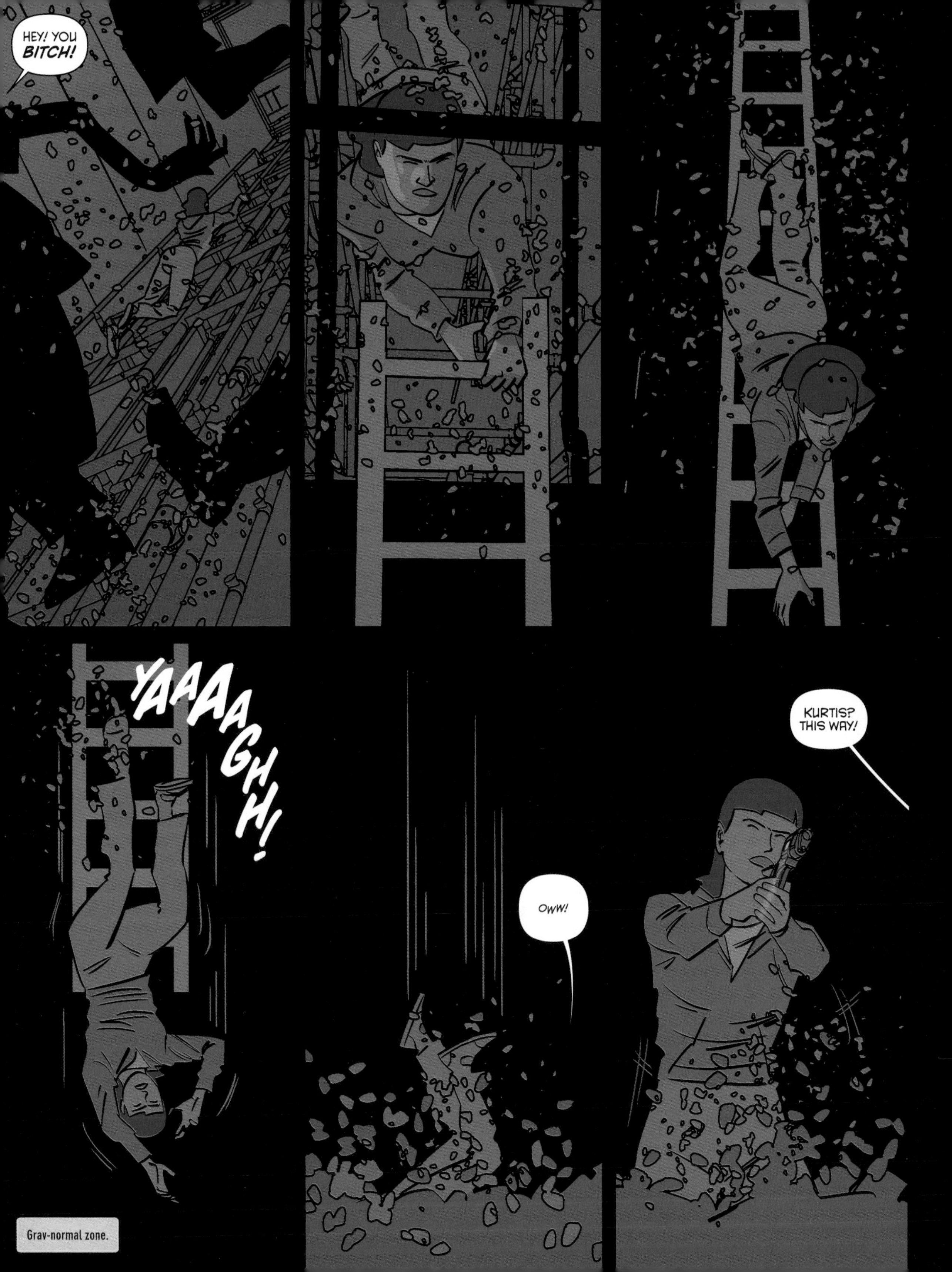
HEY! YOU BITCH!
YAAAAGHH!
OWW!
KURTIS? THIS WAY!
Grav-normal zone.

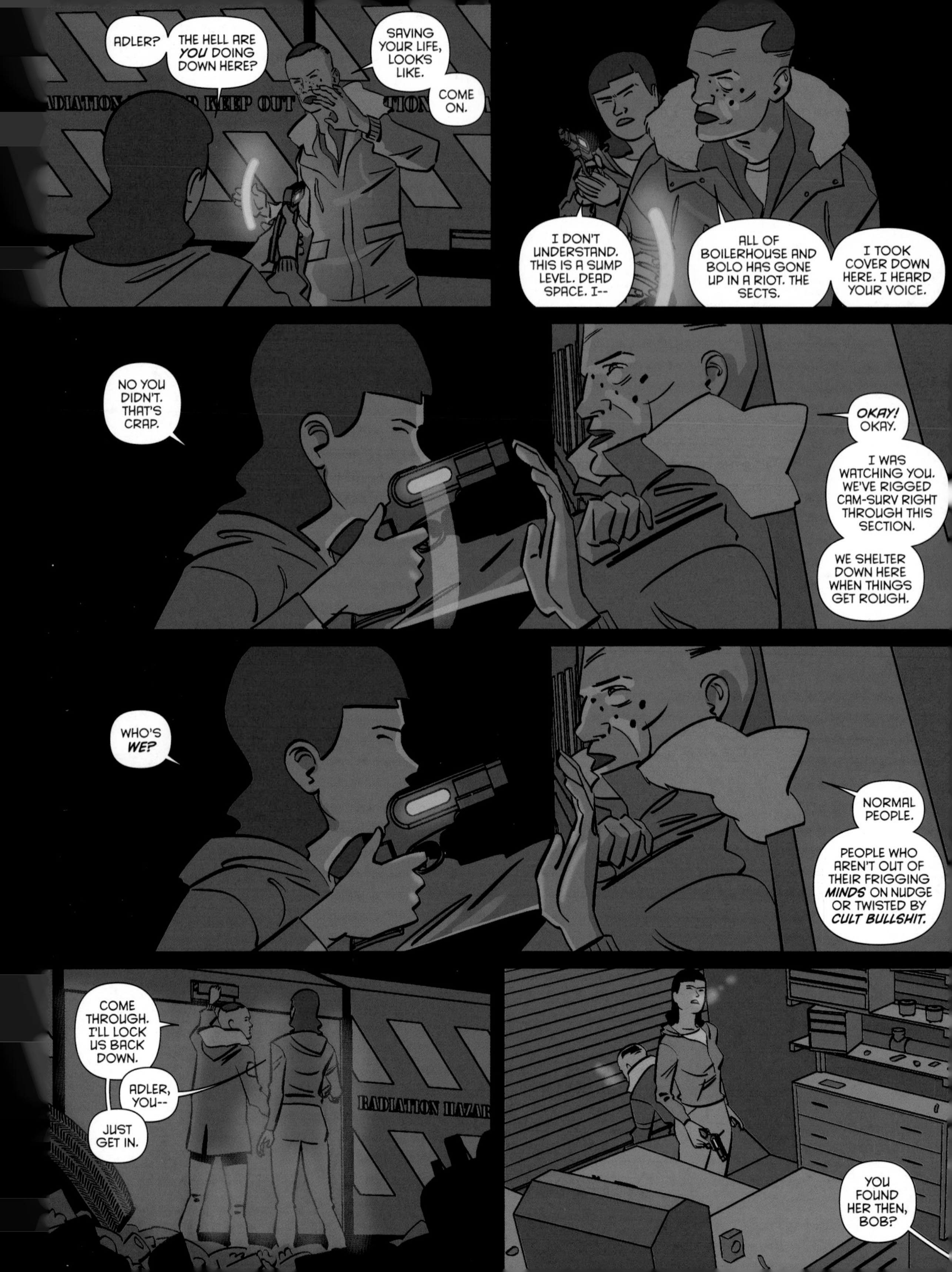

ADLER?
THE HELL ARE *YOU* DOING DOWN HERE?
SAVING YOUR LIFE, LOOKS LIKE.
COME ON.
RADIATION HAZARD KEEP OUT
I DON'T UNDERSTAND. THIS IS A SUMP LEVEL. DEAD SPACE. I--
ALL OF BOILERHOUSE AND BOLO HAS GONE UP IN A RIOT. THE SECTS.
I TOOK COVER DOWN HERE. I HEARD YOUR VOICE.
NO YOU DIDN'T. THAT'S CRAP.
OKAY! OKAY.
I WAS WATCHING YOU. WE'VE RIGGED CAM-SURV RIGHT THROUGH THIS SECTION.
WE SHELTER DOWN HERE WHEN THINGS GET ROUGH.
WHO'S *WE?*
NORMAL PEOPLE.
PEOPLE WHO AREN'T OUT OF THEIR FRIGGING *MINDS* ON NUDGE OR TWISTED BY *CULT BULLSHIT.*
COME THROUGH. I'LL LOCK US BACK DOWN.
ADLER, YOU--
JUST GET IN.
RADIATION HAZAR
YOU FOUND HER THEN, BOB?

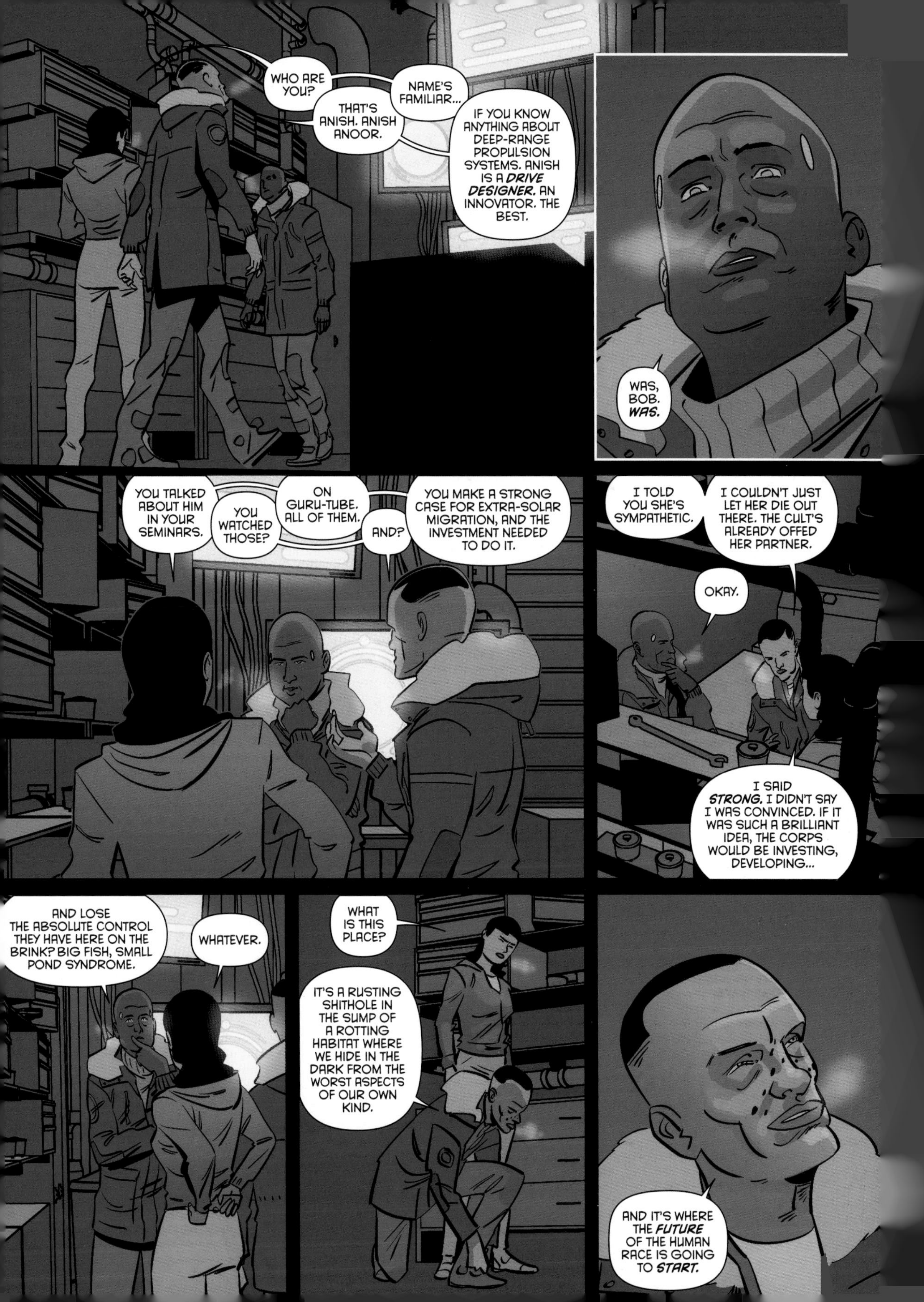
WHO ARE YOU?
THAT'S ANISH. ANISH ANOOR.
NAME'S FAMILIAR...
IF YOU KNOW ANYTHING ABOUT DEEP-RANGE PROPULSION SYSTEMS. ANISH IS A DRIVE DESIGNER. AN INNOVATOR. THE BEST.
WAS, BOB. WAS.
YOU TALKED ABOUT HIM IN YOUR SEMINARS.
YOU WATCHED THOSE?
ON GURU-TUBE. ALL OF THEM.
AND?
YOU MAKE A STRONG CASE FOR EXTRA-SOLAR MIGRATION, AND THE INVESTMENT NEEDED TO DO IT.
I TOLD YOU SHE'S SYMPATHETIC.
I COULDN'T JUST LET HER DIE OUT THERE. THE CULT'S ALREADY OFFED HER PARTNER.
OKAY.
I SAID STRONG. I DIDN'T SAY I WAS CONVINCED. IF IT WAS SUCH A BRILLIANT IDEA, THE CORPS WOULD BE INVESTING, DEVELOPING...
AND LOSE THE ABSOLUTE CONTROL THEY HAVE HERE ON THE BRINK? BIG FISH, SMALL POND SYNDROME.
WHATEVER.
WHAT IS THIS PLACE?
IT'S A RUSTING SHITHOLE IN THE SUMP OF A ROTTING HABITAT WHERE WE HIDE IN THE DARK FROM THE WORST ASPECTS OF OUR OWN KIND.
AND IT'S WHERE THE FUTURE OF THE HUMAN RACE IS GOING TO START.

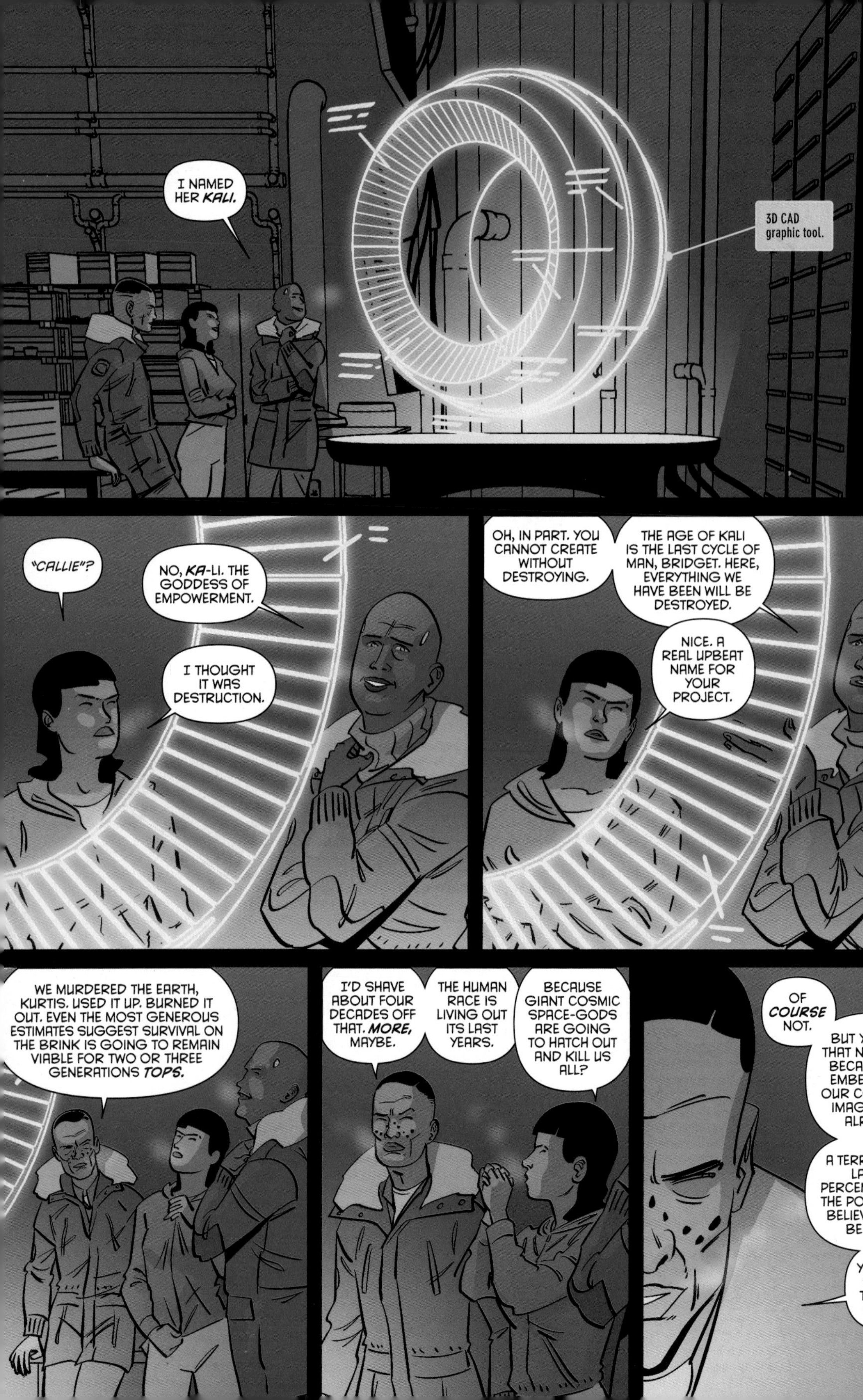
I NAMED HER KALI.
3D CAD graphic tool.
"CALLIE"?
NO, KA-LI. THE GODDESS OF EMPOWERMENT.
I THOUGHT IT WAS DESTRUCTION.
OH, IN PART. YOU CANNOT CREATE WITHOUT DESTROYING.
THE AGE OF KALI IS THE LAST CYCLE OF MAN, BRIDGET. HERE, EVERYTHING WE HAVE BEEN WILL BE DESTROYED.
NICE. A REAL UPBEAT NAME FOR YOUR PROJECT.
WE MURDERED THE EARTH, KURTIS. USED IT UP. BURNED IT OUT. EVEN THE MOST GENEROUS ESTIMATES SUGGEST SURVIVAL ON THE BRINK IS GOING TO REMAIN VIABLE FOR TWO OR THREE GENERATIONS TOPS.
I'D SHAVE ABOUT FOUR DECADES OFF THAT. MORE, MAYBE.
THE HUMAN RACE IS LIVING OUT ITS LAST YEARS.
BECAUSE GIANT COSMIC SPACE-GODS ARE GOING TO HATCH OUT AND KILL US ALL?
OF COURSE NOT.
BUT YOU SAY THAT NONSENSE BECAUSE IT IS EMBEDDED IN OUR COLLECTIVE IMAGINATION ALREADY.
A TERRIFYINGLY LARGE PERCENTAGE OF THE POPULATION BELIEVES IT TO BE FACT.
YOU'VE MET SOME OF THEM FACE TO FACE.

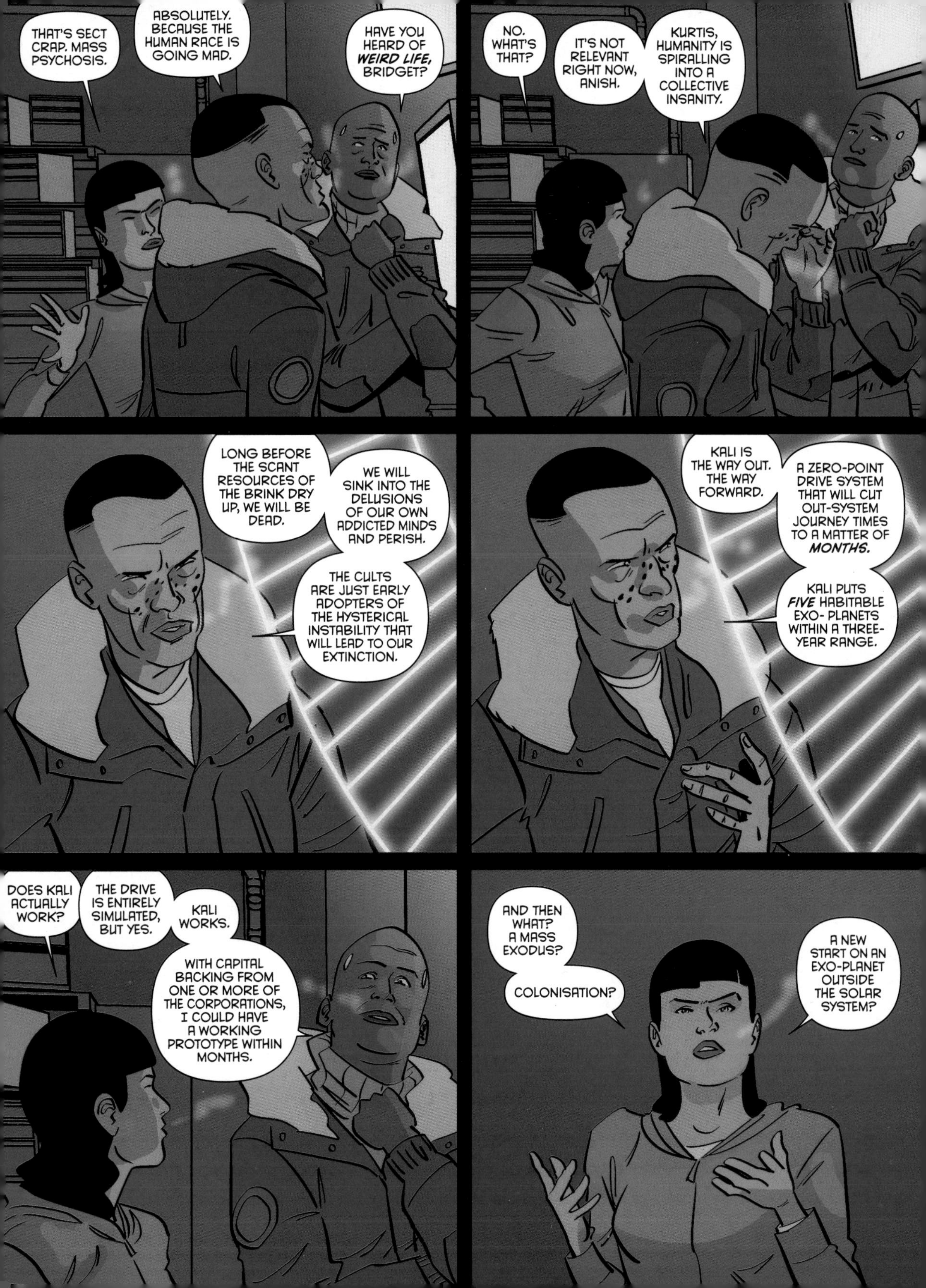
THAT'S SECT CRAP. MASS PSYCHOSIS.
ABSOLUTELY. BECAUSE THE HUMAN RACE IS GOING MAD.
HAVE YOU HEARD OF *WEIRD LIFE,* BRIDGET?
NO. WHAT'S THAT?
IT'S NOT RELEVANT RIGHT NOW, ANISH.
KURTIS, HUMANITY IS SPIRALLING INTO A COLLECTIVE INSANITY.
LONG BEFORE THE SCANT RESOURCES OF THE BRINK DRY UP, WE WILL BE DEAD.
WE WILL SINK INTO THE DELUSIONS OF OUR OWN ADDICTED MINDS AND PERISH.
THE CULTS ARE JUST EARLY ADOPTERS OF THE HYSTERICAL INSTABILITY THAT WILL LEAD TO OUR EXTINCTION.
KALI IS THE WAY OUT. THE WAY FORWARD.
A ZERO-POINT DRIVE SYSTEM THAT WILL CUT OUT-SYSTEM JOURNEY TIMES TO A MATTER OF *MONTHS.*
KALI PUTS *FIVE* HABITABLE EXO- PLANETS WITHIN A THREE-YEAR RANGE.
DOES KALI ACTUALLY WORK?
THE DRIVE IS ENTIRELY SIMULATED, BUT YES.
KALI WORKS.
WITH CAPITAL BACKING FROM ONE OR MORE OF THE CORPORATIONS, I COULD HAVE A WORKING PROTOTYPE WITHIN MONTHS.
AND THEN WHAT? A MASS EXODUS?
COLONISATION?
A NEW START ON AN EXO-PLANET OUTSIDE THE SOLAR SYSTEM?

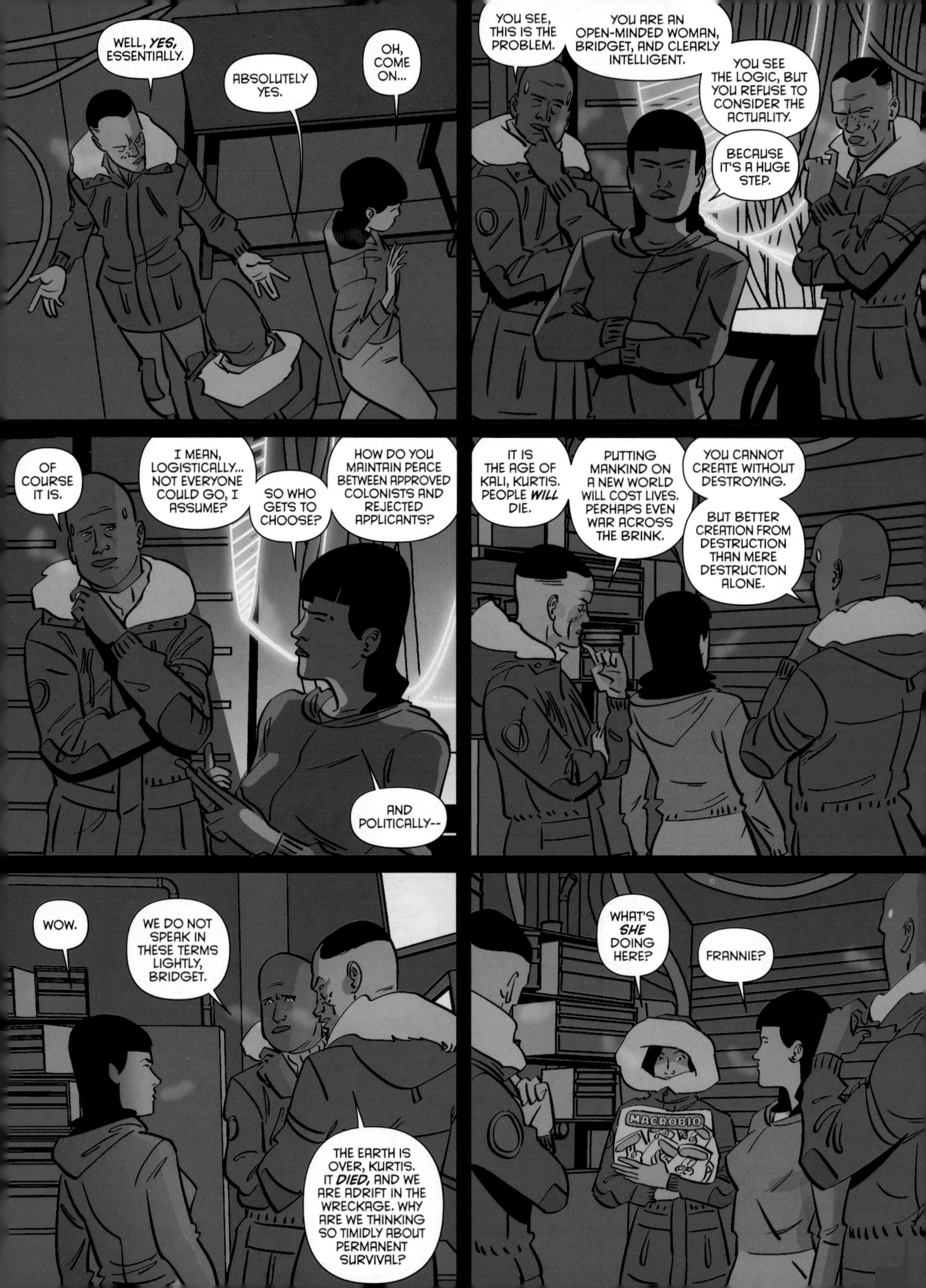
WELL, *YES,* ESSENTIALLY.
ABSOLUTELY YES.
OH, COME ON...
YOU SEE, THIS IS THE PROBLEM.
YOU ARE AN OPEN-MINDED WOMAN, BRIDGET, AND CLEARLY INTELLIGENT.
YOU SEE THE LOGIC, BUT YOU REFUSE TO CONSIDER THE ACTUALITY.
BECAUSE IT'S A HUGE STEP.
OF COURSE IT IS.
I MEAN, LOGISTICALLY... NOT EVERYONE COULD GO, I ASSUME?
SO WHO GETS TO CHOOSE?
HOW DO YOU MAINTAIN PEACE BETWEEN APPROVED COLONISTS AND REJECTED APPLICANTS?
AND POLITICALLY--
IT IS THE AGE OF KALI, KURTIS. PEOPLE *WILL* DIE.
PUTTING MANKIND ON A NEW WORLD WILL COST LIVES. PERHAPS EVEN WAR ACROSS THE BRINK.
YOU CANNOT CREATE WITHOUT DESTROYING.
BUT BETTER CREATION FROM DESTRUCTION THAN MERE DESTRUCTION ALONE.
WOW.
WE DO NOT SPEAK IN THESE TERMS LIGHTLY, BRIDGET.
THE EARTH IS OVER, KURTIS. IT *DIED,* AND WE ARE ADRIFT IN THE WRECKAGE. WHY ARE WE THINKING SO TIMIDLY ABOUT PERMANENT SURVIVAL?
WHAT'S *SHE* DOING HERE?
FRANNIE?
MACROBIO

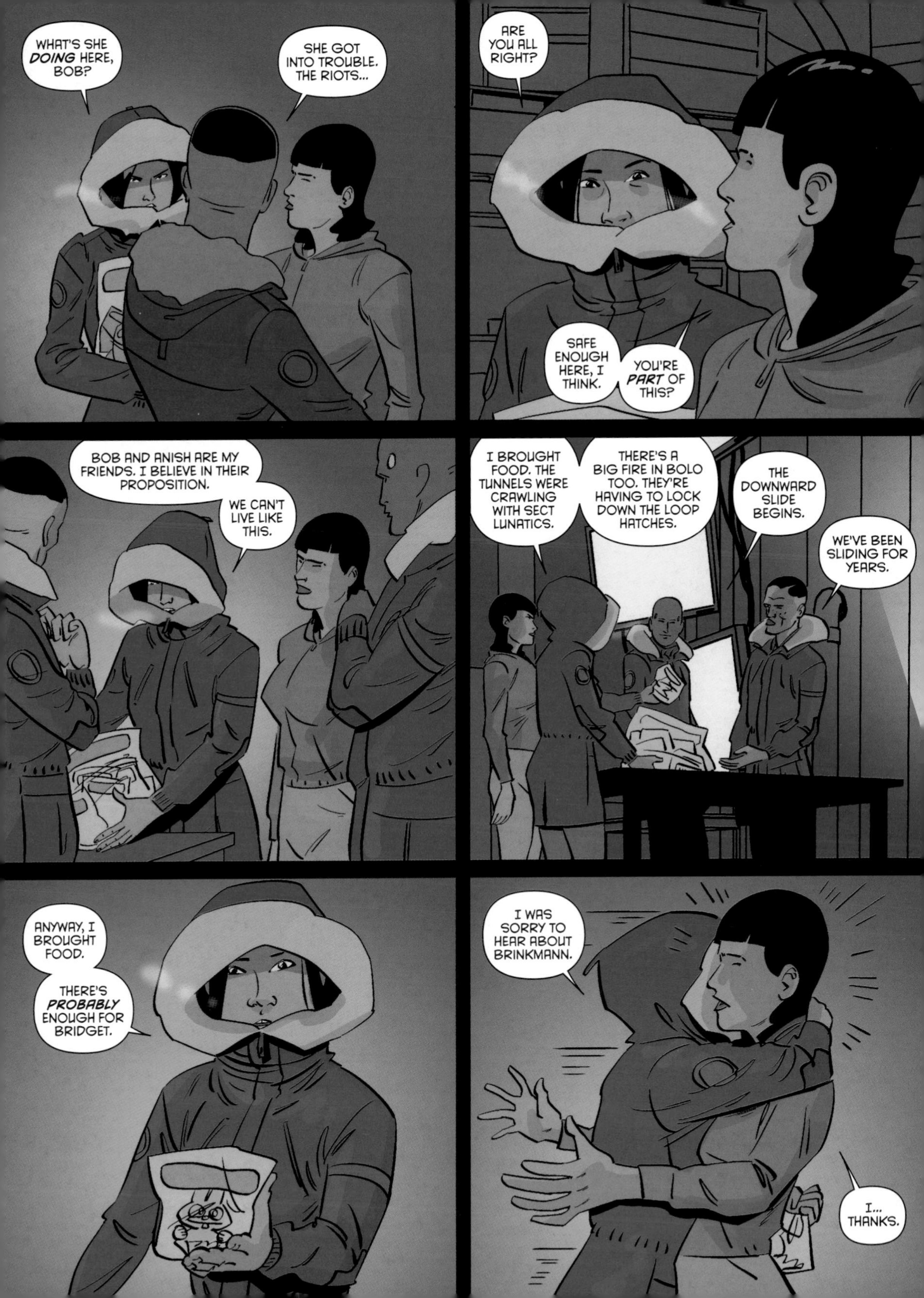
WHAT'S SHE *DOING* HERE, BOB?
SHE GOT INTO TROUBLE. THE RIOTS...
ARE YOU ALL RIGHT?
SAFE ENOUGH HERE, I THINK.
YOU'RE *PART* OF THIS?
BOB AND ANISH ARE MY FRIENDS. I BELIEVE IN THEIR PROPOSITION.
WE CAN'T LIVE LIKE THIS.
I BROUGHT FOOD. THE TUNNELS WERE CRAWLING WITH SECT LUNATICS.
THERE'S A BIG FIRE IN BOLO TOO. THEY'RE HAVING TO LOCK DOWN THE LOOP HATCHES.
THE DOWNWARD SLIDE BEGINS.
WE'VE BEEN SLIDING FOR YEARS.
ANYWAY, I BROUGHT FOOD.
THERE'S *PROBABLY* ENOUGH FOR BRIDGET.
I WAS SORRY TO HEAR ABOUT BRINKMANN.
I... THANKS.

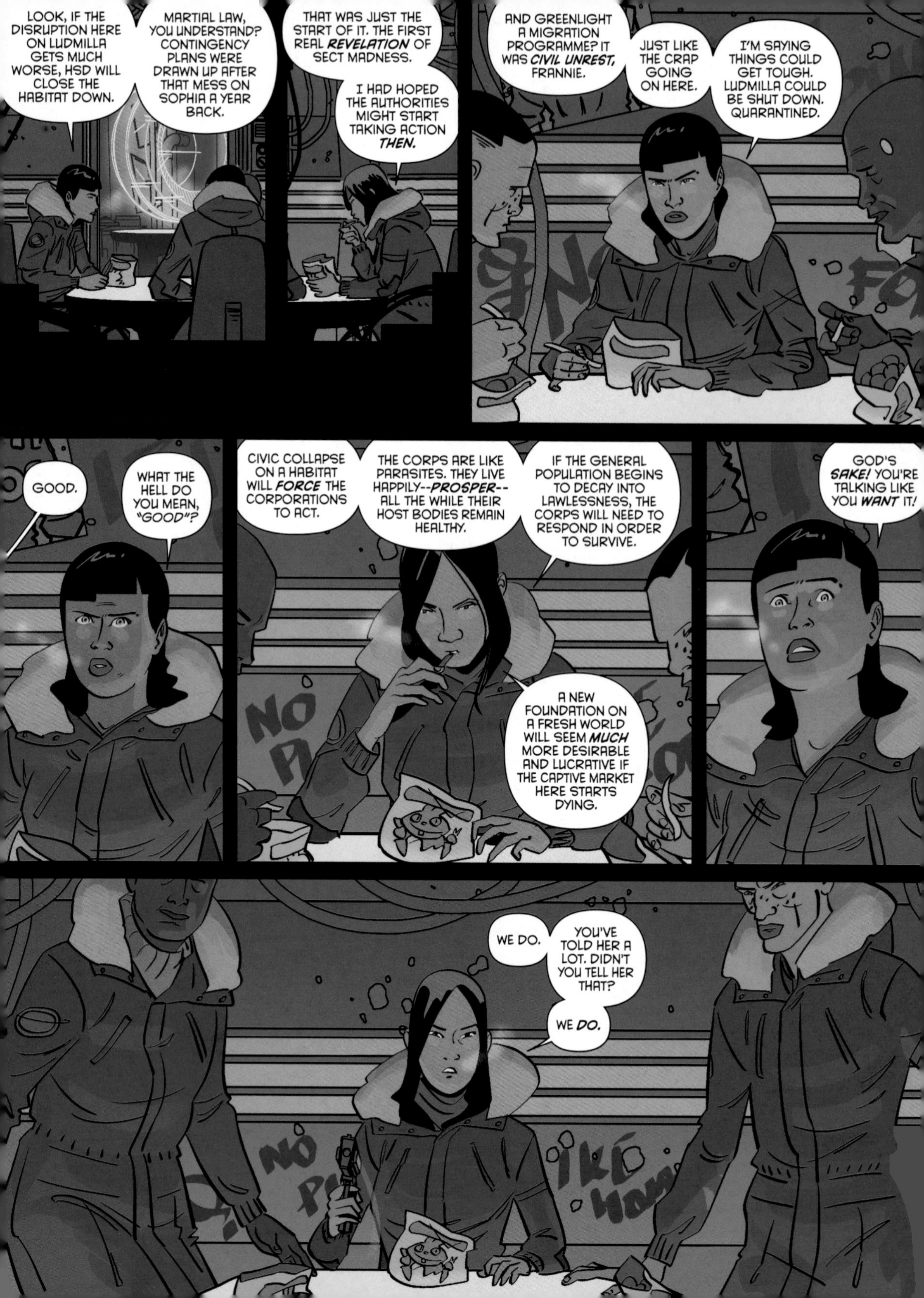
LOOK, IF THE DISRUPTION HERE ON LUDMILLA GETS MUCH WORSE, HSD WILL CLOSE THE HABITAT DOWN.
MARTIAL LAW, YOU UNDERSTAND? CONTINGENCY PLANS WERE DRAWN UP AFTER THAT MESS ON SOPHIA A YEAR BACK.
THAT WAS JUST THE START OF IT. THE FIRST REAL *REVELATION* OF SECT MADNESS.
I HAD HOPED THE AUTHORITIES MIGHT START TAKING ACTION *THEN.*
AND GREENLIGHT A MIGRATION PROGRAMME? IT WAS *CIVIL UNREST,* FRANNIE.
JUST LIKE THE CRAP GOING ON HERE.
I'M SAYING THINGS COULD GET TOUGH. LUDMILLA COULD BE SHUT DOWN. QUARANTINED.
GOOD.
WHAT THE HELL DO YOU MEAN, *"GOOD"*?
CIVIC COLLAPSE ON A HABITAT WILL *FORCE* THE CORPORATIONS TO ACT.
THE CORPS ARE LIKE PARASITES. THEY LIVE HAPPILY--*PROSPER*--ALL THE WHILE THEIR HOST BODIES REMAIN HEALTHY.
IF THE GENERAL POPULATION BEGINS TO DECAY INTO LAWLESSNESS, THE CORPS WILL NEED TO RESPOND IN ORDER TO SURVIVE.
A NEW FOUNDATION ON A FRESH WORLD WILL SEEM *MUCH* MORE DESIRABLE AND LUCRATIVE IF THE CAPTIVE MARKET HERE STARTS DYING.
GOD'S *SAKE!* YOU'RE TALKING LIKE YOU *WANT* IT!
WE DO.
YOU'VE TOLD HER A LOT. DIDN'T YOU TELL HER THAT?
WE *DO.*

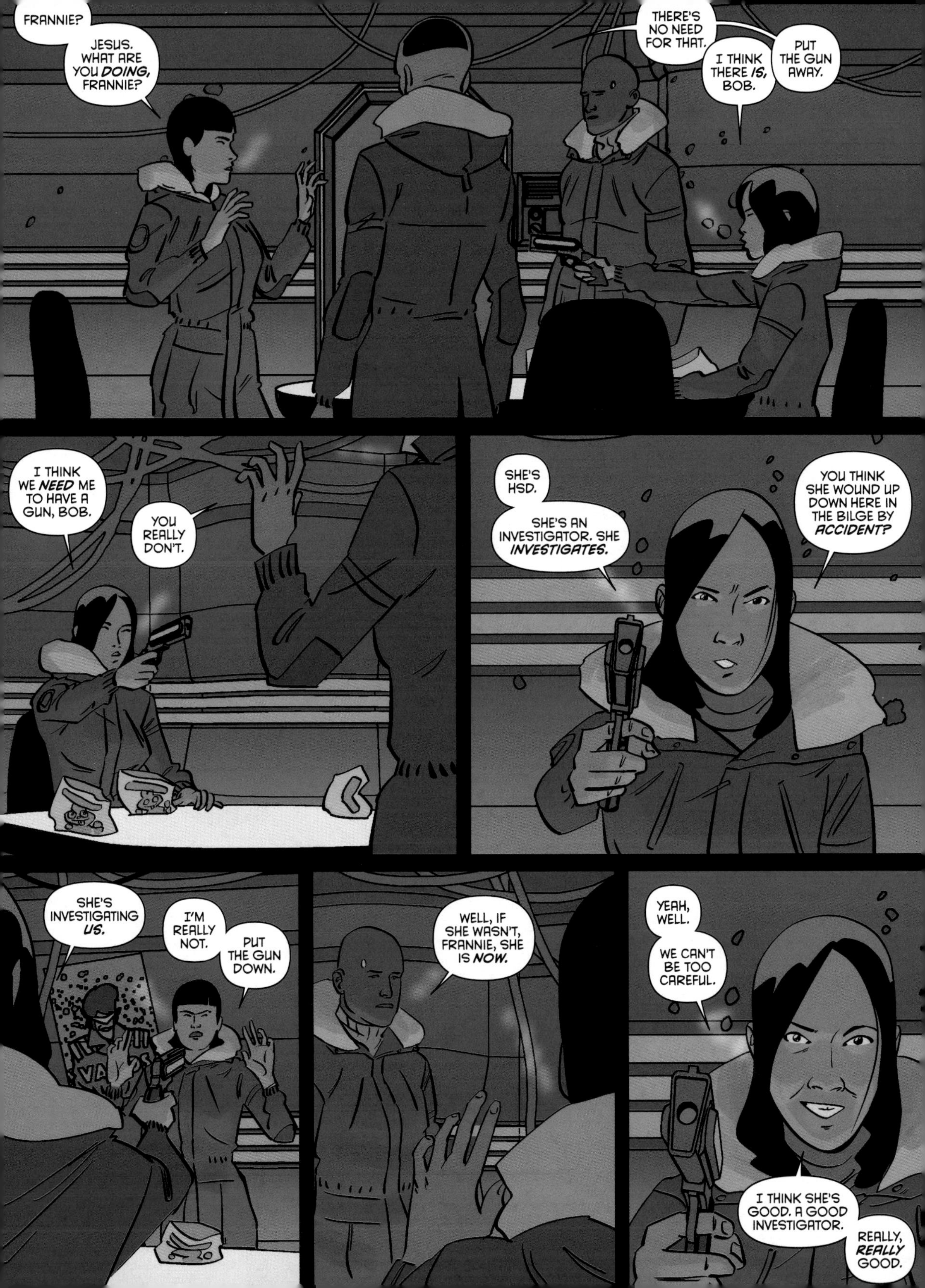
FRANNIE?
JESUS. WHAT ARE YOU *DOING,* FRANNIE?
THERE'S NO NEED FOR THAT.
PUT THE GUN AWAY.
I THINK THERE *IS,* BOB.
I THINK WE *NEED* ME TO HAVE A GUN, BOB.
YOU REALLY DON'T.
SHE'S HSD.
SHE'S AN INVESTIGATOR. SHE *INVESTIGATES.*
YOU THINK SHE WOUND UP DOWN HERE IN THE BILGE BY *ACCIDENT?*
SHE'S INVESTIGATING *US.*
I'M REALLY NOT.
PUT THE GUN DOWN.
WELL, IF SHE WASN'T, FRANNIE, SHE IS *NOW.*
YEAH, WELL.
WE CAN'T BE TOO CAREFUL.
I THINK SHE'S GOOD. A GOOD INVESTIGATOR.
REALLY, *REALLY* GOOD.

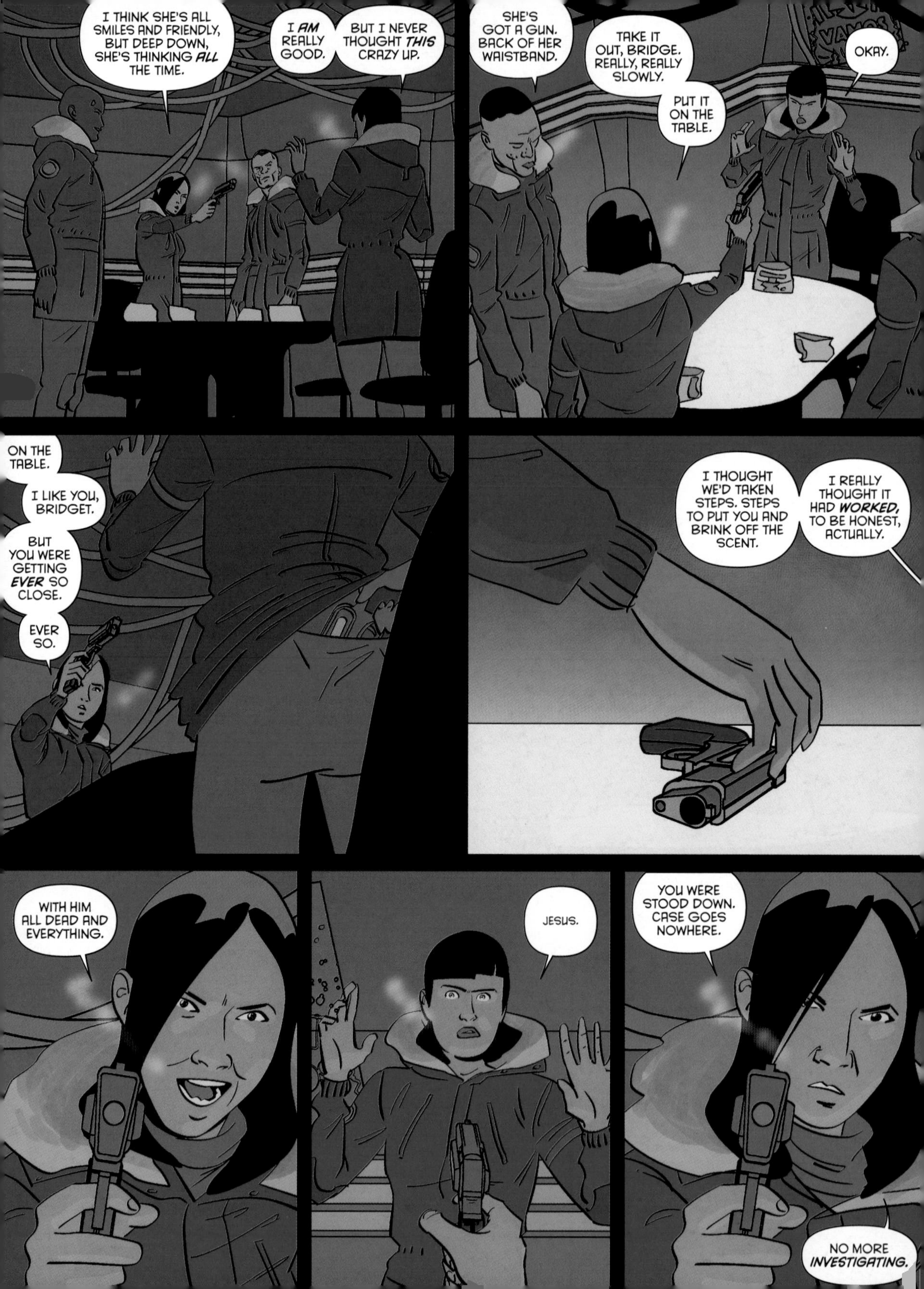
I THINK SHE'S ALL SMILES AND FRIENDLY, BUT DEEP DOWN, SHE'S THINKING *ALL* THE TIME.
I *AM* REALLY GOOD.
BUT I NEVER THOUGHT *THIS* CRAZY UP.
SHE'S GOT A GUN. BACK OF HER WAISTBAND.
TAKE IT OUT, BRIDGE. REALLY, REALLY SLOWLY.
PUT IT ON THE TABLE.
OKAY.
ON THE TABLE.
I LIKE YOU, BRIDGET.
BUT YOU WERE GETTING *EVER* SO CLOSE.
EVER SO.
I THOUGHT WE'D TAKEN STEPS. STEPS TO PUT YOU AND BRINK OFF THE SCENT.
I REALLY THOUGHT IT HAD *WORKED,* TO BE HONEST, ACTUALLY.
WITH HIM ALL DEAD AND EVERYTHING.
JESUS.
YOU WERE STOOD DOWN. CASE GOES NOWHERE.
NO MORE *INVESTIGATING.*

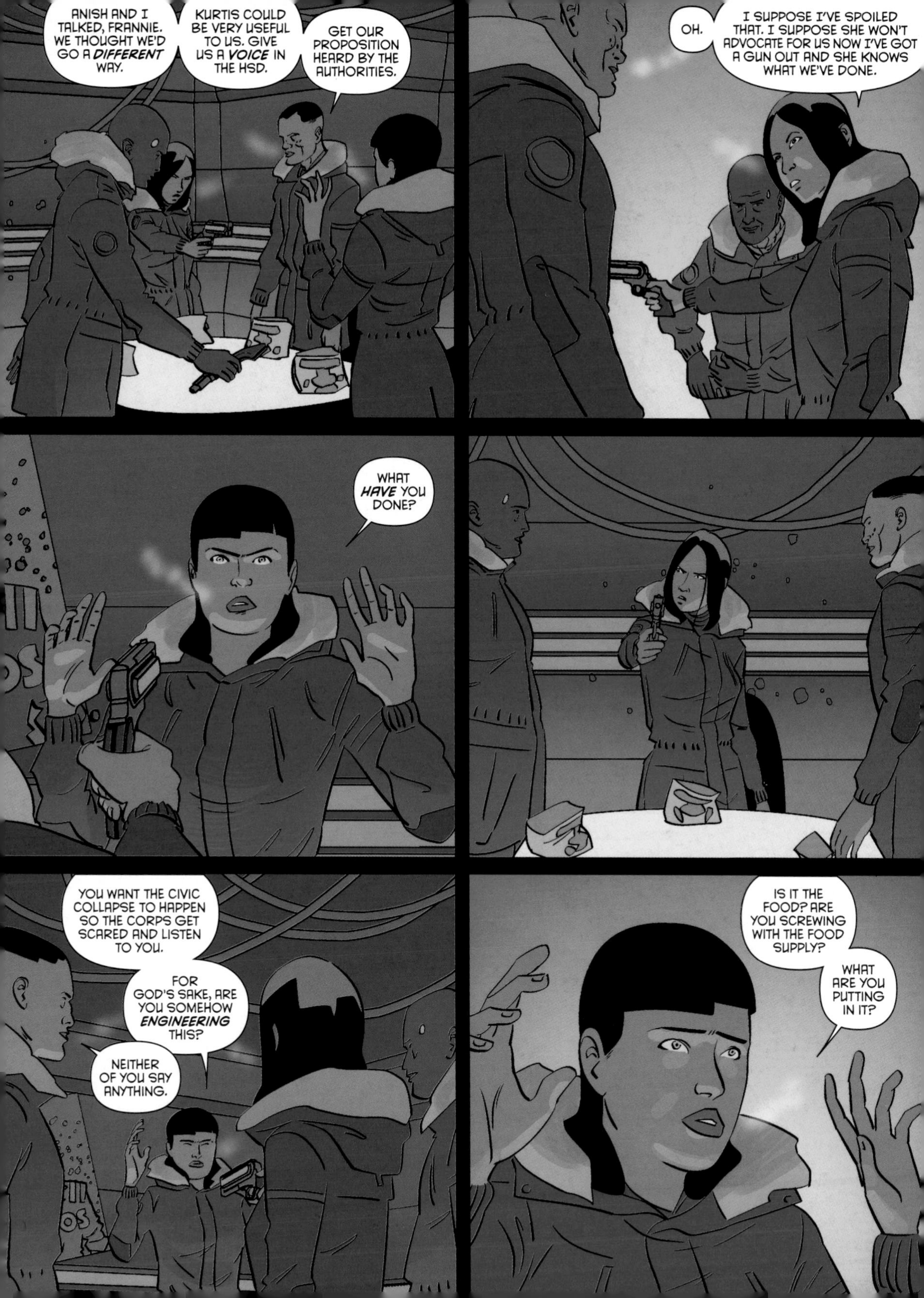
ANISH AND I TALKED, FRANNIE. WE THOUGHT WE'D GO A *DIFFERENT* WAY.
KURTIS COULD BE VERY USEFUL TO US. GIVE US A *VOICE* IN THE HSD.
GET OUR PROPOSITION HEARD BY THE AUTHORITIES.
OH.
I SUPPOSE I'VE SPOILED THAT. I SUPPOSE SHE WON'T ADVOCATE FOR US NOW I'VE GOT A GUN OUT AND SHE KNOWS WHAT WE'VE DONE.
WHAT *HAVE* YOU DONE?
YOU WANT THE CIVIC COLLAPSE TO HAPPEN SO THE CORPS GET SCARED AND LISTEN TO YOU.
FOR GOD'S SAKE, ARE YOU SOMEHOW *ENGINEERING* THIS?
NEITHER OF YOU SAY ANYTHING.
IS IT THE FOOD? ARE YOU SCREWING WITH THE FOOD SUPPLY?
WHAT ARE YOU PUTTING IN IT?

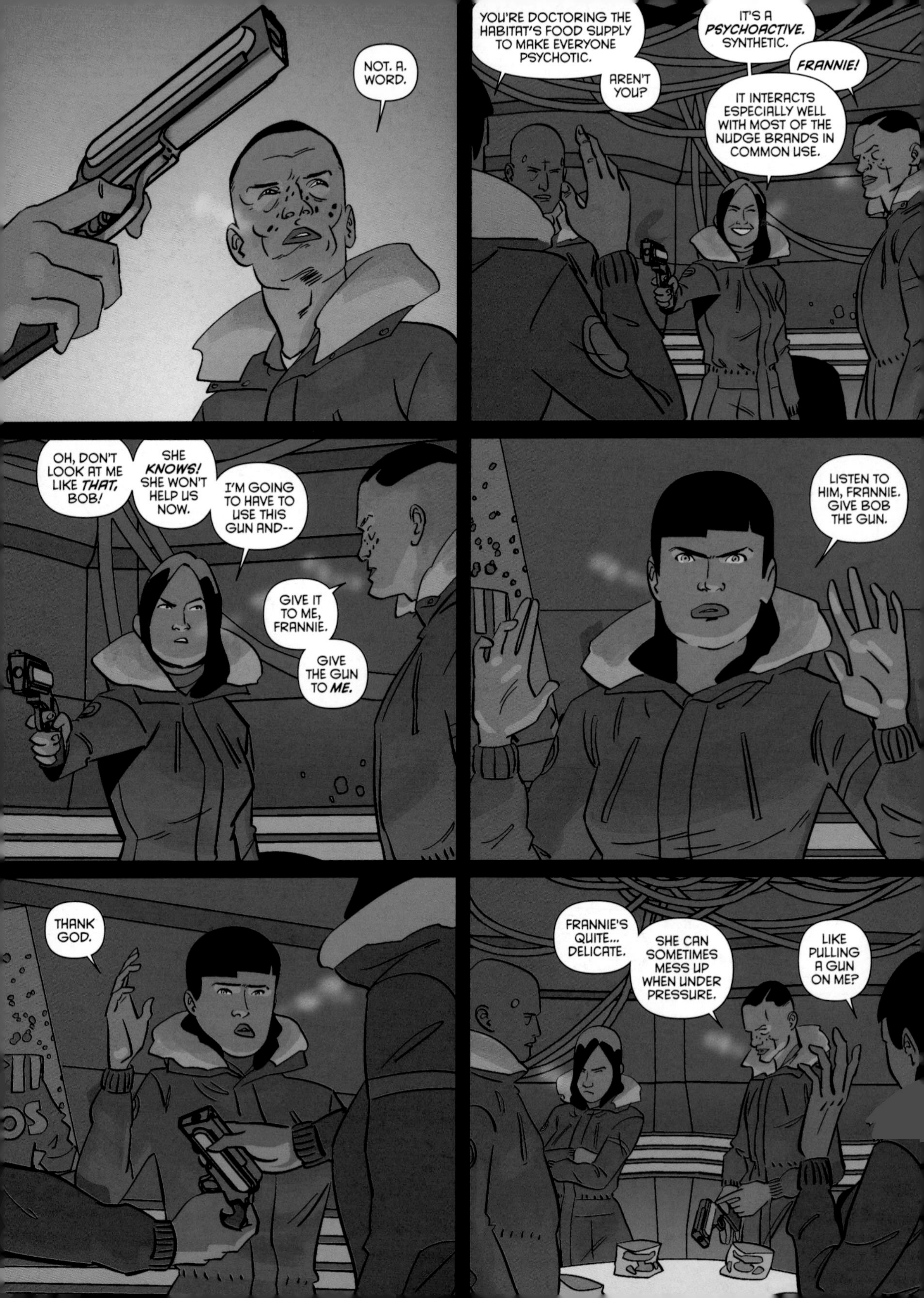
NOT. A. WORD.
YOU'RE DOCTORING THE HABITAT'S FOOD SUPPLY TO MAKE EVERYONE PSYCHOTIC.
AREN'T YOU?
IT'S A PSYCHOACTIVE. SYNTHETIC.
FRANNIE!
IT INTERACTS ESPECIALLY WELL WITH MOST OF THE NUDGE BRANDS IN COMMON USE.
OH, DON'T LOOK AT ME LIKE THAT, BOB!
SHE KNOWS! SHE WON'T HELP US NOW.
I'M GOING TO HAVE TO USE THIS GUN AND--
GIVE IT TO ME, FRANNIE.
GIVE THE GUN TO ME.
LISTEN TO HIM, FRANNIE. GIVE BOB THE GUN.
THANK GOD.
FRANNIE'S QUITE... DELICATE.
SHE CAN SOMETIMES MESS UP WHEN UNDER PRESSURE.
LIKE PULLING A GUN ON ME?

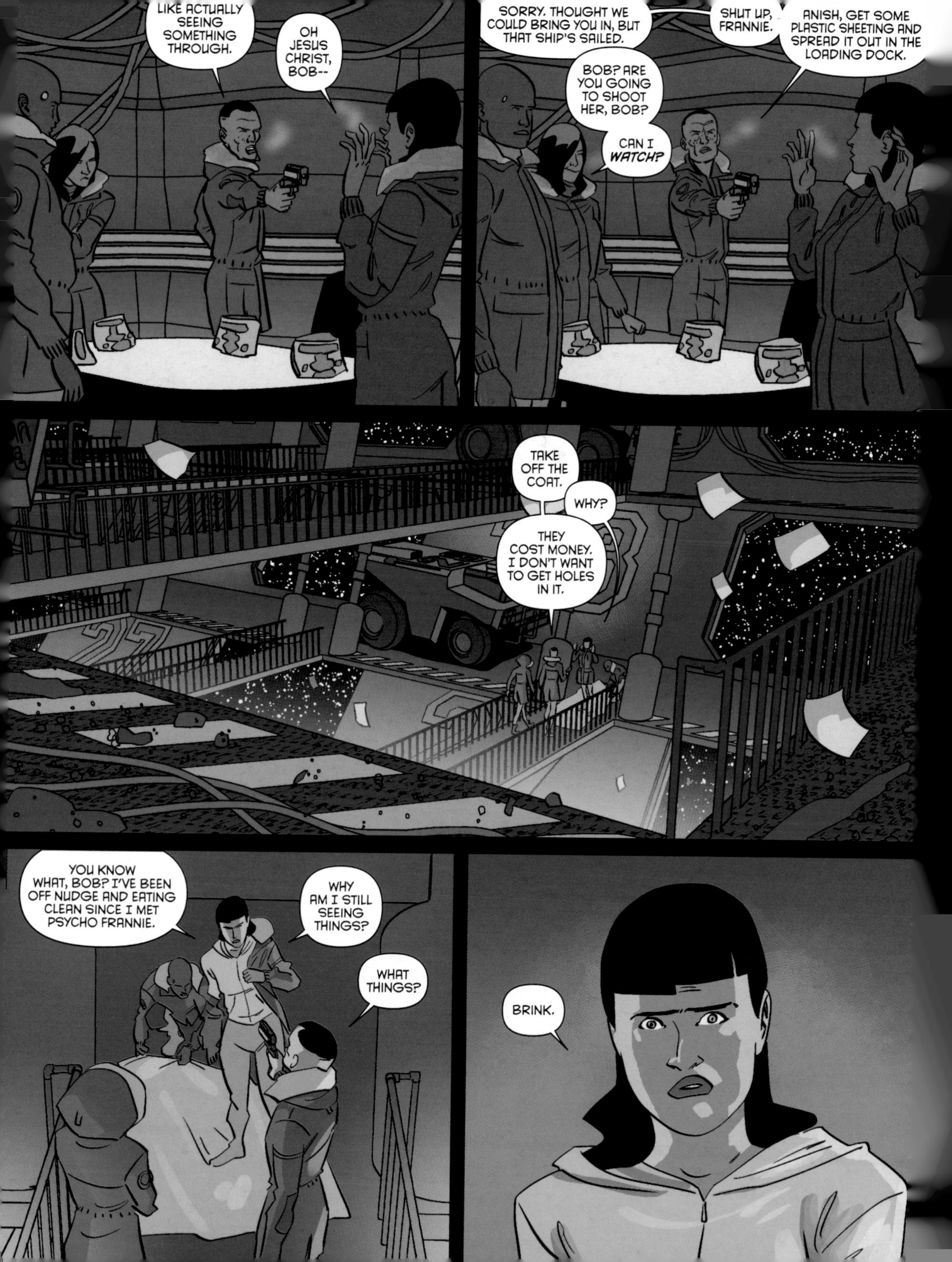
LIKE ACTUALLY SEEING SOMETHING THROUGH.
OH JESUS CHRIST, BOB--
SORRY. THOUGHT WE COULD BRING YOU IN, BUT THAT SHIP'S SAILED.
SHUT UP, FRANNIE.
ANISH, GET SOME PLASTIC SHEETING AND SPREAD IT OUT IN THE LOADING DOCK.
BOB? ARE YOU GOING TO SHOOT HER, BOB?
CAN I WATCH?
TAKE OFF THE COAT.
WHY?
THEY COST MONEY. I DON'T WANT TO GET HOLES IN IT.
YOU KNOW WHAT, BOB? I'VE BEEN OFF NUDGE AND EATING CLEAN SINCE I MET PSYCHO FRANNIE.
WHY AM I STILL SEEING THINGS?
WHAT THINGS?
BRINK.

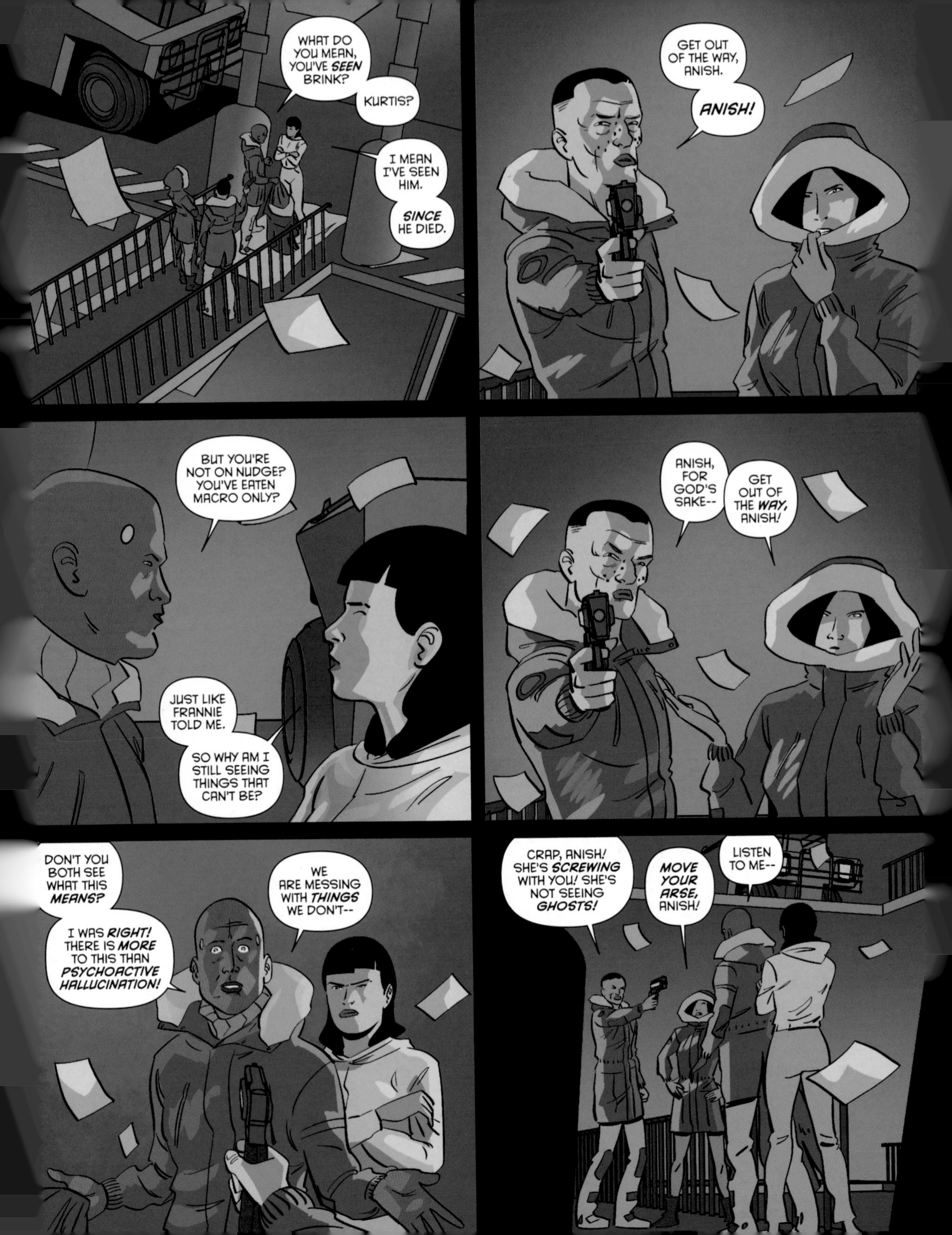
WHAT DO YOU MEAN, YOU'VE SEEN BRINK?
KURTIS?
I MEAN I'VE SEEN HIM.
SINCE HE DIED.
GET OUT OF THE WAY, ANISH.
ANISH!
BUT YOU'RE NOT ON NUDGE? YOU'VE EATEN MACRO ONLY?
JUST LIKE FRANNIE TOLD ME.
SO WHY AM I STILL SEEING THINGS THAT CAN'T BE?
ANISH, FOR GOD'S SAKE--
GET OUT OF THE WAY, ANISH!
DON'T YOU BOTH SEE WHAT THIS MEANS?
I WAS RIGHT! THERE IS MORE TO THIS THAN PSYCHOACTIVE HALLUCINATION!
WE ARE MESSING WITH THINGS WE DON'T--
CRAP, ANISH! SHE'S SCREWING WITH YOU! SHE'S NOT SEEING GHOSTS!
MOVE YOUR ARSE, ANISH!
LISTEN TO ME--

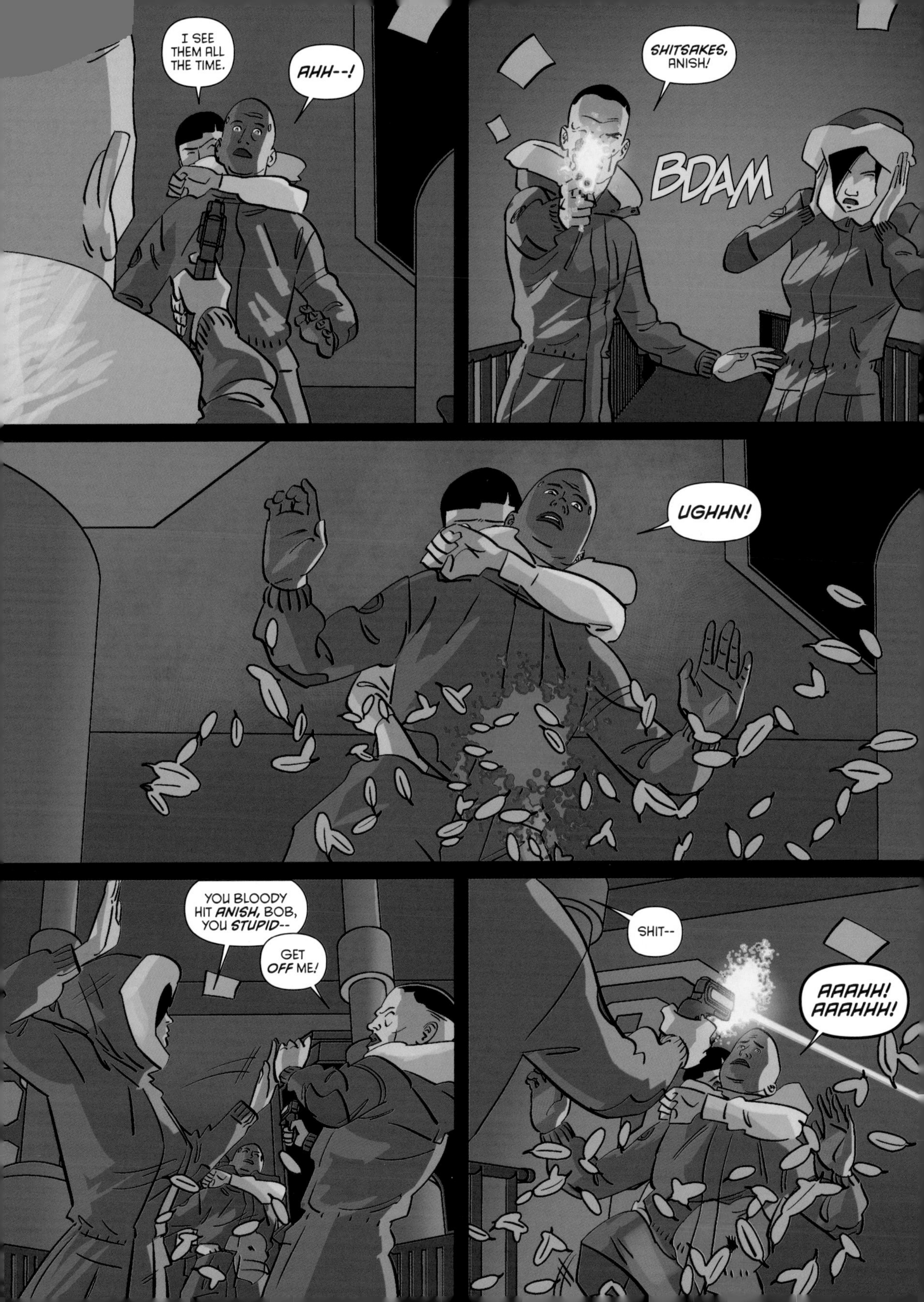
I SEE THEM ALL THE TIME.
AHH--!
SHITSAKES, ANISH!
BDAM
UGHHN!
YOU BLOODY HIT ANISH, BOB, YOU STUPID--
GET OFF ME!
SHIT--
AAAHH! AAAHHH!

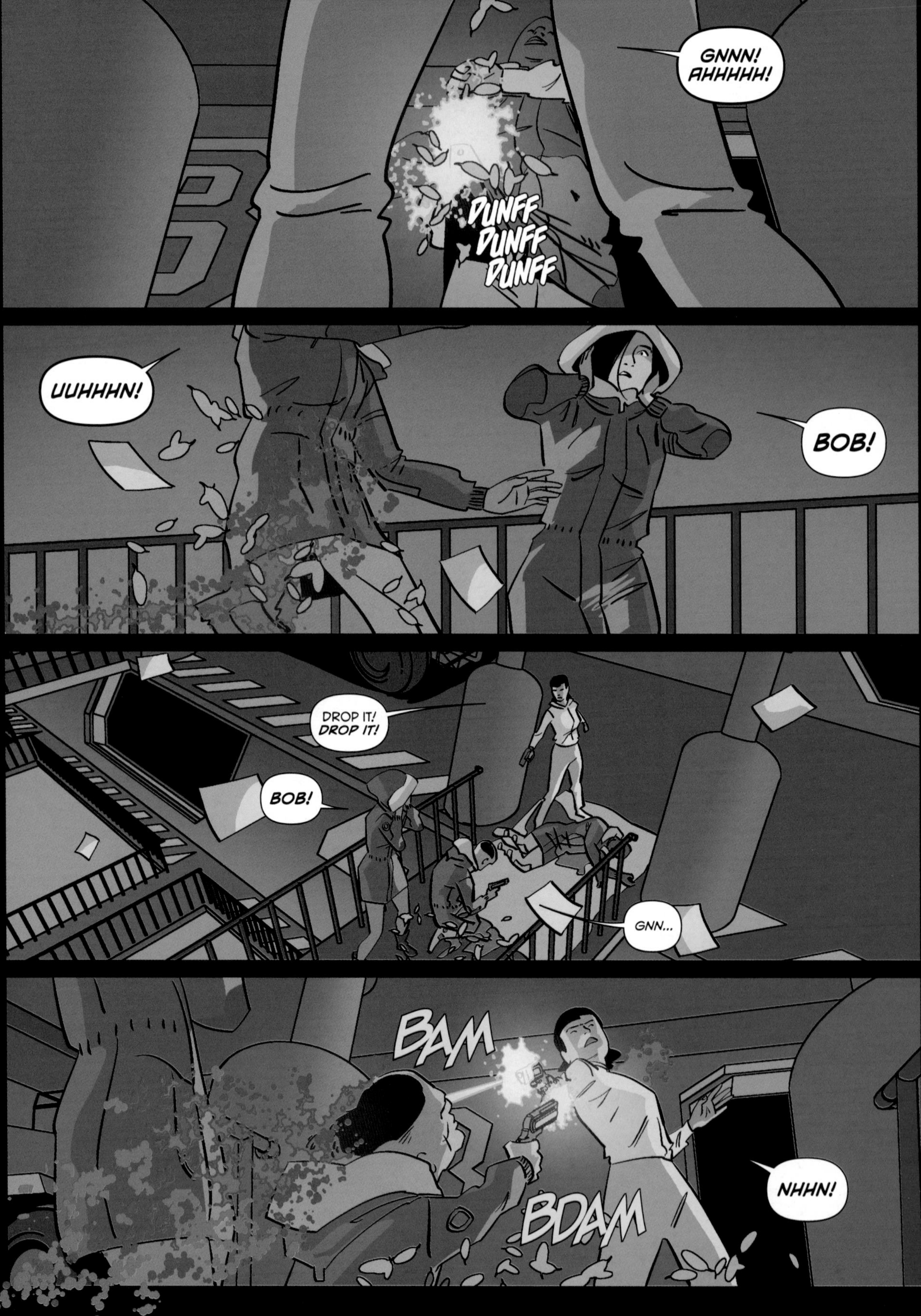
GNNN! AHHHHH!
DUNFF DUNFF DUNFF
UUHHHN!
BOB!
DROP IT! DROP IT!
BOB!
GNN...
BAM
BDAM
NHHN!

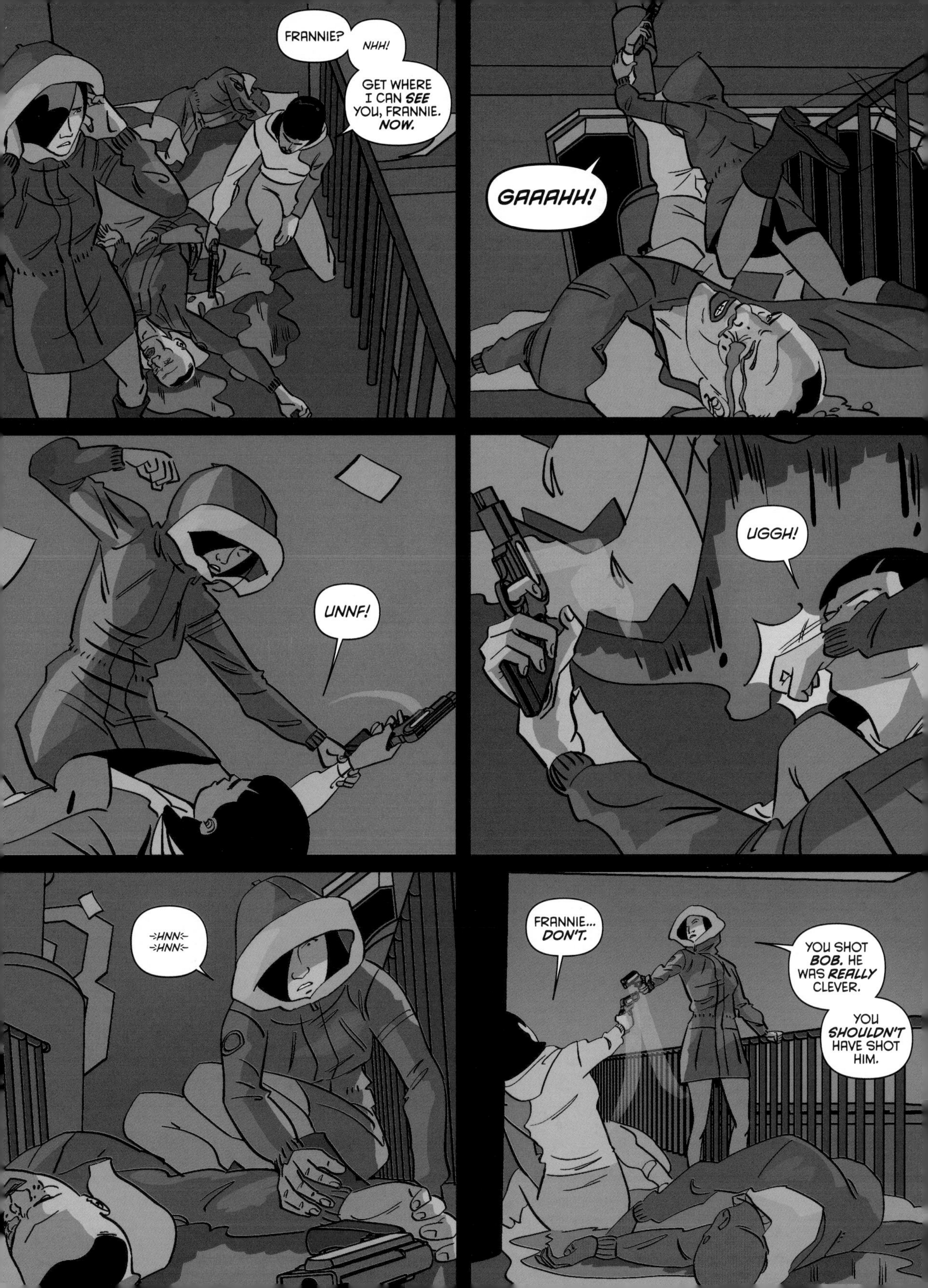

FRANNIE?
NHH!
GET WHERE I CAN SEE YOU, FRANNIE. NOW.
GAAAHH!
UNNF!
UGGH!
HNN HNN
FRANNIE... DON'T.
YOU SHOT BOB. HE WAS REALLY CLEVER.
YOU SHOULDN'T HAVE SHOT HIM.

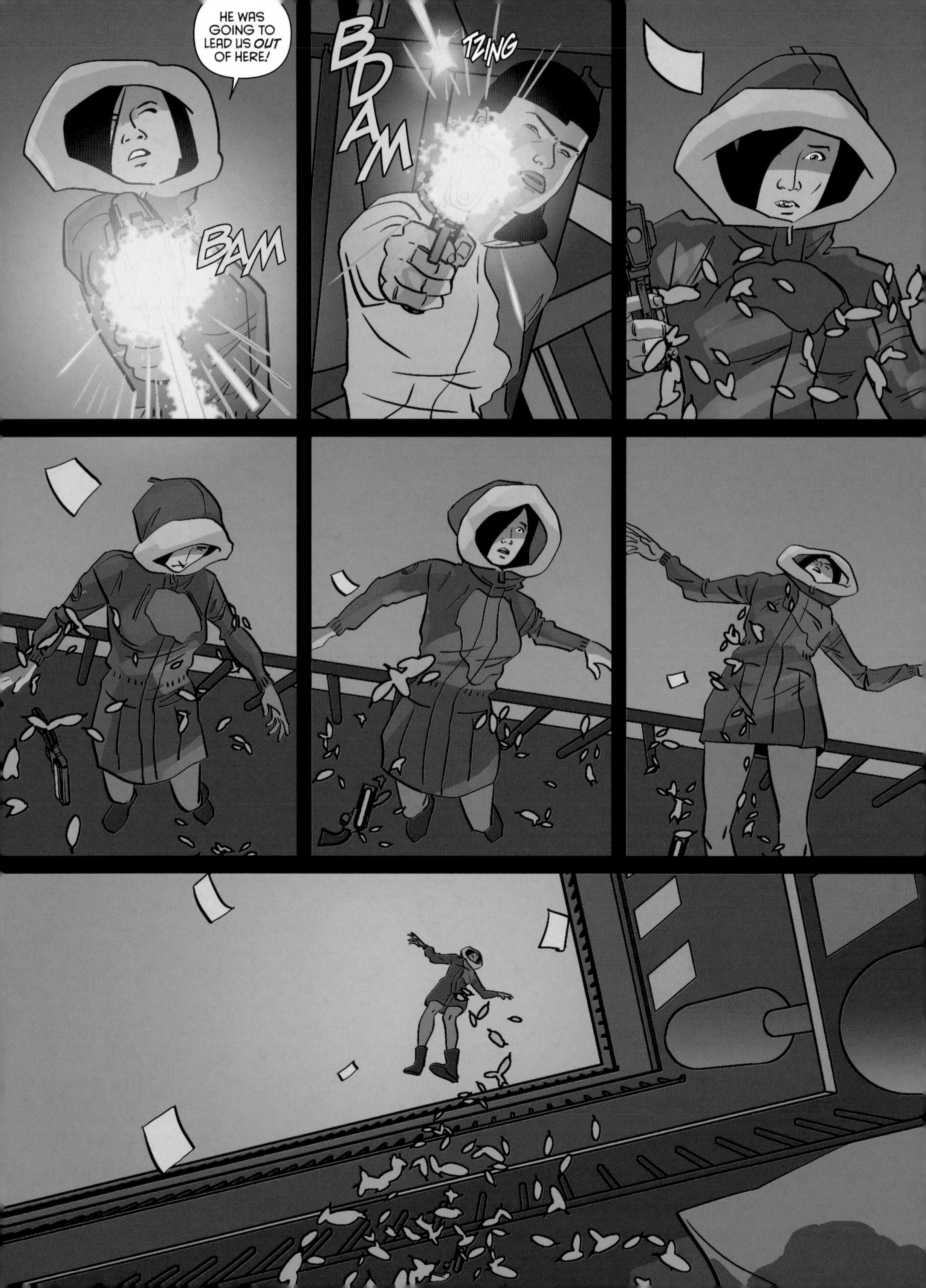
HE WAS GOING TO LEAD US OUT OF HERE!
BAM
BDAM
TZING

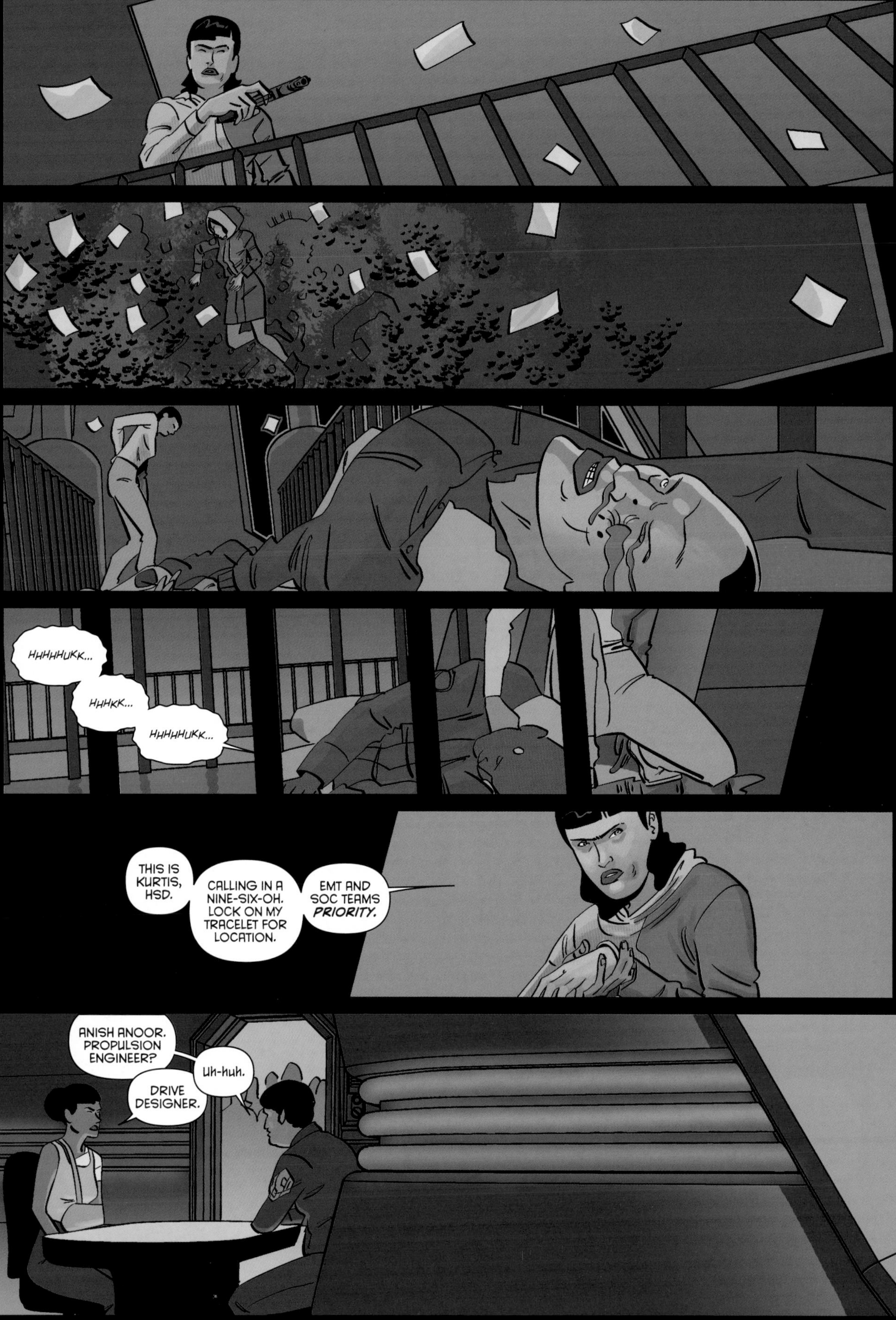
HHHHHUKK...
HHHKK...
HHHHHUKK...
THIS IS KURTIS, HSD.
CALLING IN A NINE-SIX-OH. LOCK ON MY TRACELET FOR LOCATION.
EMT AND SOC TEAMS PRIORITY.
ANISH ANOOR. PROPULSION ENGINEER?
UH-HUH.
DRIVE DESIGNER.

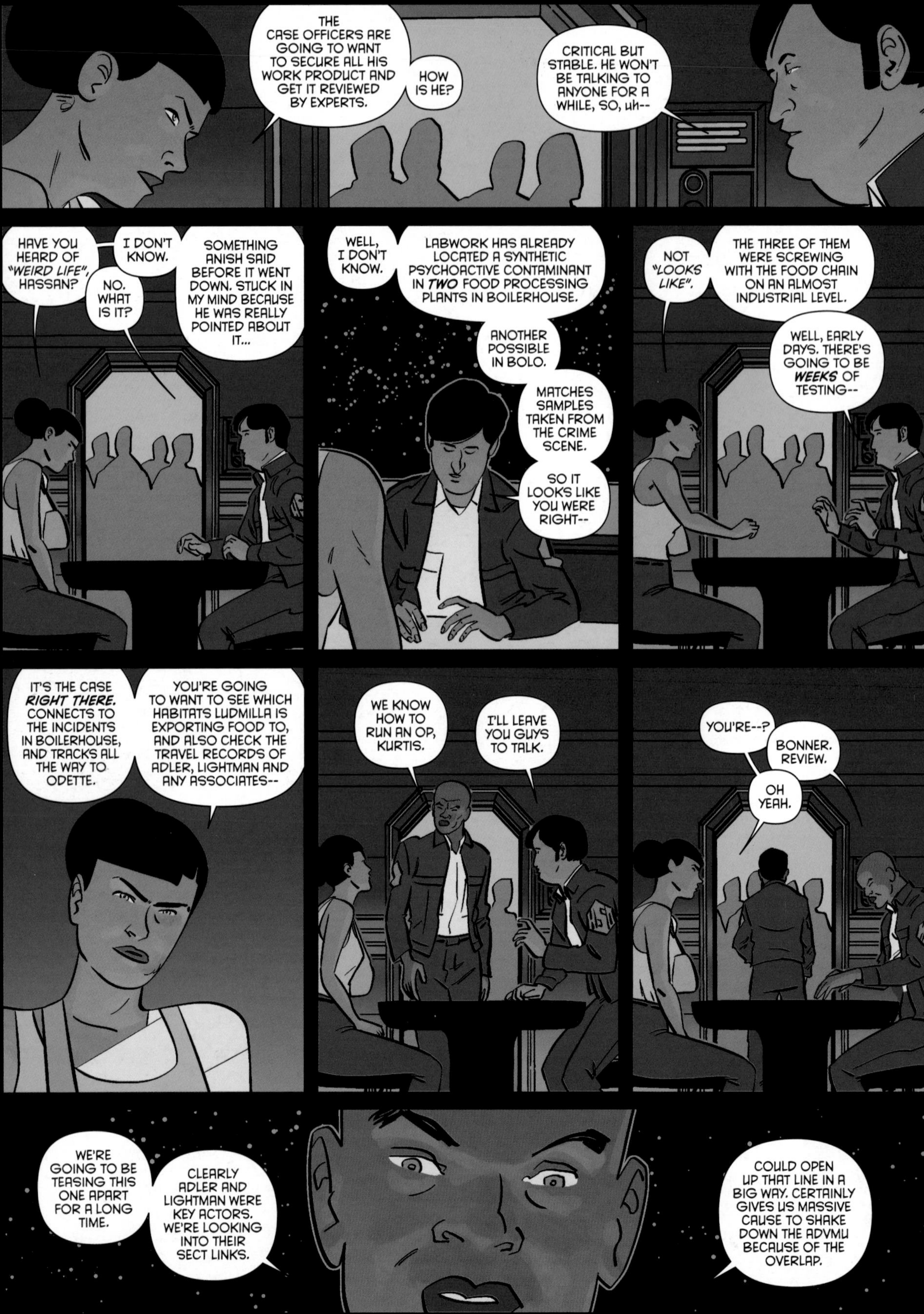
THE CASE OFFICERS ARE GOING TO WANT TO SECURE ALL HIS WORK PRODUCT AND GET IT REVIEWED BY EXPERTS.
HOW IS HE?
CRITICAL BUT STABLE. HE WON'T BE TALKING TO ANYONE FOR A WHILE, SO, uh--
HAVE YOU HEARD OF "WEIRD LIFE", HASSAN?
I DON'T KNOW.
NO. WHAT IS IT?
SOMETHING ANISH SAID BEFORE IT WENT DOWN. STUCK IN MY MIND BECAUSE HE WAS REALLY POINTED ABOUT IT...
WELL, I DON'T KNOW.
LABWORK HAS ALREADY LOCATED A SYNTHETIC PSYCHOACTIVE CONTAMINANT IN TWO FOOD PROCESSING PLANTS IN BOILERHOUSE.
ANOTHER POSSIBLE IN BOLO.
MATCHES SAMPLES TAKEN FROM THE CRIME SCENE.
SO IT LOOKS LIKE YOU WERE RIGHT--
NOT "LOOKS LIKE".
THE THREE OF THEM WERE SCREWING WITH THE FOOD CHAIN ON AN ALMOST INDUSTRIAL LEVEL.
WELL, EARLY DAYS. THERE'S GOING TO BE WEEKS OF TESTING--
IT'S THE CASE RIGHT THERE. CONNECTS TO THE INCIDENTS IN BOILERHOUSE, AND TRACKS ALL THE WAY TO ODETTE.
YOU'RE GOING TO WANT TO SEE WHICH HABITATS LUDMILLA IS EXPORTING FOOD TO, AND ALSO CHECK THE TRAVEL RECORDS OF ADLER, LIGHTMAN AND ANY ASSOCIATES--
WE KNOW HOW TO RUN AN OP, KURTIS.
I'LL LEAVE YOU GUYS TO TALK.
YOU'RE--?
BONNER. REVIEW.
OH YEAH.
WE'RE GOING TO BE TEASING THIS ONE APART FOR A LONG TIME.
CLEARLY ADLER AND LIGHTMAN WERE KEY ACTORS. WE'RE LOOKING INTO THEIR SECT LINKS.
COULD OPEN UP THAT LINE IN A BIG WAY. CERTAINLY GIVES US MASSIVE CAUSE TO SHAKE DOWN THE ADVMU BECAUSE OF THE OVERLAP.

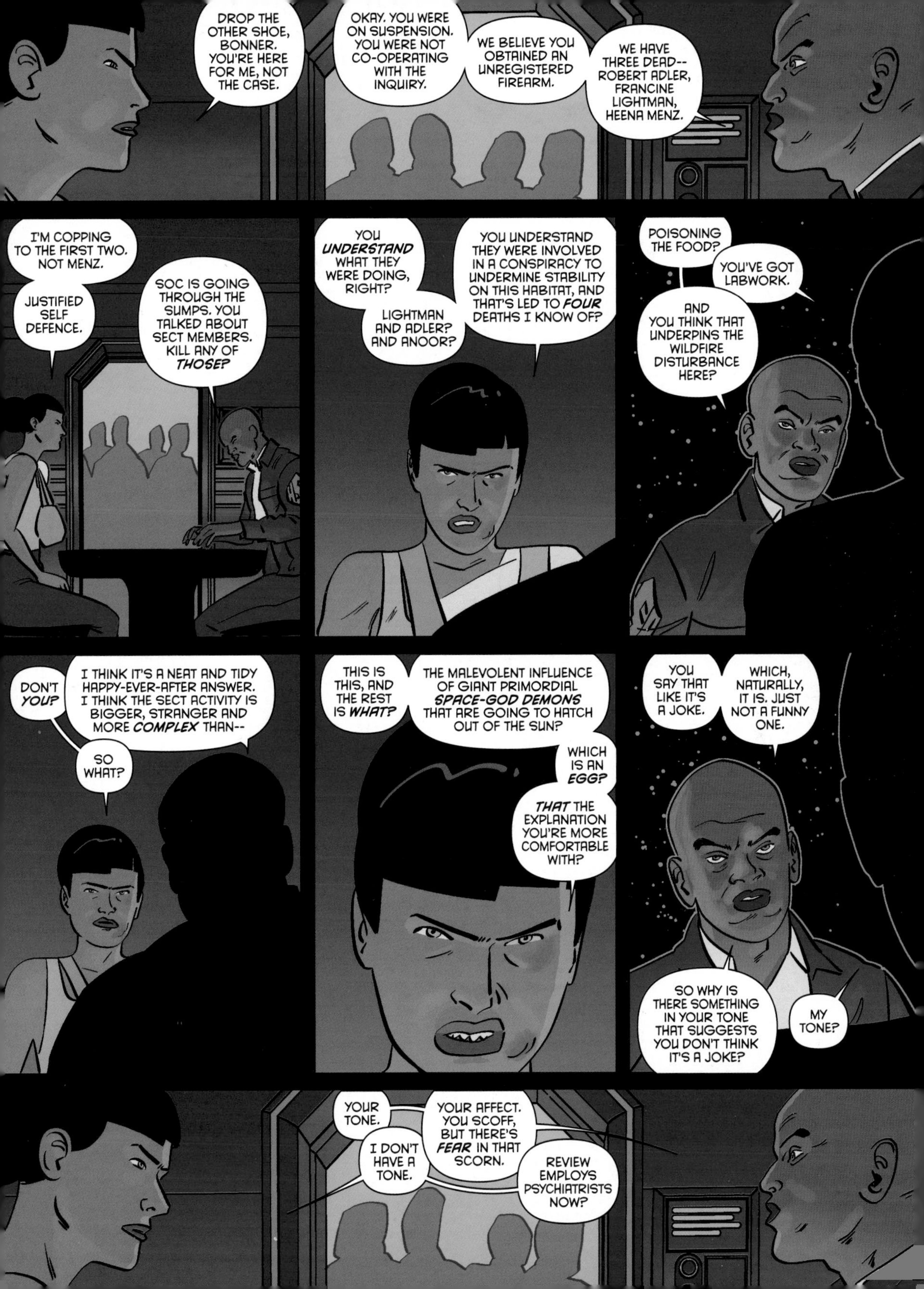

DROP THE OTHER SHOE, BONNER. YOU'RE HERE FOR ME, NOT THE CASE.
OKAY. YOU WERE ON SUSPENSION. YOU WERE NOT CO-OPERATING WITH THE INQUIRY.
WE BELIEVE YOU OBTAINED AN UNREGISTERED FIREARM.
WE HAVE THREE DEAD-- ROBERT ADLER, FRANCINE LIGHTMAN, HEENA MENZ.
I'M COPPING TO THE FIRST TWO. NOT MENZ.
JUSTIFIED SELF DEFENCE.
SOC IS GOING THROUGH THE SUMPS. YOU TALKED ABOUT SECT MEMBERS. KILL ANY OF THOSE?
YOU UNDERSTAND WHAT THEY WERE DOING, RIGHT?
LIGHTMAN AND ADLER? AND ANOOR?
YOU UNDERSTAND THEY WERE INVOLVED IN A CONSPIRACY TO UNDERMINE STABILITY ON THIS HABITAT, AND THAT'S LED TO FOUR DEATHS I KNOW OF?
POISONING THE FOOD?
YOU'VE GOT LABWORK.
AND YOU THINK THAT UNDERPINS THE WILDFIRE DISTURBANCE HERE?
I THINK IT'S A NEAT AND TIDY HAPPY-EVER-AFTER ANSWER. I THINK THE SECT ACTIVITY IS BIGGER, STRANGER AND MORE COMPLEX THAN--
SO WHAT?
DON'T YOU?
THIS IS THIS, AND THE REST IS WHAT?
THE MALEVOLENT INFLUENCE OF GIANT PRIMORDIAL SPACE-GOD DEMONS THAT ARE GOING TO HATCH OUT OF THE SUN?
WHICH IS AN EGG?
THAT THE EXPLANATION YOU'RE MORE COMFORTABLE WITH?
YOU SAY THAT LIKE IT'S A JOKE.
WHICH, NATURALLY, IT IS. JUST NOT A FUNNY ONE.
SO WHY IS THERE SOMETHING IN YOUR TONE THAT SUGGESTS YOU DON'T THINK IT'S A JOKE?
MY TONE?
YOUR TONE.
I DON'T HAVE A TONE.
YOUR AFFECT. YOU SCOFF, BUT THERE'S FEAR IN THAT SCORN.
REVIEW EMPLOYS PSYCHIATRISTS NOW?

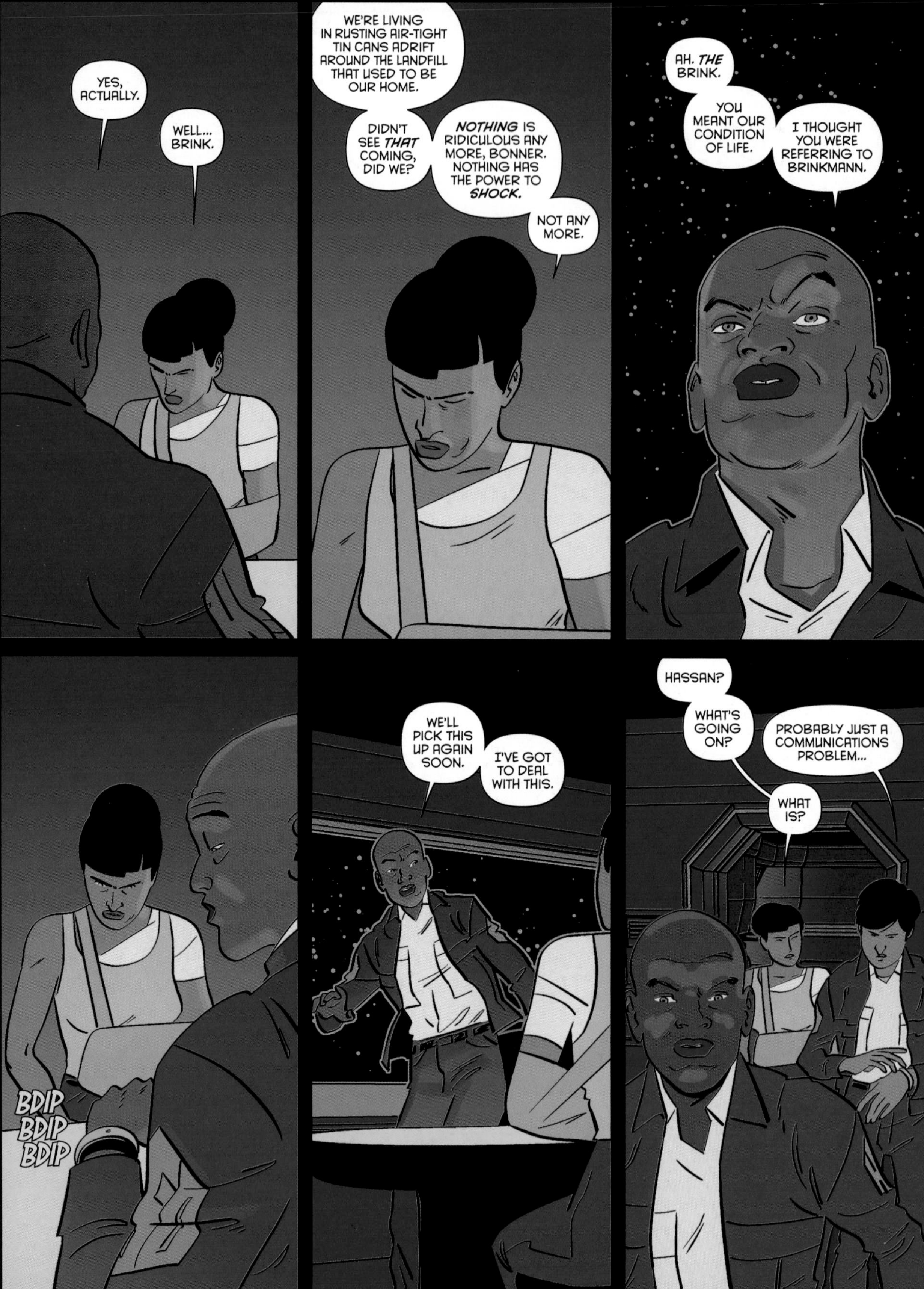
YES, ACTUALLY.
WELL... BRINK.
WE'RE LIVING IN RUSTING AIR-TIGHT TIN CANS ADRIFT AROUND THE LANDFILL THAT USED TO BE OUR HOME.
DIDN'T SEE *THAT* COMING, DID WE?
NOTHING IS RIDICULOUS ANY MORE, BONNER. NOTHING HAS THE POWER TO *SHOCK.*
NOT ANY MORE.
AH. *THE* BRINK.
YOU MEANT OUR CONDITION OF LIFE.
I THOUGHT YOU WERE REFERRING TO BRINKMANN.
BDIP BDIP BDIP
WE'LL PICK THIS UP AGAIN SOON.
I'VE GOT TO DEAL WITH THIS.
HASSAN?
WHAT'S GOING ON?
PROBABLY JUST A COMMUNICATIONS PROBLEM...
WHAT IS?

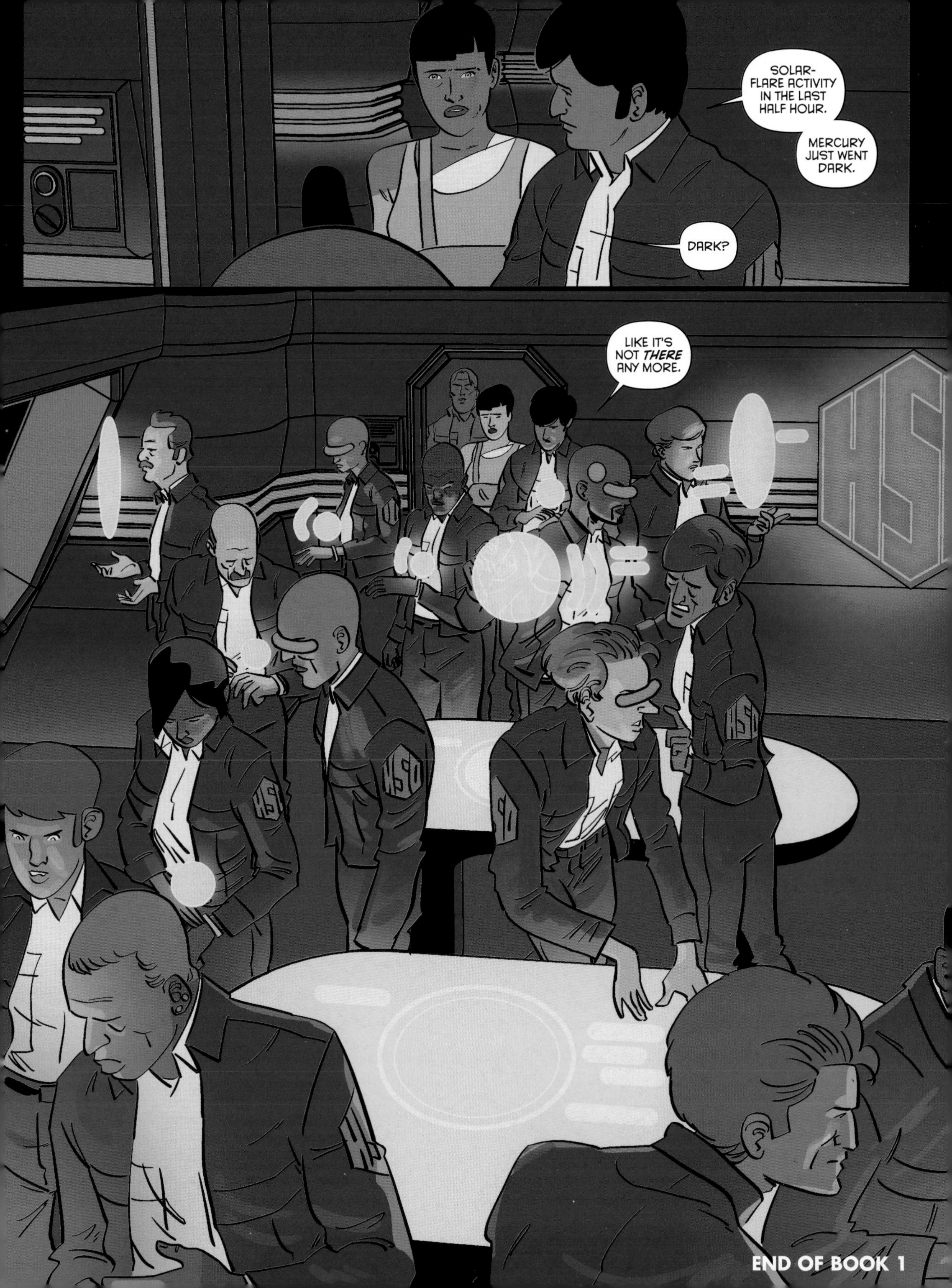
SOLAR-FLARE ACTIVITY IN THE LAST HALF HOUR.
MERCURY JUST WENT DARK.
DARK?
LIKE IT'S NOT *THERE* ANY MORE.
HSD
END OF BOOK 1

COVER GALLERY, SKETCHES & DAN ABNETT SCRIPT

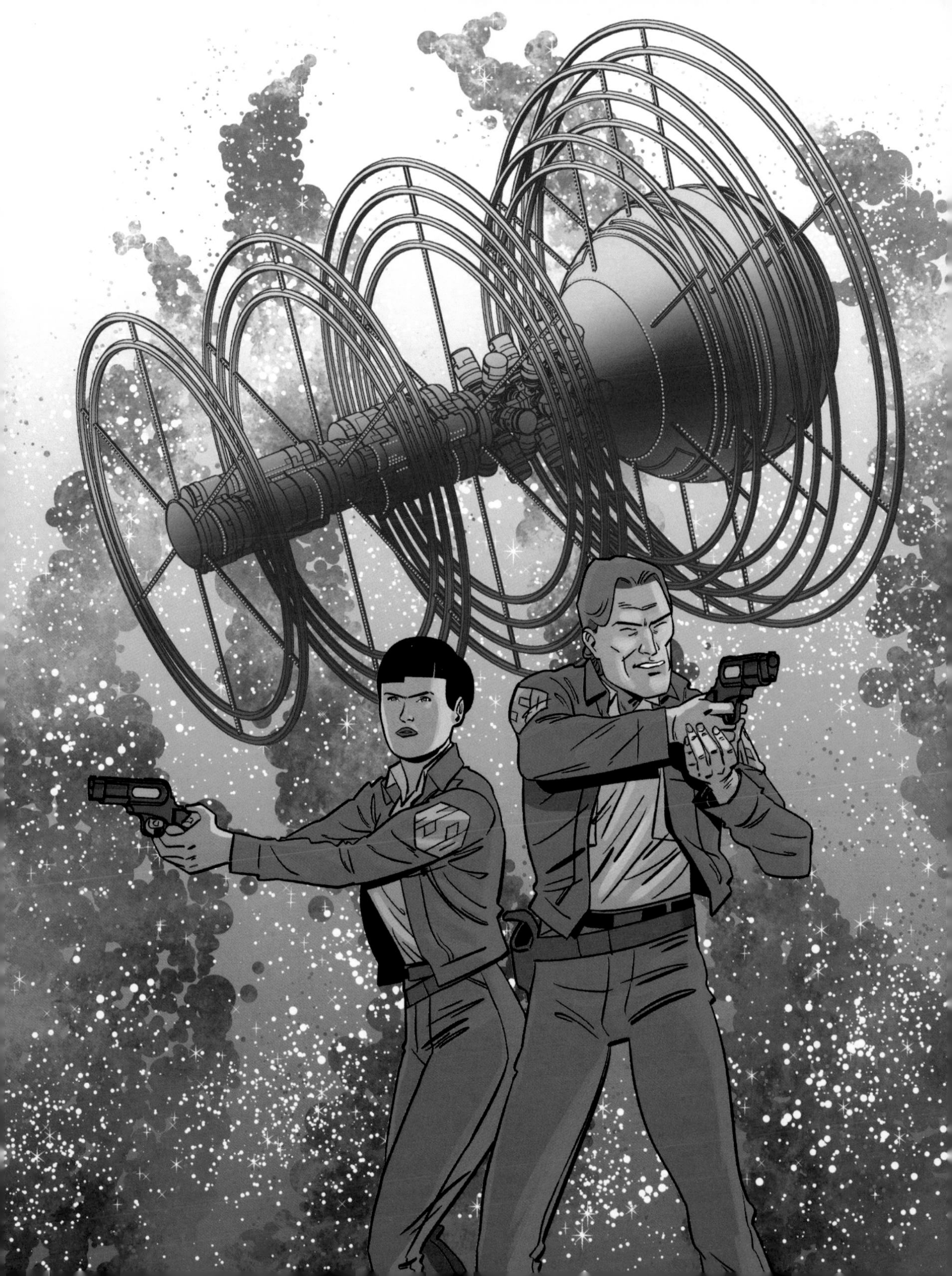

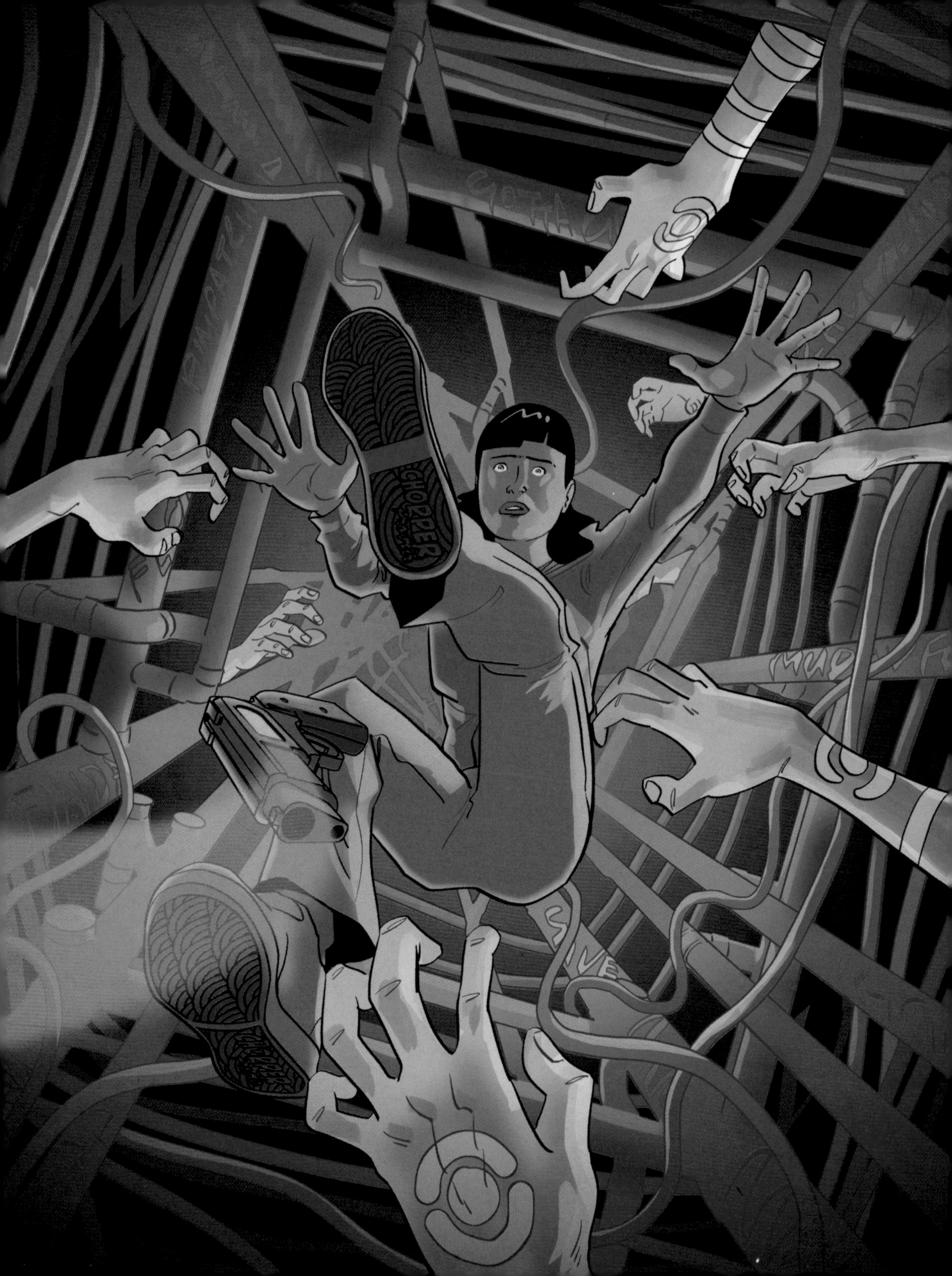
CHOPPER

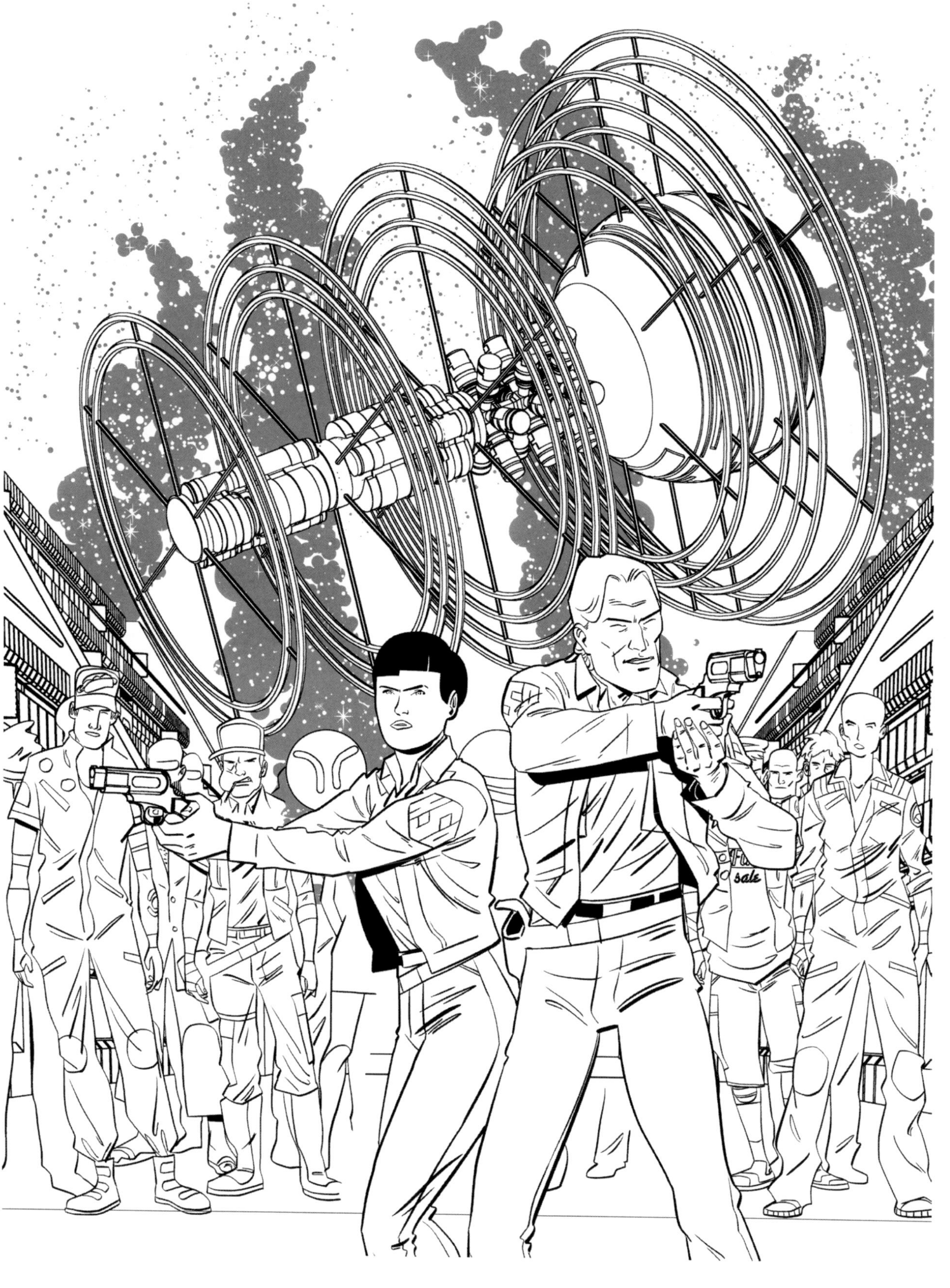
sale

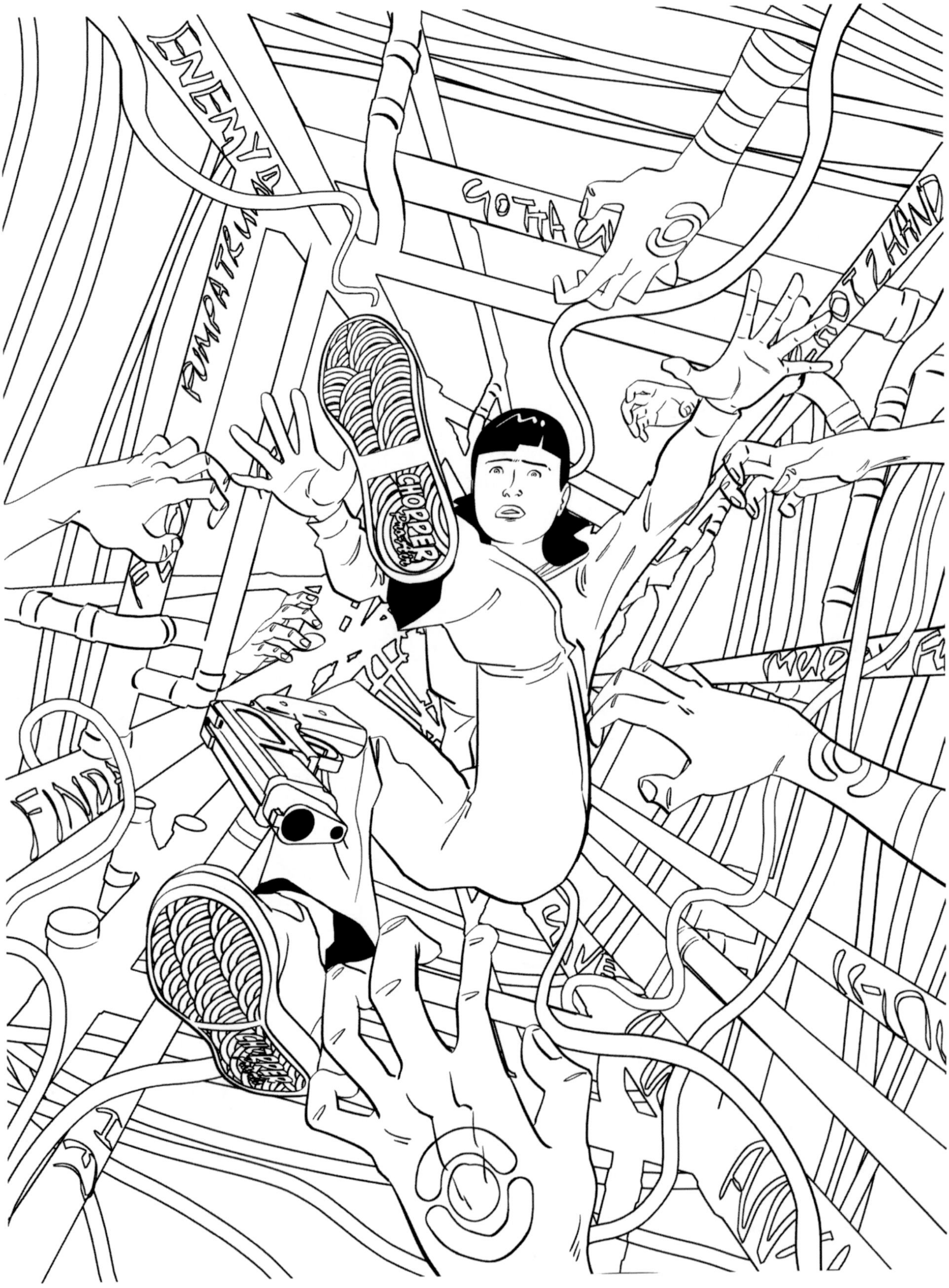
GOTTA
CHOPPER
FIND

ODETTE DESIGN

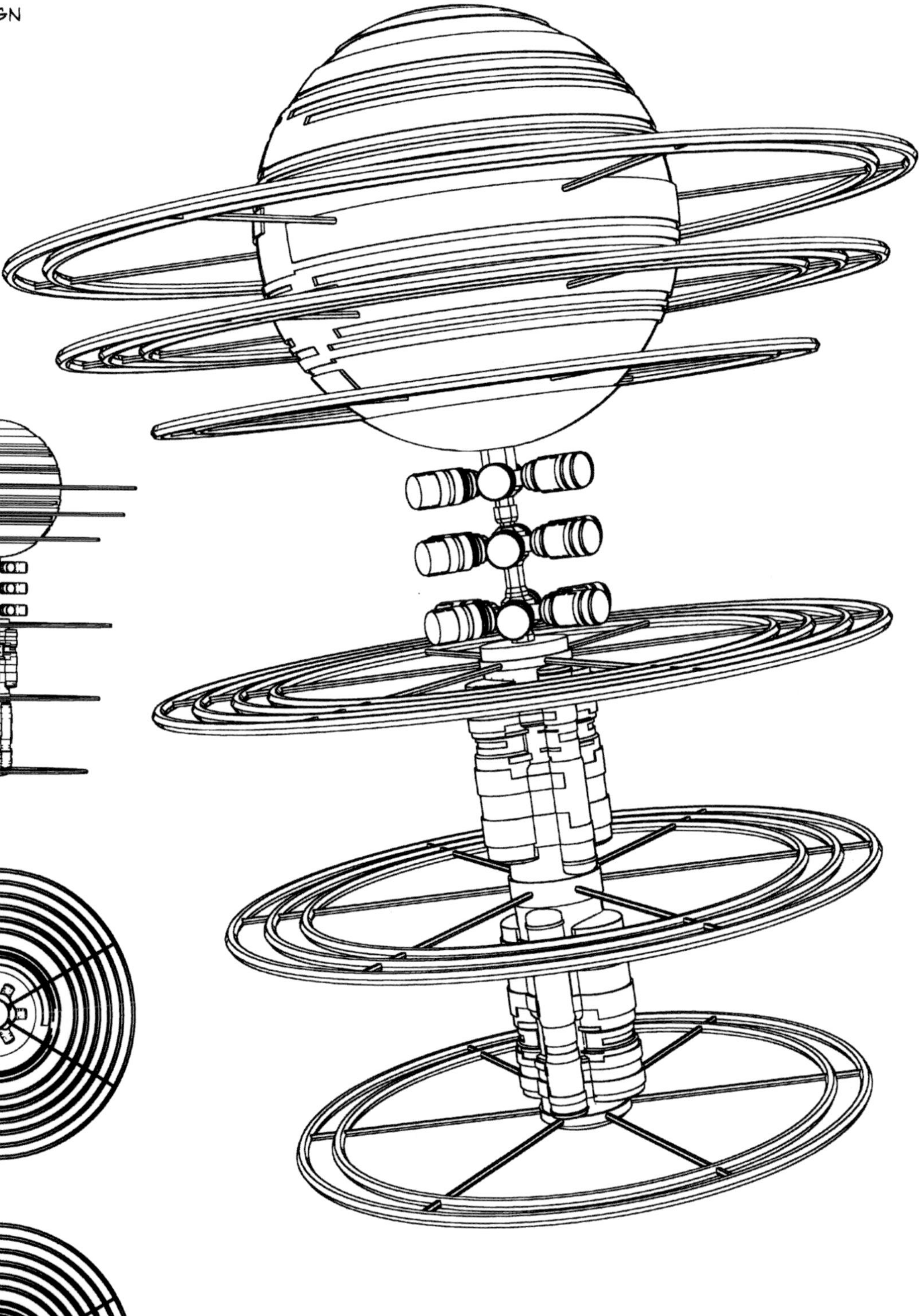

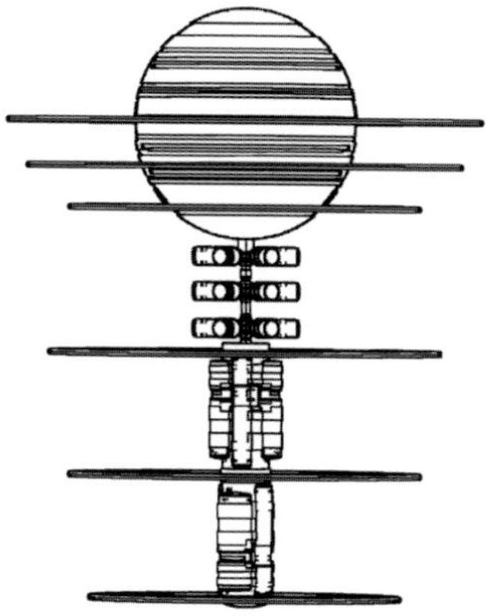

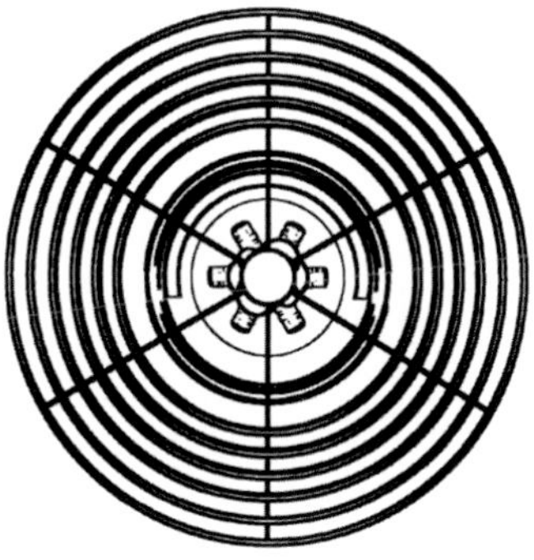

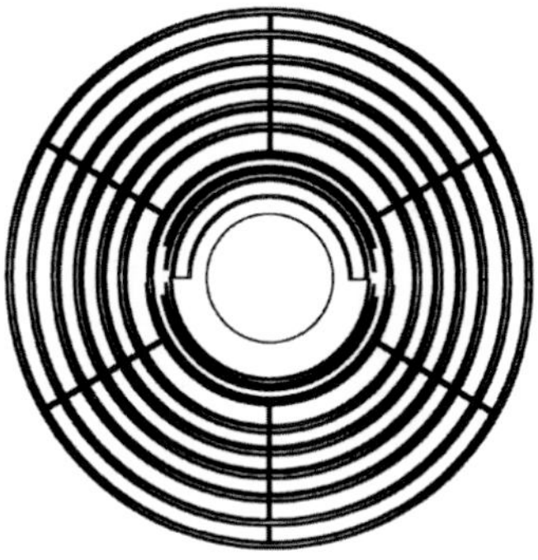

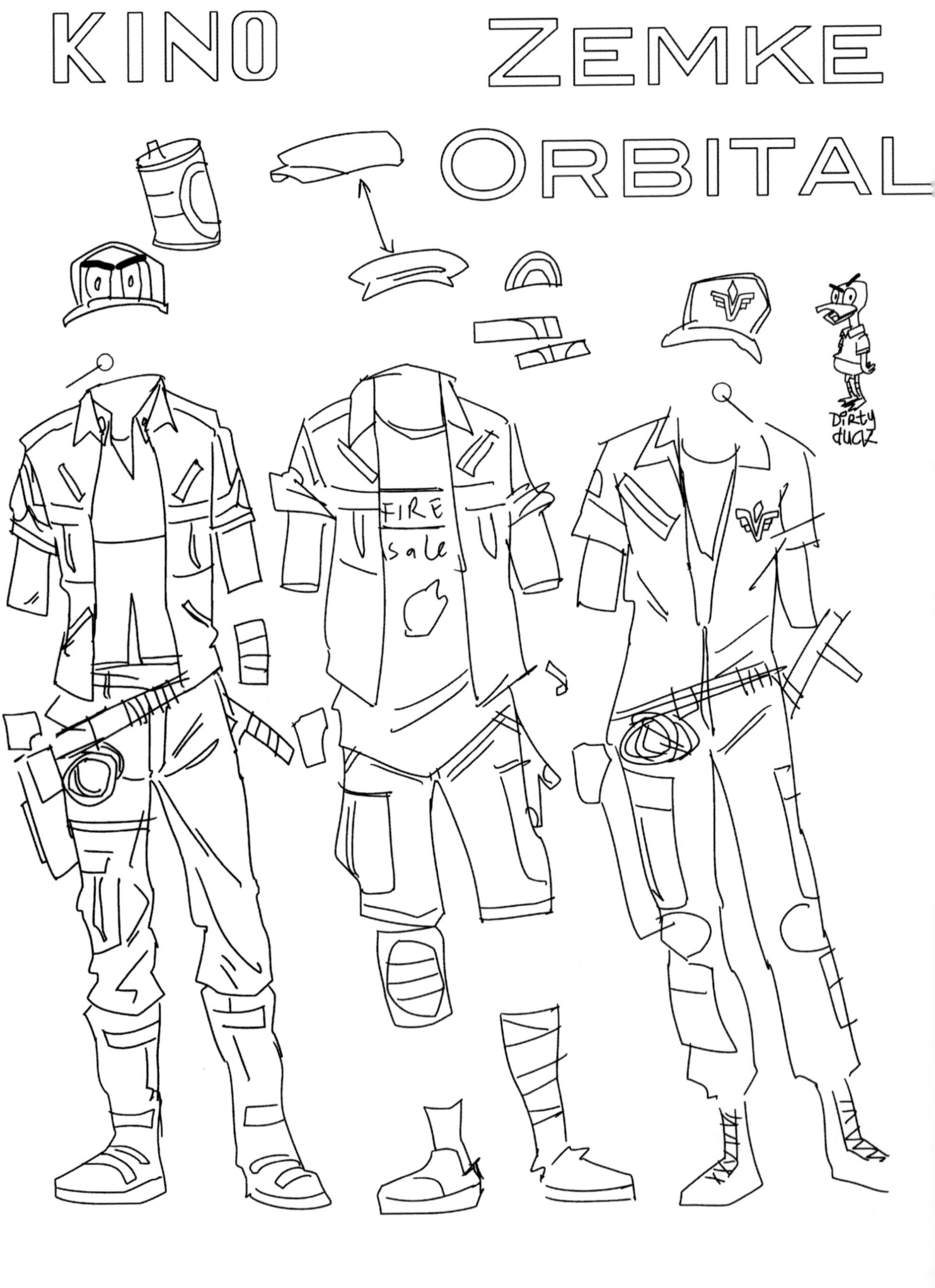
KINO
ZEMKE
ORBITAL
FIRE
sale
Dirty
duck

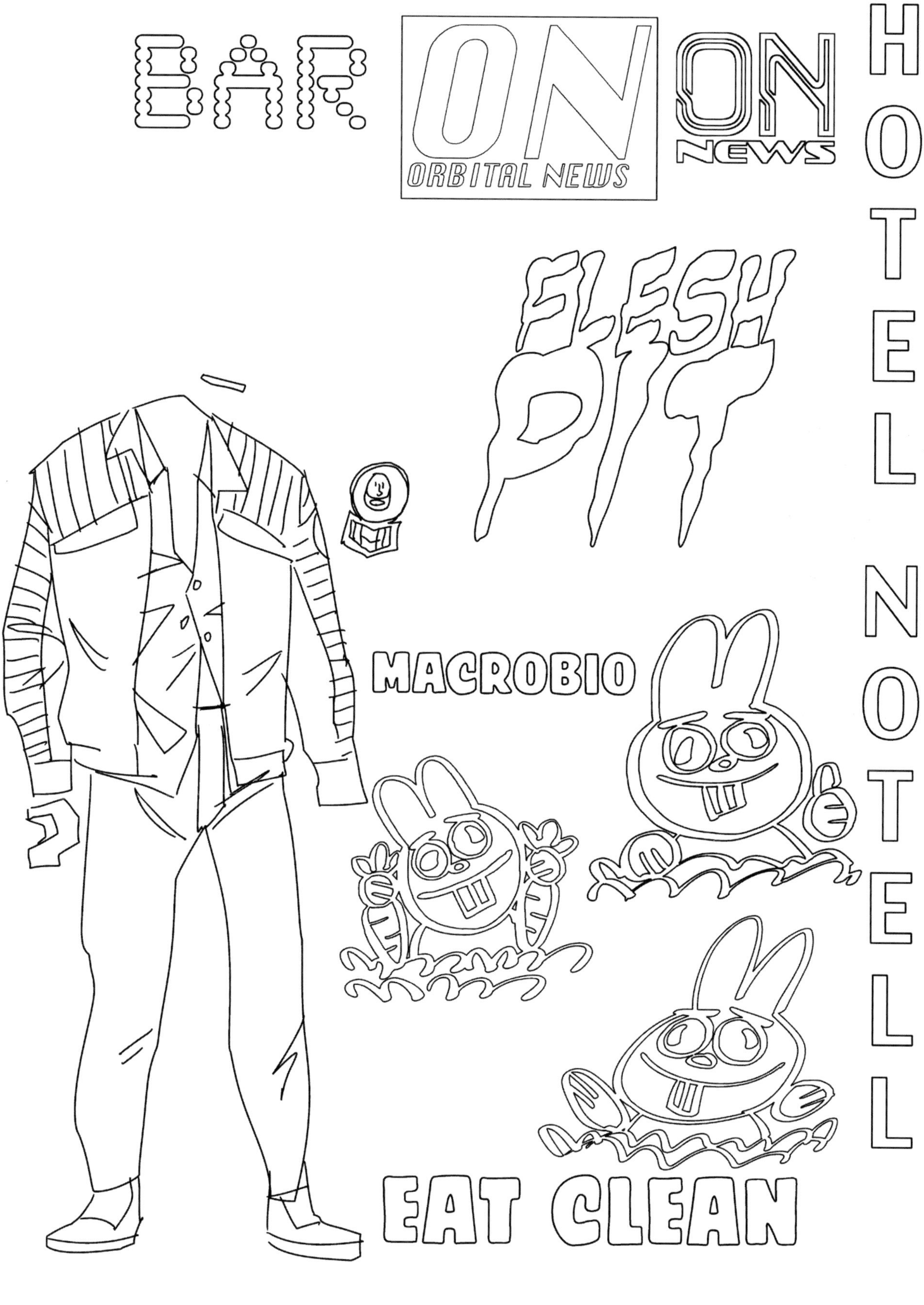
BAR
ON
ORBITAL NEWS
ON
NEWS
HOTEL
FLESH
PIT
MACROBIO
NOTELL
EAT CLEAN

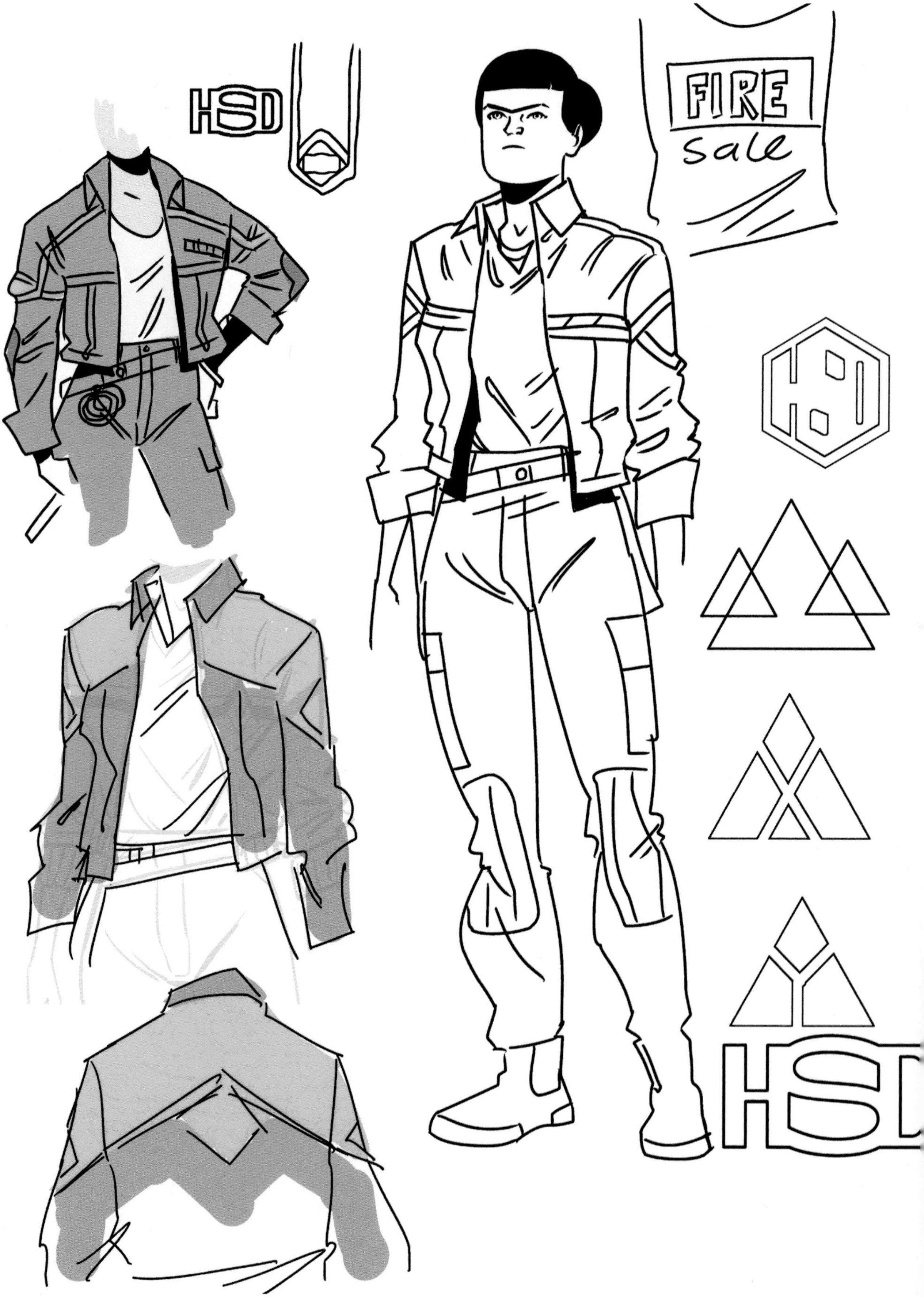
HSD
FIRE
sale
HSD

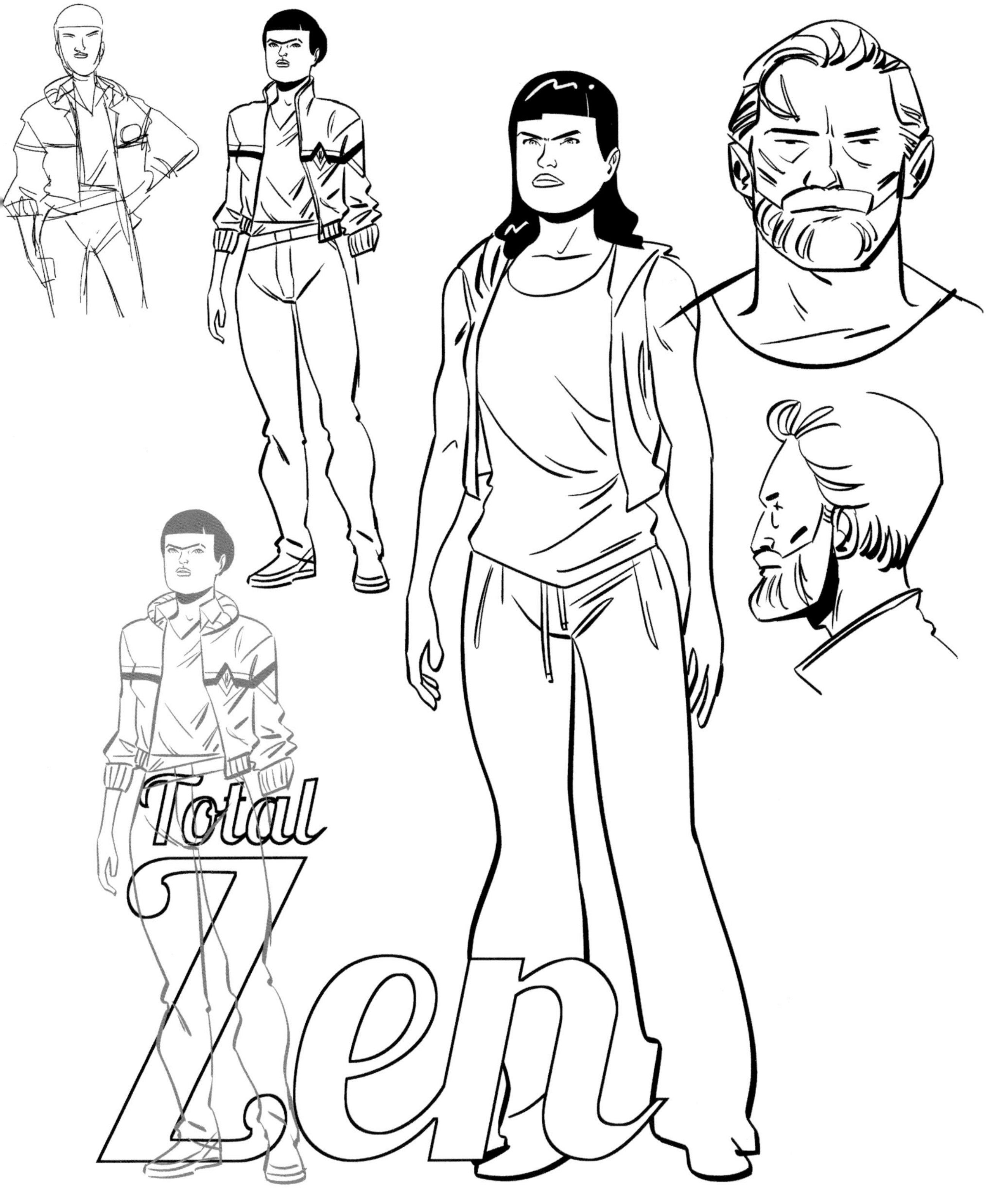
Total
Zen

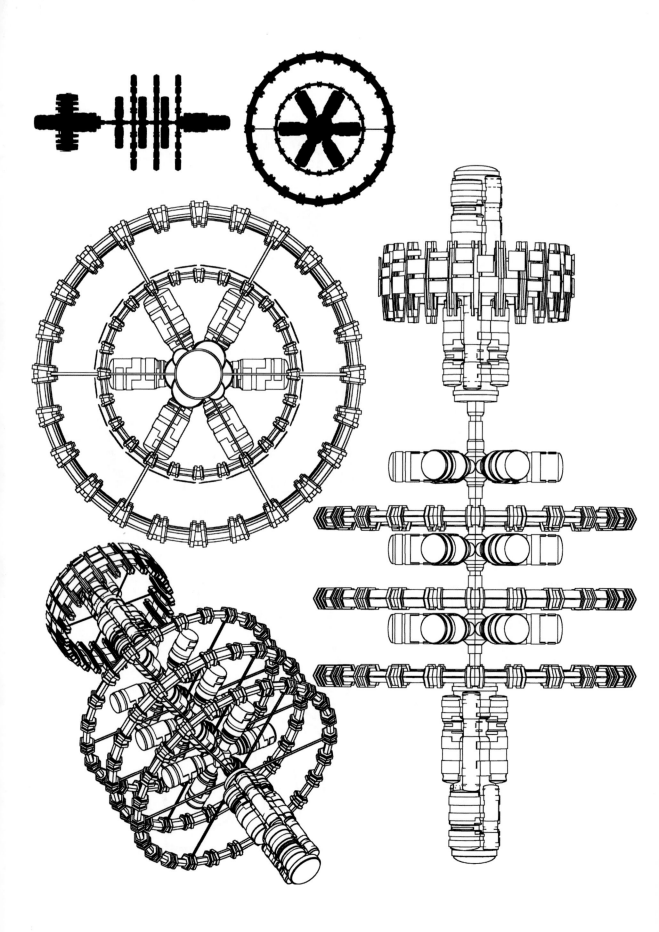

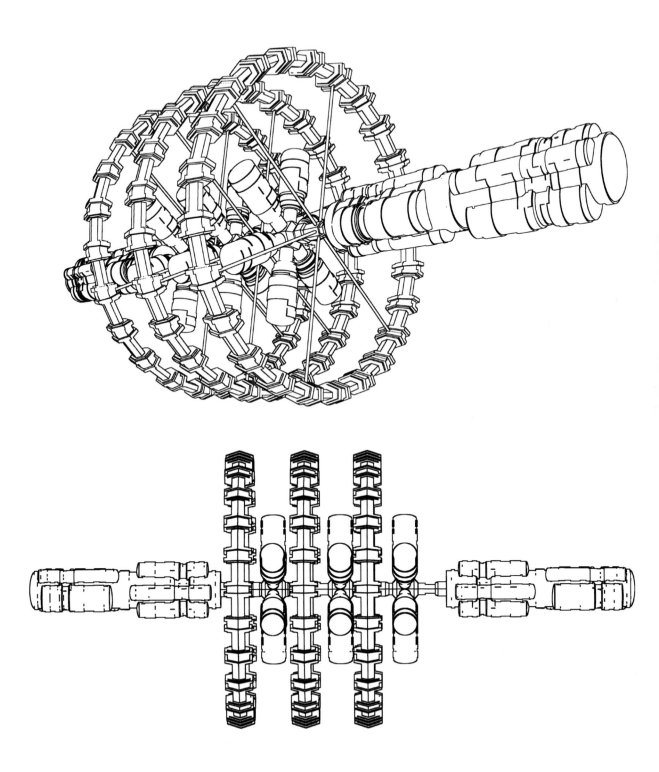

Odette Habitat concept art

BRINK: Part One Script

PAGE ONE

1. Page wide panel. <u>To shock</u>. In a gloomy, artificially lit 'cabin' on a habitat: a personal space, cluttered, mechanical, busy, dirty, worn, like the interior of Soyuz capsule. Junk. Porn pin-ups on the wall. Weare looking directly at the head and shoulders of a dead man. What's left of him stares at us, slack-jawed, as if disappointed or bored. Something has bored clean through one side of his face, taking the cheek and the eye, digging a blood-black hole of chewed bone and tissue that goes <u>right through his head</u>. Deliberately, provocatively shocking, like the final shot of Gus in Breaking Bad, or the dead Indian scientist/astronaut in Gravity. He is sitting, propped up. Realistic, messy, human, shocking: not horror movie staged gore, but news-footage clumsy and un-glamorously real.

NO DIALOGUE

2. Page wide. Reverse angle. BRIDGET and BRINK face us in the doorway, sidearms drawn, but lowering them. Probably a waist up establishing shot. Both should look, at this point, pasty and sick, bad skin, lank hair, like they have flu (everyone looks like that), but they're also horrified by what they see.

Bridge looks like she is trying not to vomit. The dead guy could be in the foreground, facing them. Just for detail, there's a small window port looking out into space in the back wall of the room, opposite the hatch into the common hallway.

> **BRINK**
> Bridge?
> **BRIDGE**
> Mnm,yeah.
> **BRINK**
> Might you be sick?
> **BRIDGE**
> <u>Nope</u>. Mmn.

NEW PANEL 3

> **BRINK** (FROM OFF)
> Let's secure the scene.
> **FX**
> KLK
> **TAG** (to unit)
> Environmental ambi-grav setting to 9.807 m/s sq (Earth Normal)

NEW PANEL 4

> **FC**
> Splpsh

3. Brink peers at the dead guy, distastefully. Bridge glances around the grubby room.

> **BRINK**
> Someone opened his face with a machine drill.

4. Brink checks the dead guy's "tracelet", a wristband like a sleek rubber charity wristband. Everyone wears one. Maybe they're all orange. When you tap them, they project a display like an iPhone screen onto the skin of your forearm or the back of your hand. See this: http://www.gizmag.com/cicret-bracelet/35109/ ...but fully functional. Brink is making it project on the man'shand, but we can't read the display, just the orangy glow of it.

> **BRINK**
> According to his tracelet, he's Xan Harbin.

5. Bridge is checking her own tracelet, adjusting the display like a touchscreen.

> **BRIDGE**
> Snap. The caller.
> **TAG** (her display)

Harbin, Xan
inhab 412 loop 343 Odette
Call of complaint regarding neighbours logged 03:56

6. Brink glances at her. She shrugs.

>**BRINK**
>Are we going to feel bad for getting here too late?
>**BRIDGE**
>Yes, Brink. <u>Forever</u>.
>**BRINK**
>Long time, forever.

PAGE TWO

1. Page wide, large shot, exterior, establishing the ODETTE HABITAT, a long chain of clumped together habitat drums and pods, 'weather-beaten' and dirty, hanging ina vast darkness of space, Big in the foreground, trailing away smaller as the chain grows distant. Maybe have some small shuttle docking for scale, or two guys in space suits working on the exterior with welding torches (nowhere near where the voices are coming from).

>**BRIDGE** (from)
>Not <u>these</u> days.

TITLE Brink
SUB Episode one

>**TAG** (habitat)
>Odette Habitat
>Owned: Sugarsurf Pharma
>Completed: 2076 AD
>**TAG** (habitat)
>Population: 209,000
>First occupied 2077, five years after the final evacuation of Earth

2. Now maybe we're looking in through the grubby window port into the crime scene cabin, seeing them searching.

>**TAG** (that cabin)
>Habitation compartment 412
>Loop 343 Odette
>**BRINK**
>Check the lockers.

3. Interior, they start to search, opening lockers, moving stained seat cushions etc. She's finding a packet of pills in one of the lockers.

>**TAG** (Bridge)
>Bridget Kurtis
>Investigator, Habitat Security Division
>born: Salma Habitat 2067
>**TAG** (Brink)
>Carl Brinkmann
>Investigator, Habitat Security Division
>born: Xiang Habitat 2061
>**BRIDGE**
>Harbin was on double-scrip nudge.
>**TAG** (drugs)
>High-dose selective seratonin reuptake inhibitor antidepressants

4. From the window side of the room as Bridge shoots a glance at Brink, finger to her lips. Both are moving to cover. Someone's approaching outside.

>**FROM OFF**
>...that crackwipe Cruz done <u>now</u>? (joined)
>I <u>told</u> him to be chill.

5. Match shot, but Bridge and Brink are either side of the door, pressed to the wall, guns drawn

and ready, so neither can be seen by the two men stepping into the room. Both are workers, grubby, very shifty and sick looking. Both stare at the corpse without much reaction except tiredness. One (Bremer) is further into the room than the other (Nold) who is still half-out in the corridor. Both, as an incidental detail, are wearing creepy-weird, home-made necklaces, little 'symbols' of their dark cult. Maybe a star-shaped design, disturbing, which we'll use again. Both maybe wear several variations of the same, and we don't have to see the detail here.

> **BREMER**
> Oh, for crap's <u>sake</u>.
> (joined)
> We're gonna need sheet wrap and access to the waste plant--

6. Match shot as Brink and Bridge both step out, guns aimed. Their guns are dark, blunt functional modern firearms - Sig Sauer pistols blended with Blade Runner's handgun. Retrofitted, solid slug, moulded grips. Bremer freezes in terror, but Nold starts to run.

> **BRINK**
> <u>Freeze</u>.
> (joined)
> Security.
> **BREMER**
> <u>Shit</u>!
> **TAG** (gun, either)
> .40 SIGlock automatic, H.S.S. field issue flatnose rounds

PAGE THREE

1. Continuous. Bridge is bundling the panicking Bremer down hard, arm lock. Brink is flying out the door after the otherone.

> **BRIDGE**
> Down! <u>Down</u>! Get <u>down</u>!
> **BREMER**
> <u>Shit</u>! <u>No</u>! <u>Shit</u>!
> **BRIDGE**
> <u>Get the other one</u>!

2. Exterior, the hallway. Nold sprinting desperately towards us, glancing back, Brink sprinting in pursuit. Other habitat dwellers get out of the way, shrink back, or watch with grim fascination.

> **BRINK**
> <u>Halt</u>!
> (joined, small)
> Damn it.

3. Back on Bridge, struggling with the arm-locked Bremer, getting cuffs on him.

> **BRIDGE**
> <u>Quit it</u>! You're <u>under arrest</u>!
> **BREMER**
> This <u>ain't</u> the way! This <u>ain't</u> the way!
> (joined)
> The Leper Heart will see you for what you <u>are</u>! <u>See</u> your disrespect! <u>See</u> your bruises upon my body!
> **BRIDGE**
> <u>Shut up</u>!

4. Back on Brink. He's vaulting down a metal staircase using the handrails into a filthy, steamy kitchen galley. Nold is already running and barging his way through the workers, knocking them aside, cookpots spilling, etc. Shots, angry complaints.

TAG (room)
Loop 343 communal galley

> **SHOVED COOK**
> Hey! <u>Retard</u>!

5. Continuous. Brink slams through the galley in pursuit, shouting, gun raised high so it isn't aimed at anyone. People are getting in his way (accidentally).

> **BRINK**
> Security!
> (joined)
> Move aside!
> (joined)
> Come on!

6. Back on Bridge, the cuffs now in place. Bremer's still struggling, on his knees, and she having to shove his shoulders down.

> **BREMER**
> Promises were made! You're spoiling it! The Leper Heart promised!
> (joined)
> Took the soil and the air, and left us in the dark with a promise it would come back for us too!
> **BRIDGE**
> Shut the hell up!
> **BREMER**
> Swelling up, swelling up out of the unreach, keeping its whispered promises!
> (joined)
> Low Theta, hanging inside the sun, Melancholema, and Phale Chronozon--

PAGE FOUR

1. Continuous. Bridge halts, for a second, shocked, suddenly looking very very pasty and unwell.

> **BRIDGE**
> (small)
> Hell did you just say?
> **BREMER**
> Phale Chronozon!

2. Continuous. She keeps him pinned as before but, involuntarily, vomits violently, either aside onto the deck or (I prefer this) accidentally all over his shoulders and the back of his head.

> **BRIDGE**
> -WHHHULLPP-
> **BREMER**
> Gaaah! Jesus, bitch!

3. Cut back to Brink. Kinetic impact shot as he flying tackles the fleeing Nold as they come out of the galley exit onto a metal gantry pavement above a huge engineering space. This impact is painful for both of them. This engineering space is a large chamber, perhaps where two habitat modules join. Below, we can see a curving wall of cabin or apartment windows, showing the density of the living space, a tower block wrapped into a drum. Maybe washing lines loop between the railings and walkways as people use the space for maximum efficiency.

> **BRINK**
> GRnaaaah!
> **NOLD**
> Nuuhhhk!
> **TAG** (chamber)
> Loop 343/Loop 344 junction ring

4. Continuous. They rolling, grappling. A painful frenzy. Brink is throwing a punch that is snapping Nold's head around and slamming it towards the pavement guardrail.

> **BRINK**
> Enough of your shit!
> **NOLD**
> Boohkk!

5. Continuous. Driven by the punch, Nold's head ricochets nastily off the railing.
> FX
> **BLANG!**

6. Panting, sick and out of shape, Brink kneels on (straddles) the very unconscious Nold, trying to cuff him. He's facing us through the guardrail. He doesn't see (but we do) the terrifying figure coming up behind him fast, appearing like LEATHERFACE in TCM.

This is a big guy, filthy, dirty work clothes, wearing a scary rebreather mask from a space suit and maybe some creepy-weird necklaces like Nold and Bremer. He has a massive dirty wrench raised to brain Brink.

> **BRINK**
> -nnh!- -nhh!- -nhh!-
> (joined)
> Asshole!
> **MASK** (muffled)
> Mmmll Krmmnnzznnn!

PAGE FIVE

1. Brink dives to one side as the wrench comes down and deeply dents, deforms the railing instead of his head.

> **FX**
> WHUNNGG!
> **BRINK**
> AAAH!

2. Brink is sprawling, trying to raise his sidearm, but the brute swings the wrench and smashes out of his hand, breaking fingers.

> **FX**
> KRKK!
> **BRINK**
> Nyaaaghh!

3. Brink falls back, the brute over him. We're looking up at it, from 'over Brink's shoulder' as it raises the wrench to pulp him (and us).

> **MASK** (muffled)
> Mmmll Krmmnnzznnn!
> **BRINK**
> Son of a--

4. Match shot, but the brute spasms, one of his mask's eye lenses suddenly cracked and full of blood (he's been shot from behind in the back of the head).

> **FX**
> KBAMMM!

5. Brink looks up, the brute slumped face down across him, heavy and dead, the back of his head a bloody pulp. Bridge is standing back aways down the pavement, her sidearm still aimed in a braced, two-handed stance, muzzle smoking.

> **BRINK**
> Jesus.
> (joined)
> Thanks.
> (joined)
> You going to be sick now?

6. He clambers up, letting the body roll aside. In the foreground, she is turning aside, lowering her gun, sagging and fatigued as the tension release shivers through her, looking pale and sick.

> **BRIDGE**
> No.
> (joined)
> Nothing left to come up.

CAP
Next: case study